"WITH DISARMING HONESTY, WILLIAMS WRITES OF HIS RELATIONSHIPS . . . with his mother, Miss Edwina, and his sister, Miss Rose, who has been confined to mental institutions for much of her life; his homosexual love affairs, many of which lasted only a night, one of which lasted fourteen years; and his addiction to pills, liquor and 'feel-good' shots which contributed to a devastating breakdown . . . He talks candidly about his struggle to achieve recognition as a playwright . . . Throughout, Williams' story is studded with cameo appearances by such notables as Anna Magnani, Elia Kazan, Marlon Brando, Tallulah Bankhead, Ernest Hemingway, William Inge, Carson McCullers and Greta Garbo. But in the end, it is Tennessee Williams—alternately witty, outrageous and brutally frank—who dominates center stage."

# Tennessee Williams
# MEMOIRS

BANTAM BOOKS · LONDON · TORONTO · NEW YORK

MEMOIRS

*A Bantam Book / published by arrangement with
Doubleday & Company, Inc.*

*PRINTING HISTORY*
*Doubleday edition published November 1975*
*Book-of-the-Month Club edition published December 1975*
*Bantam edition / December 1976*

*Cover photo courtesy of Alex Gotfryd*

ISBN 0–553–02745–X

*Published simultaneously in the United States and Canada*

*Bantam Books are published by Bantam Books, Inc. Its trade-
mark, consisting of the words "Bantam Books" and the por-
trayal of a bantam, is registered in the United States Patent
Office and in other countries. Marca Registrada. Bantam
Books, Inc., 666 Fifth Avenue, New York, New York 10019.*

PRINTED IN THE UNITED STATES OF AMERICA

# CONTENTS

Foreword      vii

Memoirs      1

Index      321

"Of what is past, or passing, or to come."
—WILLIAM BUTLER YEATS

# FOREWORD

A fairly short while ago I happened to be in the city of
New Haven, Connecticut, in connection with what
was imposingly announced as the "world premiere" of
an "adventure in drama," a play called *Out Cry*, about
which I will write from time to time in this book. *Out
Cry* was irrevocably committed to its first public exposure on-stage in the early season of 1973, at that
grand old maternity ward of the Broadway theatre
called the Shubert.

I suspect the reader may know that New Haven is
distinguished as the site not only of the Shubert but
also of one of the largest of our old Ivy League schools,
known as Yale.

At *this* point I will not go into my nervous and physical condition at *that* point except to say that I was recuperating much too gradually from a bout with
London and/or Hong Kong flu, complicated by that
condition whose name is derived from the name of
"Pan" and whose first name isn't Peter.

Never mind these feeble attempts at humor, so pathetically characteristic of old crocodiles and old playwrights. Scratching the hide of the latter, you will discover that it can only be noticeably indented by the
cutting edge of a diamond or by a bit of dandelion fluff
in the atmosphere of a late summer afternoon.

Well, anyhow, as they say so often in my plays, I had
been invited to appear before a collection of Yale
drama students the afternoon before the aforemen-

tioned "world premiere" of this adventure in drama. I
remembered the Shubert as a building that contained
a great many seats, upstairs and down, and also I remembered that quite a number of these seats are likely
to be unoccupied even on the occasion of a "world
premiere." And it occurred to me that if I made a seductive impression upon Yale students some of those
seats not booked for that same evening might be ad-
venturously snatched from the dreadful maw of va-
cuity.

I have now covered the geographic and social and
physical and mental background of the impending occurrence so let's now cut directly to story.

I was invited to hold a symposium with Yale drama
students. The symposium was arranged by the genial
head of the Department of Theatre Arts at Yale. I
found myself entering (through a door marked EXIT)
an auditorium considerably smaller than the Shubert
but containing a more than proportionately small audience. I would say roughly about twoscore and ten, not
including a large black dog which was resting in the
lap of a male student in the front row. My own position
was in a folding chair behind a folding table on which
was set a tumbler of what appeared to be plain water
and which I immediately discovered to be just that.
Furthermore, the young faces before me were uniform-
ly inexpressive of any kind of emotional reaction to
my entrance through that side door marked EXIT. In
fact, the only face that betrayed a real interest was
that of the dog.

I am not much good at disguising my feelings, and
after a few moments I abandoned all pretense of feeling less dejection than I felt. I was talking. I was making these tired old jokes that come off like the destitute
man's Bob Hopeless at an encampment in some failed
war. I found myself sinking lower in the folding chair,
and that slumped position, combined with fits of
wheezing, sniffling and coughing, encouraged some of
the small assemblage to get up and walk out on me,

a thing that stirred in my heart no sense of the favorably providential. Still I continued to hear myself talking but no longer telling old jokes. I heard myself describing an encounter, then quite recent, with a fellow playwright in the Oak Room Bar at Manhattan's Plaza Hotel. I told them that this encounter had been inadvertent on both his part and mine, but since he happened to be my old friend Gore Vidal, I had embraced him warmly. However, Mr. Vidal is not a gentleman to be disarmed by a cordial embrace, and when, in response to his perfunctory inquiries about the progress of rehearsals of *Out Cry* I told him that its two performers, Michael York and Cara Duff-MacCormick, and the director, Peter Glenville, and the producer, David Merrick, all seemed a dream come true after many precedent nightmares, he smiled at me with a sort of rueful benevolence and said, "Well, Bird, it won't do much good, I'm afraid, you've had too much bad personal exposure for anything to help you much anymore."

Well, then, for the first time, I could see a flicker of interest in the young faces before me. It may have been the magic word Vidal or it hay have been his prophecy of my professional doom. At any rate, a young lady student of drama in the diminished group stood up to ask me if I regarded Gore's assessment of my present situation in my profession here in the States as a reliable one.

I looked at her in silence for a moment while wondering if I did so regard it, and I came to no conclusion about the question.

My eyes drifted from her face to that of the young man in the front row with the big black dog in his lap.

Laughter has always been my substitute for lamentation and I laugh as loudly as I would lament if I hadn't discovered a useful substitute for weeping. Usually I laugh longer than I should, as well as more loudly than I should. This time I cut short my travesty of mirth and said to the young lady, "Ask the dog."

The truth is that I don't know whether or not I can ever again receive a persuasively favorable critical response to my theatre work in this country, I know the answer no more than does the dog.

But I am not embittered nor even greatly disconcerted by this dilemma in which I find myself. In a way, it does seem that I have almost asked for it. There is a duality in my attitude toward an audience now. Of course I want their approval, I want their understanding and their empathy. But there is much about them that strikes me as obdurately resistant to my kind of theatre these days. They seem to be conditioned to a kind of theatre which is quite different from the kind I wish to practice.

Actually my own theatre is also in a state of revolution: I am quite through with the kind of play that established my early and popular reputation. I am doing a different thing which is altogether my own, not influenced at all by other playwrights at home or abroad or by other schools of theatre. My thing is what it always was: to express my world and my experience of it in whatever form seems suitable to the material.

Since *The Night of the Iguana,* the circumstances of my life have demanded of me a continually less traditional style of dramatic writing: I am referring to such works as *The Gnadiges Fraulein, In the Bar of a Tokyo Hotel,* and, most recently, the latest production of *Out Cry.* And, to an extent, the style of these memoirs.

I want to admit to you that I undertook this memoir for mercenary reasons. It is actually the first piece of work, in the line of writing, that I have undertaken for material profit. But I want to tell you, too, that soon after I started upon the work I forgot the financial angle and became more and more pleasurably involved in this new form, undisguised self-revelation.

This whole book is written by something like the process of "free association," which I learned to practice during my several periods of psychoanalysis. It concerns the reportage of present occurrences, both trivial and important; and of memories, mostly much more important. At least to me.

I will frequently interrupt recollections of the past with an account of what concerns me in the present because of many of the things which concerned me in the past continue to preoccupy me today.

Whether or not it will be acceptable to you will depend in part upon your tolerance for an aging man's almost continual scuttling back and forth between his recollections and his present state.

This "thing," as I have come to call it, will need your interpretation. I have to ask you to remember what you can of the history of the man who wrote it.

In the course of the book I will talk a great deal about love and much of the talk will be about carnal love as well as spiritual love. I have had, for a man so nearly destroyed so often, a remarkably fortunate life which has contained a great many moments of joy, both pure and impure.

"That sensual music . . ."

I still hear it clearly.

Is this book, then, with its rather unusual structure, a professional matter? Has any of my writing been "a professional matter"? I have always written for deeper necessities than the term "professional" implies, and I think that this has sometimes been to the detriment of my career. But more of the time to its advantage. Career? The wrong word. I should have said—no, nothing so pretentious as "vocation." But truly, I never had any choice but to a writer.

And so what's next on the agenda? Or, quoting Anna Magnani, "What is the program now?"

Success in the theatre came to me pretty late by prevailing standards, but whether good fortune comes to you early or late, if it comes at all, you have to know you've been lucky. And the rest is a question to be put to "the dog."

# MEMOIRS

# 1

To begin this "thing" on a socially impressive note, let me tell you that one recent fall, before the leaves had fallen, I happened to be weekending at one of the last great country houses in England, an estate so close to Stonehenge that one of the stones was dropped on the lady's estate before it got to that pre-historical scene of druidical worship and, probably due to collapse or revolt of slave labor, it was not picked up but allowed to rest where it fell, and this bit of information has only the slightest and most oblique connection with the material which follows.

It was bedtime and the lady of the manor, giving me a sharp look, inquired if I didn't want to retire with a good book since she knew I was a restless sleeper. "Go in the library and pick out something," she advised me, pointing to a huge, chilly room in the left wing of the Palladian mansion. Since she was already on her way upstairs, I had no recourse but to follow her suggestion. I entered the library and discovered it to contain almost nothing but very large leather-bound volumes of an ancient vintage almost comparable to that stone which didn't quite make it to Henge. Incidentally, I also discovered a secret doorway, floor to ceiling, rather amateurishly disguised by false book fronts, and this was not the only touch of deception that I encountered. There was a real book

in there which was titled *International Who's Who* or
something of the sort. Quite naturally I snatched it out
of its case and turned immediately to the index to see
if I had made that scene. I was gratified to discover
that there was considerable data upon that nonexistent
personage who bears my professional name: the data
contained a number of harmless inaccuracies but one
of those inaccuracies was distinctly unfortunate in its
effect upon my humor.

Among the list of my honors and awards was the
astonishing announcement that in a certain year of the
early forties I had received a grant of one thousand
dollars, yes, what is called à "big one," from the National Institute of Arts and Letters. It is the year, not
the donor, of the alleged grant that stands out so
prominently in my mind, for that was the year (several years before my life was changed irrevocably
by the success of *The Glass Menagerie*) in which I
had to hock literally everything I owned, including an
old borrowed portable typewriter and everything else
old and new and portable, including all clothes except
a dirty flannel shirt, riding breeches and a pair of boots
which were relics of a term in the study of equitation
I had taken in preference to regular ROTC at the
University of Missouri. And it was the year when I
was bounced from lodging to lodging for nonpayment
of rent, which was a minimal rent, and it was the year
when I had to go out on the street to bum a cigarette,
that absolutely essential cigarette that a living and
smoking writer must have to start work in the morning.
And it was even the year when I usually had what the
French call *"papillons d'amour"* because I did not have
the price of a bottle of Cuprex, the standard pubic
pesticide in those days, and when I was once embarrassed by this outcry on a crowded street corner in
daylight, "You bastard, you gave me crabs last night!"
—an outcry which cut short my social season in the
French Quarter of New Orleans and sent me packing
—well, packing is hardly the word, since I had no

luggage—on my thumb to Florida. And presenting upon the highways such a spooky appearance that motorists would push their accelerators to the floorboards when they sighted me in the light of day and so I had to try to catch rides mostly at night. I have journals to prove these specific recollections of that year when I was supposed to be the hilarious recipient of that "big one" from the institute of which I am now a tolerated member.

In the course of my early years as a skimpy youth infatuated with a theatre which was hugely oblivious of him, I knew and associated closely with a good many other young writers and/or artists and all of us were disregarding the small craft warnings in the face of which we were continually sailing our small crafts, each with his crew of one, himself that crew and its captain. We were sailing along in our separate small crafts but we were in sight of each other and sometimes in touch, I mean like huddling in the same inlet of the rocky, storm-ridden shoreline, and this gave us a warm sense of community, not too different from that which has been felt in recent years by kids called "longhairs" whom the inclement weather of society backed into what are called communes.

To have a problem in common is much like love and that kind of love was often the bread that we broke among us. And some of us survived and some of us didn't, and it was sometimes a matter of what's called luck and sometimes a matter of having or not having the gift to endure and the will to. I mean that none of us were voluntary dropouts, just occasional push-outs, and none of us had breath to waste on the totally fruitless complaint that we were not being fed with spoons of precious metal.

I am sure that when we had time to think of it, we must have suspected that a society whose elite was so grossly affluent, I mean a society that numbered its billions of dollars as we counted our nickels, could have and possibly should have exhibited a bit more concern for the fate of its young artists who might plausibly be expected, if they chanced to mature, to have some influence on the (very protean) culture of a nation which was then, as it remains now, a nation ruled by that numerically tiny gang which has fitted itself on the top of the totem pole and is scared of getting dizzy if it glances down.

Now to be fair, there were, in the forties, certain fabulously fat pocketbooks that scattered bits of much-publicized dole to young talents. There were the Guggenheim fellowships to be had, sometimes at the last ditch by such a tremendous and yet fragile artist as Hart Crane. Perhaps it could never have come early enough to have saved Hart from his own destruction, but it came, when it did, much too late. And there were in the thirties the WPA projects, and, oh, God, did I ever try to make that scene in Chicago and New Orleans and was I ever slapped down! And a bit later, there were the Rockefeller grants of a thousand dollars with a possible but improbable future increase by half the original big one. That one and its half-size addition did come my way, eventually.

*The very rich have such a touching faith in the efficacy of small sums.*

I should have put that observation in quotes rather than italics since it is not a remark of my own but one of (the legendary) Paul Bigelow's most succinct comments on the godly handouts, tax-exempted no doubt, of our Babylonian plutocracy.

It is only now, in retrospect, at a great distance of time, that I speak of these celebrated benefactors of the young and gifted in a tone that is something less than pietistic, but you can put that down to the acidity of oncoming age. When I was one of the young and gifted, and living among others of that kind, there was no self-pity among us, at least no degree of it that distinguished us from the rest of humankind. Of course we all know that self-pity is one of those root emotions of mankind, a feeling of self-respect, sometimes carried to the excess of pride, and I have observed and have felt and still feel and observe a lot more self-respect carried to the excess of pride than I've felt or observed self-pity, which is, after all, only a slight variation on self-contempt, a feeling that's better left to the naturally contemptuous.

In 1939 I found myself employed as a feather picker on a squab ranch in one of those little communities on the periphery of Los Angeles, which I've heard described as a lot of villages in search of a city. This job of squab picking was not very lucrative, but it had its compensations of a nonmaterial sort. Several times a week a group of young men and boys would gather in "the killing shed." The squabs were executed by slitting their throats and holding them by their frantically twitching legs over a bucket in which to bleed out their lives. For each squab that each of us plucked and prepared for the L.A. markets we would drop a feather in the milk bottle that bore our particular name and we were paid according to the number of feathers in our bottles when we knocked off for the day. It was, for me, a distasteful thing: the compensation, besides the small pay, was the wonderful rapping among us feather pickers in that shed, and I remember, never to forget, a homely bit of philosophy that was voiced by one of the more sophisticated kids.

"You know," he said, "that if you hang out long enough on a corner of this coast, sooner or later a sea gull is going to fly over and shit a pot of gold on you." (I have quoted this line a couple of times, once in a play and once in a film script, but have yet to hear it delivered from stage or screen. However—)

While I was out there at that occupation, a great piece of luck did hit me. I received a telegram from the Group Theatre in New York informing me that I had received a "special award" of one hundred dollars for a group of one-act plays called *American Blues*. This wire was signed by Harold Clurman, Irwin Shaw and the late Molly Day Thacher Kazan.

Most people no longer remember that a hundred dollars in the late thirties was a pretty big slice of bread, since now, you know, you can hardly get a good girl to spend the night with you on it. But at that time it was not only a big slice of bread but it was a huge piece of encouragement and boost of morale and, even in those days, encouragement in my "sullen craft and art" was far more important to me than anything convertible into cash.

You know, I can never be a true misanthrope, looking back on the totally sincere and nonenvious congratulations which I received from my colleagues and also from my employers on the squab ranch. They all knew that I was a writer, and consequently a kook, and here, all of a sudden, this sea gull had flown over my corner and crowned me with this heavenly manna, and I had not even been waiting out there on that particular corner for a long time.

I could, of course, have purchased a bus ticket immediately and directly to Manhattan and had enough left over for a week or two at the "Y," but instead I bought for less than ten dollars a secondhand bicycle which was in good shape, and the lighthearted nephew of the squab ranchers bought a bike too and, to celebrate, we set out southward on a highway called the Camino Real and we pedaled our way from Los Angeles County—Hawthorne, to be exact—down to and across the Mexican border. We went to Tijuana and to Agua Caliente, both of which were quite primitive in those days. The places were primitive and we were innocent and in a border-town *cantina* we met with—well, let's say we discovered that the little kewpie-type god has a predatory nature, sometimes, and we were considerably less enchanted with Mexican cantinas and their clientele when we started back north on the camino very real. In fact, we no longer had the price of nightly lodging along the way, but there were comfortable fields to sleep in under big stars.

Then in a canyon near Laguna Beach—a lovely town in those days—we happened to pass a chicken ranch at the entrance of which was a sign that said "Help Needed." And since we needed help, too, we turned onto the dirt road and presented ourselves to the ranchers, an elderly couple who wanted to hire custodians for their poultry for a couple of months while they went on vacation somewhere. (I don't know why I was so committed to occupations involving poultry in those days; no analyst has ever explained that to me.)

The old, respectably married couple of chicken ranchers had not struck it rich on the ranch, in fact they were barely able to keep the chickens in feed, and they said, with touching apologies, that all they could offer us in the way of remuneration was the occupancy of a little cabin at the back of the chicken run. We assured them that our passion for poultry was quite enough to make the job attractive, and they set out on their vacation and we moved into the cabin and established friendly relations with the chickens the first time we scattered their feed.

I don't know what the beach of Laguna is like now but in the thirties it was a fine place to pass summer days. There was constant volleyball, there was surfing and surfers, there was an artist colony and there was so on and so forth and all of it was delightful. It seems to me that the best part of all was riding our bikes up the canyon at first dark in those days when the sky was still a poem. And dogs at every ranch along the way barked at us, not threateningly, but just to let us know they were on duty.

I suppose that summer was the happiest and healthiest and most radiant time of my life. I know that I kept a journal, then, and in this journal I referred to that season as *Nave Nave Mahana*, which is the title of my favorite (Tahitian) painting by Gauguin and which means "The Careless Days."

So it went that way till the month of August, which is the month when the sky goes crazy at night, full of shooting stars which undoubtedly have an effect on human fate, even when the sun's up.

To put it in two words: disaster struck. It struck first the chickens and caromed off them onto us. We came out of our cabin one crystal-clear morning to discover about a third of this feathered flock lying on their backs and sides with legs extended in a state of *rigor mortis,* and the survivors of this flash epidemic were not in much better condition. They were wandering dizzily about their enclosure as if in shock of sorrow for their defunct companions and now and then one of them would squawk and fall over and not get up again. We never did learn what the disease was. But this was the end of *Nave Nave Mahana.*

My friend had somehow legitimately acquired a beat-up old Ford and late that day of disaster he split the scene and I was alone with the plague-stricken poultry, and almost envied their lot. This was, I believe, the longest time in my life that I went hungry. I went without nourishment for about ten days except for some remnants of dried peas and some avocados that I stole now and then from a grove in the canyon. I subsisted on these meager rations, since the heroically surviving but diseased chickens did not appear fit for the frypan or stewpot, and I myself was afflicted with a curious inertia that made me disinclined to leave the ranch, and anyhow I hadn't a dime left on me, nor even postage for a letter of supplication if I had been in the mood for such an embarrassing thing.

I learned, however, that after about three days of semistarvation you stop feeling hungry. The stomach contracts, the gastric spasms subside, and God or somebody drops in on you invisibly and painlessly injects you with sedation, so that you find yourself drifting into a curiously, an absolutely inexplicably, peaceful condition, and this condition is ideal for meditation on things past and passing and to come, in just that sequence.

After a fortnight in that condition, mostly horizontal, I heard my friend's scatter-bolt sputtering with exhaustion toward the cabin and he entered grinning casually as if he had left ten minutes before.

During his absence he had played his clarinet in a night spot near L.A., had received a week's salary, and that sum was sufficient to get us into the San Bernardino Mountains for a time of recuperation from our respective ordeals.

I was receiving letters that summer from various agents on Broadway who had seen my name in the theatre columns as winner of that Group Theatre "special award." One agent said she was not interested in serious plays but was looking for a good "vehicle." I wrote her that the only vehicle I had to offer was a secondhand bike. But another lady, Audrey Wood, expressed a more serious interest, and on the advice of Molly Day Thacher Kazan I chose Miss Wood to represent me, and this dainty little person whom her husband called "The Little Giant of the American Theater"—both of them were of small physical stature —took me on, sight unseen, as a client and she continued to represent me for a long, long time.

In the late autumn of 1939, during a period of confinement to the attic of the family residence in a suburb of St. Louis, I received a wire from Miss Luise M. Sillcox, executive secretary of the Dramatists Guild at that time, and a phone call from Audrey Wood informing me that I was the recipient of a thousand-dollar grant, on which the ladies urged me to catch the first Greyhound to the city of New York, where the action was in those days, and possibly still is.

When this bit of information first came through, it was my mother, the indomitable Mrs. Edwina (Cornelius C.) Williams, who received it. She practically collapsed. I think it was the first time that I saw her in tears and it was a very startling sight and one which still touches me deeply, that sight and her outcry: "Oh, Tom, I'm so happy!"

Of course I was just as happy as she was but for some reason a piece of good fortune has never moved me to tears, nor has a piece of bad fortune, for that matter. I only cry at sentimental movies which are usually bad ones.

St. Louis is not a large part of the world and yet the fact that the Rockefellers had invested a thousand dollars in my talent as a writer, which lacked a great deal in the way of substantial evidence at that time and probably for some time thereafter, was a matter of considerable local interest. All three of the St. Louis newspapers invited me to their offices for interviews on the subject of this grant.

Now we hadn't always been so favorably noticed in the cold city of St. Louis; in fact my sister Rose and I had been quite lonely there during our childhood and adolescence. Also, although my father had early on acquired a sort of underground reputation as a fairly big wheel in the International Shoe Company, he had suffered a remarkable misadventure during an all-night poker party at the Hotel Jefferson not long before the Rockefellers noticed me, and this misadventure had not been openly publicized but there had been a good deal of gossip about it. Somebody in the poker game had called Dad a "son of a bitch" and my father, being of legitimate and distinguished lineage in East Tennessee, had knocked the bastard down and the bastard had scrambled back up and had bit off my father's ear, or at least he had bit off most of the external part of it, and "C.C." had been hospitalized for plastic surgery. Cartilage was removed from his ribs and skin from his behind and the bitten-off portion of his ear was not exactly restored but rather ineptly approximated. The gossip concerning this incident had given the family a certain notoriety in St. Louis and the county, which rubbed off on me when I got this grant from the Rockefellers, and I think it is fairly safe to say that there has been public and private interest in the ups and downs of our fortunes ever since . . .

On Sunday I had lunch with the "great" Russian poet Yevtushenko. He came to me at "The Victorian Suite" about an hour late and was accompanied by a very fat, silent man whom he said he brought along as interpreter—which seemed extraordinary since he has full command of English.

He had gone as my guest, the evening before, to see my play *Small Craft Warnings* and he immediately launched an attack upon the play.

"You put only about thirty per cent of your talent into it, and that's not just my opinion but that of people seated around me."

I was distressed but I kept my composure.

"I'm very happy to know," I said, with the cool of a Southern lady, "that I still have so much of my talent left."

He went on and on, he's a very voluble as well as personable young man, till it was past closing time at the restaurant in my hotel.

I don't know whether it was he or I who suggested that we go to the Plaza, which is in walking distance.

He told me, as we arrived and were seated in the Oak Room, that he was a connoisseur of wines. He proved it immediately by summoning the wine steward with that arrogance that characterizes his behavior in the States. He ordered two bottles of Château Lafite-Rothschild (they are about eighty bucks a bottle at the Plaza), and then a supplementary bottle of Margaux. Then he called over the Captain to place his order for lunch. He wanted (and got) a great bowl of beluga caviar with its appropriate trimmings, the best pâté and the most expensive steaks for himself and his equally voracious "interpreter."

I was now a bit put out. I called him a "capitalist pig"—the remark applied with a veneer of humor. Then I launched a counterassault.

"Being a homosexual," I told him, "I am very concerned over your [Russia's] treatment of my kind in your country."

"Absolute nonsense. In Russia we have no homosexual problem."

"Oh, is that so! How about, say, Diaghilev, Nijinsky or some of the other artists who have left the Soviet Union to avoid imprisonment for being one of my kind?"

"We have absolutely no homosexual problem," he still insisted.

The wine was excellent, of course, and our humors improved under its influence. He told me that I was a millionaire in Russia from the accrued royalties of my plays there and that I should come over and live off them like a king.

I said, "Be that as it may, I'd rather stay out of Russia."

The lunch continued till closing time in the Oak Room and then came the bill and it was so big it required three pages for itemization . . .

He presented me with his most recent collection of verse, inscribing it to me with great flourish and expression of esteem and affection.

During our controversy over whether there was, or was not, any homosexual problem in the Soviet Union, I said to him, "I hope you don't think I've brought the subject up because I plan to seduce you."

I believe he thinks I'm quite mad, and I believe I have the same opinion of him, as well as "esteem and affection."

After the local fanfare over the Rockefeller grant, I left St. Louis to come to New York, and arrived in

New York City by Greyhound at daybreak. I had not rested or shaved, and looked pretty disreputable when I presented myself at the imposing offices of Liebling-Wood, Inc., way, way up in the RCA Building at 30 Rockefeller Plaza.

The reception room was full of girls seeking chorus jobs in a musical that Mr. Liebling, husband of my new agent, Audrey Wood, was casting; they were milling about, chattering like birds on a locoweed high, when Mr. Liebling came charging out of his inner sanctum and shouted, "Okay, girls, line up now!" and everybody lined up except me. I remained on a chair in a corner. A number of girls were selected for auditions, the others gently discouraged, and they rushed chattering off. Then Liebling noticed me and he said, "Nothing for you today."

I said, "I don't want anything today except to meet Miss Wood."

And dead on that cue she entered the outer office, a very small and dainty woman with red hair, a porcelain complexion and a look of cool perspicacity in her eyes which remains there today.

I figured that this was the lady I'd come to see and I was not mistaken. I got up and introduced myself to her and she said, "Well, well, you've finally made it," to which I replied, "Not yet." I meant this not as a witticism but quite literally, and I was rather discountenanced by her frivolous peal of laughter.

# 2

I guess it hardly needs stating that I had been the victim of a particularly troubled adolescence. The troubles had started before adolescence: I think they were clearly rooted in childhood.

My first eight years of childhood in Mississippi were the most joyously innocent of my life, due to the beneficent homelife provided by my beloved Dakin grandparents, with whom we lived. And to the wild and sweet half-imaginary world in which my sister and our beautiful black nurse Ozzie existed, separate, almost invisible to anyone but our little cabalistic circle of three.

That world, that charmed time, ended with the abrupt transference of the family to St. Louis. This move was preceded, for me, by an illness diagnosed by a small Mississippi town doctor as diphtheria with complications. It lasted a year, was nearly fatal, and changed my nature as drastically as it did my physical health. Prior to it, I had been a little boy with a robust, aggressive, almost bullying nature. During the illness, I learned to play, alone, games of my own invention.

Of these games I recall vividly one that I played with cards. It was not solitaire. I had already read *The Iliad* and I turned the black and red cards into two opposite armies battling for Troy. The royalty, the face cards of both Greeks and Trojans, were the kings, princes and heroes; the cards merely numbered were the common soldiers. They would battle in this fashion: I would slap a red and black card together and the one that fell upon the bedspread face up was the victor. By ignoring history, the fate of Troy was decided solely by these little tournaments of the cards.

During this period of illness and solitary games, my mother's overly solicitous attention planted in me the makings of a sissy, much to my father's discontent. I was becoming a decided hybrid, different from the family line of frontiersmen-heroes of east Tennessee.

My father's lineage had been an illustrious one, now gone a bit to seed, at least in prominence. He was directly descended from Tennessee's first senator, John Williams, hero of King's Mountain; from the brother Valentine of Tennessee's first Governor John (Nollichucky Jack) Sevier; and from Thomas Lanier Williams I, the first Chancellor of the Western Territory (as Tennessee was called before it became a state). According to published genealogies, the Seviers could be traced back to the little kingdom of Navarre, where one of them had been a ward of the Bourbon monarch. The family then became divided along religious lines: between Roman Catholics and Huguenots. The Catholics remained Xaviers; the Huguenots changed their name to Sevier when they fled to England at the time of St. Bartholomew's Massacre. St. Francis Xavier, credited with the conversion of many Chinese —a valiant but Quixotic undertaking, in my opinion— is the family's nearest claim to world renown.

My paternal grandfather, Thomas Lanier Williams II, proceeded to squander both his own and his wife's fortunes on luckless campaigns for the governorship of Tennessee.

Now the imposing old Williams residence in Knoxville has been turned into a black orphanage—a good ending for it.

The question I'm asked with most tedious frequency by interviewers and talk-show hosts is "How did you get the name Tennessee when you were born in Mississippi?" So that's the justification for my professional monicker—and I've also just indulged myself in the Southern weakness for climbing a family tree.

My father, Cornelius Coffin Williams, grew up mostly without the emolient influence of a mother, as the beautiful Isabel Coffin Williams died of TB at the age of twenty-eight. Consequently he had a rough and tough character. It was not softened at the military academy of Bellbuckle, where he spent much of his time in the guardhouse for infractions of rules; there he was fed only turnips, a vegetable which he never permitted to appear on our family table. After a year or two studying law at the University of Tennessee, he became a second lieutenant during the Spanish-American War, caught typhoid fever, and lost all his hair. Mother claims that he remained good-looking till he took to drink. I never saw him during his time of abstention and good looks.

But heavy drinking was not a detriment to a Mississippi drummer. After a short career in the telephone business, he became a shoe salesman and was very popular and successful at this itinerant profession, during which he acquired a great taste for poker and for light ladies—which was another source of distress to my mother.

He was such a good salesman that he was taken off the road to become sales manager of a branch of the International Shoe Company in St. Louis—a promotion which took us to St. Louis where the wholesale shoe company's main offices were located, and which also removed my father from the freedom and wildness on which his happiness depended.

Dad went to St. Louis before Mother, Rose and I.

He met us at Union Station. We had scarcely left that curiously designed structure of gray stone, now threatened with demolition, when we happened to pass an outdoor fruit stand. In passing it, I reached out and plucked a grape. Dad delivered a stinging slap to my hand and boomed out, "Never let me catch you stealing again!"

A catalogue of the unattractive aspects of his personality would be fairly extensive, but towering above them were, I think, two great virtues which I hope are hereditary: total honesty and total truth, as he saw it, in his dealings with others.

Our first home in St. Louis was on Westminster Place, a pleasant residential street lined with great trees which made it almost Southern in appearance. Rose and I made friends and we had an agreeable children's life among them, playing "hide-and-seek" and "fly, sheep, fly," and bathing under garden hoses in the hot summer. We were only a block from the Lorelei swimming pool and the West End Lyric movie and we had bicycle races about the block. Rose's closest friend was a pretty child whose mother was a snob who made catty remarks about Mother and Dad in front of us. I recall her once saying, "Mrs. Williams always walks down the street like she was on the boardwalk at Atlantic City and Mr. Williams struts like the Prince of Wales."

I don't know why we left Westminster Place for 5 South Taylor; perhaps the apartment on South Taylor admitted more sunlight (my mother was recuperating from "a spot on her lungs"). Anyway, it was a radical step down in the social scale, a thing we'd never had to consider in Mississippi; and all our former friends dropped us completely—St. Louis being a place where location of residence was of prime importance. That, and going to a private school and belonging to the St. Louis Country Club or one of nearly corresponding prestige; attending Mahler's dancing classes and having the right sort of car.

So we had to make new friends.

I took up almost immediately with a rowdy little fellow named Albert Bedinger, he was as prankish as the Katzenjammer kids. I remember only a few of these pranks: throwing a rock at a window of a house which contained a retarded child, and sticking Limburger cheese in the radiator cap of a parked car. Then there was Guy Shaw, a tough little redheaded Mick who delighted in pushing me into the gutter, an affectionate kind of teasing which I did not appreciate at all. All free afternoons were spent, at first, with Albert, participating joyfully in his pranks. I was truly devoted to him and he to me. Then all at once Mother delivered one of her edicts. Albert was a terrible influence on me and I must never see him again.

Mrs. Bedinger was outraged and I remember her coming to see Mother about it.

"My son," she declared, "is a red-blooded American boy." Then she cast a frowning glance upon me, which clearly implied that I was quite the opposite.

I made one or two pathetic attempts to resume friendship with Albert on the sly, but Mrs. Bedinger treated me icily when I slipped over there and Albert was indifferent.

The malign exercise of snobbery in "middle American" life was an utterly new experience to Rose and to me and I think its sudden and harsh discovery had a very traumatic effect on our lives. It had never occurred to us that material disadvantages could cut us off from friends. It was about this time, age eleven or twelve, that I started writing stories—it was a compensation, perhaps . . .

But now for my first meeting with Hazel.

The Kramers lived around the corner from us on the one attractive street in the neighborhood, a street entirely of residences with a tree-planted park running down the center of it, a street called Forest Park Boulevard.

One afternoon I heard a child screaming in the alley back of this street. Some young hoods were, for some unknown reason, throwing rocks at a plump little girl. I went to her defense; we took flight into her house and all the way up to the attic. Thus began my closest childhood friendship which ripened into a romantic attachment.

I was then eleven, Hazel was nine. We started spending every afternoon in her attic. Being imaginative children, we invented many games, but the chief diversion that I recall was illustrating stories that we made up. Hazel drew better than I and I made up better stories.

Old Mrs. Kramer, Hazel's grandmother, maintained a pretty active and prominent place in the social world of St. Louis. She belonged to the Woman's Club, she drove a glossy new "electric," she bore herself with great style.

Mother was relieved, at first, that I was with Hazel, not Albert Bedinger or the other rough boys of Laclede and South Taylor.

Hazel was a redhead with great liquid brown eyes and a skin of pearly translucence. She had extraordinary beautiful legs and her breasts developed early: she was inclined toward plumpness, like her mother (who was sort of a butterball) but she had a good deal of height. In fact, when I was sixteen and Hazel fourteen, she had already outdistanced me in stature and had begun her habit of crouching over a little when she walked alongside me in public lest I be embarrassed by the disparity in our heights.

I suppose that I can honestly say, despite the homosexual loves which began years later, that she was the great extrafamilial love of my life.

My mother did not approve of my attachment to Hazel, as it developed, nor for that matter had Miss Edwina ever seemed to want me to have any friends. The boys were too rough for her delicate son, Tom, and the girls were, of course, too "common."

This also applied, I'm afraid, to Miss Edwina's attitude toward my sister's friendships and little romances. And in Rose's case, they applied with more tragic consequences.

Miss Edwina disapproved more of Hazel's mother, Miss Florence, than of Hazel. Miss Florence covered up her desperation at home by a great animation and gusto of manner when she was out. She played the piano by ear with great skill and considerable volume and she had an excellent and lusty singing voice. Whenever she entered our apartment, she would seat herself at our upright piano and go into some popular song hit of the day, which was naturally quite unpopular with Miss Edwina.

Of course Miss Edwina's put-downs of the grass widow were politely phrased.

"Miss Florence, I'm afraid that you forget we have neighbors and Mrs. Ebbs upstairs sometimes complains when Cornelius raises his voice."

Miss Florence would be likely to reply something to the effect that Mrs. Ebbs upstairs could go to hell, for all it mattered to her . . .

The last time I was in St. Louis, for a visit at Christmas, I had my brother Dakin drive me about all the old places where we had lived in my childhood. It was a melancholy tour. Westminster Place and Forest Park Boulevard had lost all semblance of their charm in the twenties. The big old residences had been converted into sleazy rooming-houses or torn down for nondescript duplexes and small apartment buildings.

The Kramer residence was gone: in fact, all of the family, including dear Hazel, were by then dead.

This can only serve as a preamble, in this "thing," to the story of my great love for Hazel, and not at all an adequate one at that . . .

In my adolescence in St. Louis, at the age of sixteen, several important events in my life occurred. It was in the sixteenth year that I wrote "The Vengeance of Nitocris" and received my first publication in a magazine and the magazine was *Weird Tales*. The story wasn't published till June of 1928. That same year my grandfather Dakin took me with him on a tour of

Europe with a large party of Episcopalian ladies from the Mississippi Delta, and about that trip, more later. And, it was in my sixteenth year that my deep nervous problems approached what might well have been a crisis as shattering as that which broke my sister's mind, lastingly, when she was in her twenties.

I was at sixteen a student at University City High School in St. Louis and the family was living in a cramped apartment at 6254 Enright Avenue.

University City was not a fashionable suburb of St. Louis and our neighborhood, while a cut better than that of the Wingfields in *Menagerie,* was only a little cut better: it was an ugly region of hive-like apartment buildings, for the most part, and fire escapes and pathetic little patches of green among concrete driveways.

My younger brother, Dakin, always an indomitable enthusiast at whatever he got into, had turned our little patch of green behind the apartment on Enright into quite an astonishing little vegetable garden. If there were flowers in it, they were, alas, obscured by the profuse growth of squash, pumpkins, and other edible flora.

I would, of course, have pre-empted all the space with rosebushes but I doubt they would have borne roses. The impracticalities, let's say the fantastic impracticalities, of my adolescence were not at all inclined to successful ends: and I can recall no roses in all the years that I spent in St. Louis and its environs except the two living Roses in my life, my grandmother, Rose O. Dakin, and, of course, my sister, Rose Isabel.

My adolescent problems took their most violent form in a shyness of a pathological degree. Few people realize, now, that I have always been and even remain in my years as a crocodile an extremely shy creature—in my crocodile years I compensate for this shyness by the typical Williams heartiness and bluster and sometimes explosive fury of behavior. In my high school days I had no disguise, no façade. And it was at University City High School that I developed the habit of blushing whenever anyone looked me in the eyes, as if I harbored behind them some quite dreadful or abominable secret.

You will have no trouble in guessing what that secret was but I shall, in the course of this "thing," provide you with some elaboration, all quite true.

I remember the occasion on which this constant blushing had its beginning. I believe it was in a class in plane geometry. I happened to look across the aisle and a dark and attractive girl was looking directly into my eyes and at once I felt my face burning. It burned more and more intensely after I had faced front again. My God, I thought, I'm blushing because she looked into my eyes or I into hers and suppose this happens whenever my eyes look into the eyes of another?

As soon as I had entertained that nightmarish speculation, it was immediately turned into a reality.

Literally, from that incident on, and almost without remission for the next four or five years, I would blush whenever a pair of human eyes, male or female (but mostly female since my life was spent mostly among members of that gender) would meet mine. I would feel my face burning with a blush.

I was a very slight youth. I don't think I had effeminate mannerisms but somewhere deep in my nerves there was imprisoned a young girl, a sort of blushing school maiden much like the one described in a certain poem or song "she trembled at your frown." Well, the school maiden imprisoned in my hidden self, I mean selves, did not need a frown to make her tremble, she needed only a glance.

This blushing made me avoid the eyes of my dear friend Hazel. This happened quite abruptly and both Hazel and her mother, Miss Florence, must have been shocked and puzzled by this new peculiarity of mine. Yet neither of them permitted me to observe their puzzlement.

Once Hazel said to me on a crowded streetcar, after

a little period of tense silence on my part, "Tom, don't you know I'd never say anything to hurt you?"

This was, indeed, the truth: Hazel never, never said a word to hurt me during the eleven years of our close companionship, which, on my part, ripened into that full emotional dependence which is popularly known as love. Miss Florence loved me as a son, I believe, and she talked to me as to an adult about her own lonely and difficult life with her tyrannical parents in their big house on the residential street around the corner from the apartment and fire escapes.

I believe it was at puberty that I first knew that I had a sexual desire for Hazel and it was in the West End Lyric, the movie-house on Delmar Boulevard. Sitting beside her before the movie began, I was suddenly conscious of her bare shoulders and I wanted to touch them and I felt a genital stirring.

Another time, we were driving down a lovers' lane in Forest Park one summer night, with Miss Florence and a bawdy lady friend of hers, when the headlights of Hazel's green Packard limousine picked up a young couple exchanging a very long wet kiss, and the lady friend shrieked with laughter and said, "I'll bet he's got a yard of tongue down her throat!"

These ladies, on summer eves, often diverted themselves by driving down lovers' lane in the park and by parking on top of Art Hill where young couples also engaged in pretty heavy "necking."

We had fun, and it was fun for me to be shocked.

One evening I took Hazel on the river steamer "J.S." —and she wore a pale green chiffon party dress with no sleeves and we went up on the dark upper deck and I put my arm about those delicious shoulders and I "came" in my white flannels.

How embarrassed I was! No mention was made between us of the tattletale wet spot on my pants front but Hazel said, "Let's stay up here and walk around the deck, I don't think we ought to dance now . . ."

Going out on excursion steamers at night was a popular diversion during the thirties in St. Louis and once I had a date with a beautiful young lady of the distinguished family of Choteau, a family that dated back to the time when St. Louis belonged to the French territory in the States. I believe it was a double date including Miss Rose.

I was quite enchanted with the beautiful Miss Choteau and the following weekend—I was in the shoe business, then—I called her to make another date and got this put-down: "Oh, thank you, Tom, but you know I'm afflicted with a very bad case of Rose fever."

I don't think she was alluding to my sister but to the actual flower but I never called her for a date again. She was a debutante and I figured that I just wasn't a socially acceptable date for this girl in her debutante season.

Somehow I cannot adhere as I should to chronology. Now I find myself jumping back to the age of sixteen when Grandfather took me to Europe—where an amazing episode occurred.

Grandfather provided my expenses for this trip to Europe. But Dad gave me a hundred dollars for spending money.

(It was stolen from me by a pickpocket in Paris, specifically at the Eiffel Tower.)

Grandfather's party set sail on the *Homeric*, which had once been the flagship of Kaiser Wilhelm's fleet of passenger vessels. We sailed at midnight and it was a gala departure with a brass band playing, or several of them, and with a great deal of colored paper ribbons tossed between vessel and dockside. I believe there were also many balloons and of course much shouting and drinking and laughing. It was all very Scott and Zelda Fitzgerald.

I particularly remember Pinkie Sikes with her dyed red bob and her spike-heeled slippers and her incredible animation (on the deck with Grandfather and

me) as the ship blew "all ashore." Pinkie, an unattached flower of the South, was, I would guess, near-
ing fifty. Surely she must have been unattached due
to legal process because in her earlier years she must
have been a stunning creature. In fact, she was still
stunning, though rather grotesque in her make-up
and the valiant minimization of her real age that she
showed in her very high heels and short skirts and her
girlish outfits.

I was very fond of Miss Pinkie. In spite of my painful shyness, I was almost not afraid of her.

It was on our first day out at sea that I took my first
alcoholic beverage. It was a green crème de menthe,
served me at the bar on deck.

Half an hour later I became violently seasick and
remained in that condition for about five days of the
voyage, in a cabin which had little ventilation and no
portholes—our party was not sailing first-class.

Among the passengers was a dancing teacher and
the happiest times I recall on this first crossing to Europe, summer of 1928, was dancing with this young
lady, especially the waltzes. I was, in those days, an
excellent dancer and we "just swept around the floor:
and swept and swept" as Zelda would put it.

The dancing teacher was a young lady of about
twenty-seven and she was enjoying a conspicuous flirtation with a certain Captain De Voe in the party. I
recall a mysterious conversation one night. I mean it
was mysterious to me, then, and also disturbing and
I recall it with singular clarity.

Captain De Voe did not like my spending so much
time with the dancing teacher. The three of us were
at a small table in the ship's bar one night, toward
the end of the voyage, when Captain De Voe looked
at me and said to the dancing teacher, "You know
his future, don't you?"

She said, "I don't think you can be sure about that
at the age of seventeen."

Well, of course you know what they were talking

about, but at the time I was mystified—at least it
seems to me now that I was mystified by it.

We are now approaching the onset of the most
dreadful, the most nearly psychotic, crisis that occurred in my early life. I'm afraid it will be hard to
comprehend.

It began when I was walking alone down a boulevard in Paris. I will try to describe it a little, for it has
significance in my psychological make-up. Abruptly,
it occurred to me that the process of thought was a
terrifyingly complex mystery of human life.

I felt myself walking faster and faster as if trying to
outpace this idea. It was already turning into a phobia. As I walked faster I began to sweat and my heart
began to accelerate, and by the time I reached the
Hôtel Rochambeau, where our party was staying, I was
a trembling, sweat-drenched wreck of a boy.

At least a month of the tour was enveloped for me
by this phobia about the processes of thought, and the
phobia grew and grew till I think I was within a hairs-
breadth of going quite mad from it.

We took a beautiful trip down the winding river
Rhine, from a city in Northern Prussia to the city of
Cologne.

On either side of our open-decked river boat were
densely forested hills of deep green and on many of
them were medieval castles with towers.

I noticed all this, even though I was going mad.

The principal tourist attraction of Cologne was its
ancient cathedral, the most beautiful cathedral I have
seen in my life. It was Gothic, of course, and for a
cathedral in Prussia, it was remarkably delicate and
lyrical in design.

My phobia about thought processes had reached its
climax.

We entered the cathedral, the interior of which
was flooded with beautifully colored light coming
through the great stained-glass windows.

Breathless with panic, I knelt down to pray.

I stayed kneeling and praying after the party had left.

Then a truly phenomenal thing happened.

Let me say that I am not predisposed to believe in miracles or in superstitions. But what happened was a miracle and one of a religious nature and I assure you that I am not bucking for sainthood when I tell you about it. It was as if an impalpable hand were placed upon my head, and at the instant of that touch, the phobia was lifted away as lightly as a snowflake though it had weighed on my head like a skull-breaking block of iron.

At seventeen, I had no doubt at all that the hand of our Lord Jesus had touched my head with mercy and had exorcised from it the phobia that was driving me into madness.

Grandfather was always terribly frightened for me when I escaped from his sight and from the party of ladies. He was not a scolder, he was never severe, but he said, when I got back, "My goodness, Tom, what a scare you gave us when we returned to the bus and you were missing. A lady said you'd run out of the cathedral and we'd find you at the hotel."

For about a week after that I was marvelously well and for the first time I began to enjoy my first trip to Europe. I still found the endless walking about art galleries to be interesting for only a few moments now and then, and dreadfully tiring, physically, for the rest.

But the phobia about "thought process" was completely exorcised for about a week and the physical fatigue began to disappear with it.

The final high-point of the tour was Amsterdam, or, more specifically, the Olympic games, which were being performed in Amsterdam that year. It was the equestrian competition that our party attended and it was at this equestrian event that my phobia had a brief and minor reprise.

Having thought it permanently exorcised by the "miracle" in the cathedral of Cologne, I was terribly troubled by its fresh, though relatively minor recurrence.

That night I went out alone on the streets of Amsterdam and this time a second "miracle" occurred to lift the terror away. It occurred through my composition of a little poem. It was not a good poem, except perhaps for the last two lines, but allow me to quote it, since it comes back easily to mind.

> Strangers pass me on the street
> in endless throngs: their marching feet,
> sound with a sameness in my ears
> that dulls my senses, soothes my fears,
> I hear their laughter and their sighs,
> I look into their myriad eyes:
> then all at once my hot woe
> cools like a cinder dropped on snow.

That little bit of verse with its recognition of being one among many of my kind—a most important recognition, perhaps the most important of all, at least in the quest for balance of mind—that recognition of being a member of multiple humanity with its multiple needs, problems and emotions, not a unique creature but one, only one among the multitude of its fellows, yes, I suspect it's the most important recognition for us all to reach now, under all circumstances but especially those of the present. The moment of recognition that my existence and my fate could dissolve as lightly as the cinder dropped in a great fall of snow restored to me, in quite a different fashion, the experience in the cathedral of Cologne. And I wonder if it was not a sequel to that experience, an advancement of it: first, the touch of the mystic hand upon the solitary anguished head, and then the gentle lesson or demonstration that the head, despite the climactic crisis which it contained, was still a single head on a street thronged with many.

When I returned from Europe, I still had a year to go at University City High School in St. Louis. Things were just a bit easier than they had been. For one thing, the high-school paper, at the suggestion of my English teacher, invited me to narrate my European travels, which I did in a series of sketches, none containing a reference to the miracles of Cologne and Amsterdam nor the crisis, but nevertheless giving me a certain position among the student body, not only as the most bashful boy in school but as the only one who had traveled abroad.

It was still almost entirely impossible for me to speak aloud in classrooms. And, teachers stopped asking me questions because when they did, I would produce a voice that was hardly intelligible, my throat would be so tight with panic.

Well, that particular phobia, the one about the terrifying nature of cerebration, has never come to me again.

Let me give you this sworn truth. I have never doubted the existence of God nor have I ever neglected to kneel in prayer when a situation in which I found myself (and there have been many) seemed critical enough in my opinion to merit the Lord's attention and, I trust, intervention.

Now some cynics among you will think that I am competing with Mary Pickford, who was the authoress of a work called *Why Not Try God?*

Never mind. I am old enough to have been in love with Miss Pickford, if that's a relevant point.

# 3

When I was about to set off for college in the early fall of 1929 suddenly there wasn't any money for the tuition; if it hadn't been for Grand coming through with a thousand dollars right in the nick of time, I couldn't have gone. This was just one of many times in my life when Grand and Grandfather Dakin brought calm and order to my usually chaotic state, or were responsible for my accomplishing something, in part because of the happy atmosphere they were able to create, in part because of their almost magical power to dispense financial aid from their own small resources.

Off I went, to the University of Missouri, in the charming town of Columbia.

I did not go for "rush week" as I could not imagine myself being accepted by a fraternity or wanting to be a fraternity member.

This was a disappointment to Dad, who had been a Pi Kappa Alpha during his years at the University of Tennessee and he was determined to do something about this in short order.

Miss Edwina accompanied me to Columbia; it did not concern her at all that I had not gone up for rush week. We spent our first night in a hotel room and the next day she selected for me what she regarded as a suitable boardinghouse. The boardinghouse was segregated, sexually, there were two buildings under the proprietorship of a very lively middle-age landlady, a widow with a bright red Buick convertible.

The boys and girls met only at meals. There was a piano and two or three of the girls could play and it was actually a pleasant arrangement for me.

I have forgotten to mention that my first night in Columbia, at the hotel and on its stationery, I wrote a letter to Hazel, who was at the University of Wisconsin, proposing marriage. In a week's time she sent me an appreciative but negative response, explaining that we were still much too young to think about such a thing . . .

I shared a room with a young somnambulist. One night he got out of his bed and crossed the room to my bed and got in with me. I recall him as a lanky farm boy, blond and a bit blemished with adolescent acne, but not unattractive.

Of course, when he crawled into bed with me, I cried out in dismay. He mumbled something and staggered back across the room to his single bed in another corner.

Now I'm going to make another confession of a comical nature.

For several nights, I waited for this fit of somnambulism to come upon him again and hoped that it would lead him in the same direction.

Well, it only happened that one time.

But one evening, before he'd come to the room, I took the bolts out of his cot so that it would collapse when he got into it.

I suppose I was not quite sane in those days. In any case, the cot did, indeed, collapse when he got into it. However, he quickly and silently reassembled it, giving me several enigmatic glances.

I had been in the boardinghouse for about a month when I was visited by three or four very well-dressed and personable young men from the Alpha Tau Omega fraternity.

Well, their visit had come about through Dad's intervention. He had a pair of young collateral cousins, the Merriwether boys, at the University of Tennessee and they were influential members of ATO there. They had written the local chapter, Gamma Rho, that the son of an executive in the International Shoe Company was "hiding out" in a boardinghouse and that this would not do, since he was descended from the Williamses and Seviers of East Tennessee, since he was a published writer and a traveler of the world.

One of the fraternity brothers laid it on with the most impressive and possibly genuine warmth of feelings; he insisted that I go straight to the fraternity house with him so that I could see at once how preferable it was to the "dismal" boardinghouse.

Nowadays, of course, I would have recognized this "brother," whom I will call "Melmoth," as what he turned out to be.

About as gay as they make them . . .

However, he merely struck me, then, as a person of exceptional grace and charm.

I went to the fraternity house. On the way to it, we passed the new house being constructed, a huge pseudo-Tudor thing that managed to look quite attractive. Before I got to the temporary quarters of the Gamma Rho chapter, I'd made up my mind to join, I mean pledge, if they really asked me to.

The next day they did, and, having observed the brothers with appreciative eyes, I was eager to accept.

The ATO chapter at Missouri U. greeted me with cordiality, at first, but then with growing and growing and growing disconcertion.

Surely, they had never encountered such an eccentric young man, let alone pledged him.

Once a week, at midnight, there was held what was called a "kangaroo court." At this court, conducted with great solemnity, the transgressions of each pledge were read aloud to the gathering and punishment was meted out in the form of paddling. The paddling was light in some cases, and heavy in others.

In my case, it was practically spine-breaking.

A brother would stand poised with a paddle at the end of the long front room. The pledge to be punished would be instructed to bend over, presenting his backside to the brother with the paddle, and to hold up his balls, since the brother did not want to include castration in the punishment.

Then the brother with the paddle would come dashing across the great chamber and swat the pledge's backside.

I was often meted out the maximum number of ten paddlings. And they were often administered with such force that I would barely be able to make my way back upstairs to bed . . .

What were my transgressions?

Various and many. In fact, they were practically innumerable.

A spirit of anarchy had entered into my being. This was partly due to nostalgia for the old boardinghouse. And it was partly due to the meagerness of my monthly allowance from Dad. I was continually out of shirts and in those days you had to appear at dinner, in a fraternity house, in a clean shirt and jacket.

The bell for dinner would ring at six and I would never be prepared for it. Hungry, yes, but always surprised by the sound.

I would wait until the other boys on the floor had descended to the great dining hall in the basement. Then I would scurry into somebody's room and snatch one of his white shirts and wear it down to dinner and return it, surreptitiously, when the meal was over.

I was not very clever at this and was soon found out.

Then, and this is really an awful confession, I had taken to the habit of "kiting checks." Whenever I would go out on a jelly-date, as afternoon dates were called, and find myself unable to pay the café bill, I would write out a check on a bank where I had no account. These bad checks would be pasted on the cashier's box of the restaurant.

What in hell was going on in my mind that year?

Nothing presently recognizable.

About once a month the chapter would give a formal dance and the pledges were given a list of sorority girls who were acceptable as dates for these grand occasions. And I would always ignore the list and bring some girl who was either not even a member of any sorority or was from a sorority that was considered of no consequence, such as Phi Mu or Alpha Delta Pi, which owned the dreadful, sub-rosa sobriquet of "After Dinner Pussy."

There was one particular girl from Alpha Delta Pi that I kept bringing to the dances. This girl was an hysterical nympho: and very, very pretty. She had only one formal dress and it was a shimmering rich brown satin that did not adequately contain her bosom and made no secret at all of her voluptuous behind.

Although her presence at the dance was regarded as a social disgrace, as the evening wore on the brothers began to cut in on us with more and more frequency until she was getting about the dance floor as dizzily as Tippy Smith from the Theta house or the queen of Kappa Kappa Gamma whose name I forget.

The boys would take over my date completely after midnight and they would each dance her into the dark little library and what went on I cannot relate with authority but I can easily conjecture. They would give her what was then called "a dry fuck."

My own intimacies with this girl were not much: once, in a car, I took hold of one of her breasts and she went into an almost epileptic spasm.

Boys and girls together. You can't put it down . . .

The summer after my first year at college I actually obtained and held legitimate employment for a short while, in St. Louis.

I was a house-to-house peddler of a big "woman's

magazine," and just how this came about I don't recall
but certainly I did it only to please, or should I say
pacify, "Big Daddy."

There were about ten of us recruited by a sort of regional sales manager who put up at a second-class hotel on Grand Avenue; and we were a motley crew.
We were paired off, and the pairs worked on opposite
sides of streets. The young fellow who was paired off
with me came from Oklahoma.

He struck me as being curiously antic in his behavior. I was not yet hip, you see, to the gay world
and I didn't know that this partner was actually an
outrageous young camp. He was blond and rather
pretty, I remember, but he interested me only as a funny companion at a very tedious job. Neither of us was
very successful at pushing the woman's magazine.
Housewives slammed their doors in our faces more
often than not: of course this was the first year of the
depression. I guess the job lasted for both me and my
gay partner about two weeks. But after we'd been
summarily dismissed, the kid from Tulsa remained in
St. Louis. One evening we went on a double date with
Hazel and a girl-friend of hers named Lucy. I was surprised at the Tulsa boy's lack of interest in having a
date with a girl; he said, "Wouldn't we have more fun
if we went to the bars?" I had never been to "the bars,"
he did not specify which kind of bars he meant and
I certainly didn't know, not having ever suspected
their existence.

After we'd collected our little commissions from the
mag subscriptions, we went on the open top of a bus
to the neighborhood of Hazel's house. It seemed to me
that the night air had made my partner a bit wacky
with exhilaration. He kept repeating the name "Lucy"
and going into soprano howls of amusement. The
howls had an hysterical note.

I believe that Hazel was much wiser about the sex
scene than I was at that time. When she admitted him
to the Kramer residence, she looked at the Oklahoma

kid with a touch of dismay in her great brown eyes. All during the evening he kept chattering like a bird and putting special emphasis on the name "Lucy." I must admit Lucy would not have rated at a fraternity dance: she looked quite a bit like what her name suggested. She was tall and angular and there was a sort of Luciness about her. But my partner's behavior was really quite overboard and the "double date" ended upon a somewhat ambiguous note. Hazel seemed more than a bit put off with me for the first time in our long relationship.

When I say that Hazel was probably much wiser about the sex scene than I, I am not altogether sure what I mean by that. For five or six years she had been a loving girl-friend but the love was what the Victorians would describe as pure. Now this will come as a rather incredible bit of news, but Hazel permitted me to kiss her only twice a year on the lips, and that was at Christmas and on her birthday. In retrospect I wonder if she was actually what the shrinks call "frigid," or if she was being coquettishly demure to bring out a more aggressive attitude in me. I am inclined to think the latter is true, since I remember an afternoon in our very early teens when we visited the St. Louis art gallery, atop Art Hill in Forest Park; she headed straight for a room of ancient statuary containing *The Dying Gaul*, who was clad only in a fig leaf. Now take my word for this, it's the absolute truth: the fig leaf could be lifted and Hazel knew it. She lifted the fig leaf and asked me, "Is yours like this?"

She got no answer but a maidenly blush . . .

I have incorporated that little occurrence in one of my best short stories, published by *The New Yorker*, no less: its title was "Three Players of a Summer Game." *The New Yorker* cut it out of the story, that incident of the fig leaf, but I restored it when the story appeared in *Hard Candy* and I think rightly so, for the little girl in the story was based upon Hazel as a child —including the bit about the old car, the "electric."

Mrs. Kramer, *grand'mère*, had an "electric" automobile and the pretentious old lady loved to sit in its square glass box tooling sedately among the more fashionable residential sections of the city. She doted on Hazel and she would sometimes allow Hazel to take me for rides. The electric only went at a speed of about twenty miles an hour, at the most. Later on the Kramers were to give Hazel a light green Packard, but that was quite a bit later . . .

I didn't know why the boy from Oklahoma kept hanging around St. Louis, which is all but intolerably hot in summer, but he did hang around and he did keep suggesting that we go to "the bars"—but I continued to decline. Something about him disturbed me and I was somewhat relieved when he finally went home. (Later I received from Tulsa a written declaration of love.)

Cut, now, back to college. And to a youth with large and luminous eyes which gleamed at night like a firecat's.

I was now an initiated member of ATO and at one point I had this roommate with the exceptional eyes, dark hair and one hell of a physique—I'll call him Smitty.

Once each autumn the ATO's would have "Old Home Week" when the great Tudor house would be packed with alumni. On these weekends, everyone doubled up in bunks for the night. I shared a bunk in the dormitory on the third floor with Smitty, sleeping under—no, not sleeping under but *lying* under—a very light blanket, the influx of alumni having put a great strain on the supply of bedclothing. Well, that night a singular adventure occurred. He and I were both sleeping in underwear. I had on shorts and a singlet and I think he only wore shorts.

After lights out in the dormitory, I began to feel his fingers caressing my upper arms and shoulders, at first almost imperceptibly and then, and then—

We were sleeping spoons and he began to press hard against my buttocks and I began to tremble like a leaf in a gale.

But that's as far as it went.

Then, a few weeks later, when we were back in our regular sleeping quarters and I had climbed into my upper bunk, the boy suddenly jumped up there with me.

Automatically, virginally, I said, "What do you want?" or "What are you doing?"

He laughed, sheepishly, and jumped back down from the upper.

I think I must have lain awake nearly all night, cursing myself for my inadvertent "put-down" of this (for those days) very daring approach. How mixed up can you be, and how ignorant!

Another boy began to visit our bedroom at night and one of those nights—they were purely for conversation, or "rapping" as the kids say now—Smitty grinned at our visitor and said, "You know what I'm going to do tonight? I'm going to corn-hole Tommy."

Well, I didn't know what that meant, in those days I had never heard of the idioms for pederasty.

There was a bit of puppy-love-play among the three of us on the lower bunk. We were all in shorts. And we sort of tangled our legs around a bit, but that's as far as it went.

Smitty and I were going on double dates with girls from Stephens College, and were both frustrated. The girls were not giving much.

Now I remember one night in particular and we were not double dating with girls from Stephens but with a couple of very wild coeds, unaffiliated with a sorority for quite apparent reasons. One of them had a roadster and we drove out toward the quarry and stopped by it in the moonlight. Then Smitty said, "Why don't you two walk down the road a piece?"

So we walked down the road—nothing happened. When we returned to the roadster, Smitty's date was

drinking some home brew and his fly was open and
his tumescent member stood straight up and I was
somewhat appalled. It looked more like a weapon than
part of a human body.

But the fire-cat eyes, and the tall and well-formed
body counteracted that aversion, and as the year went
on, we fell more and more in love yet still without any
outlet for the physical side of the attachment, at least
none that led to a release.

When spring came, I remember lying on the wide
lawn at night and he thrust his hand under my shirt
and caressed my upper torso with those big fingers of
his. I would always go into my shaking leaf bit and I
would always say or do nothing to encourage him.

Obviously, our attachment had begun to trouble the
brothers.

Smitty was dropped and he moved disconsolately
into a roominghouse. We went on seeing each other
without interruption, however, and one night we went
to a sort of open-air speakeasy, identical to the one I
later described in *Orpheus Descending*. A long-sloping
hill was dotted with little gazebos in which the home
brew was served and in which the couples would carry on. The gazebos were lighted by tissue paper lanterns, and one by one these lanterns would be
extinguished.

I think we would sometimes turn out our lantern,
too, and still nothing happened.

But one night something did.

We got quite high on the brew and we started
laughing and hooting together in a crazed condition.
Then all at once we raced out of the gazebo and down
that long-sloping hill toward the fence at its bottom.
I was too drunk to get over the fence. I sprawled in
the deep, wet grass and he sprawled on top of me.
We sort of wrestled together in an amorous way, that
was all. But he said, "Let's spend the night at my
place."

We went there by taxi and several times, making a

joke of it, he attempted to kiss me on the mouth and
each time I would push him away.

Sort of dumb, huh? I would say so . . .

Soon as we entered his bedroom, I puked on the
floor.

He swabbed up the vomited brew with a towel
and then he removed my clothes and put me to bed.
When he got in bed with me he caught me in a tight
grip with his arms and legs and I shook so violently
that the bed rattled.

He held me all night and I shook all night.

At this point I might say, "Ah, youth," and possibly
get away with it . . .

After exams (he had flunked) came the night which
was known as "Crazy Night"—the night just before the
college kids dispersed for home. Smitty and I and
some other fellows all piled into somebody's big car
and we drove about town in quest of bootleg liquor.
We got quite drunk, all of us. We ran out of booze
and drove to a house where home brew was dispensed.
Smitty, another boy and I remained in the car while
our companions went in the house to make the purchase. While we waited, Smitty dropped his hand on
my crotch. My cock stood straight up.

He made a joke of it.

"Tom thinks I'm like Melmoth," he yelled, removing
his hand from its improper position.

And this reference to Melmoth leads squarely
enough into an odd chapter-meeting which had taken
place in the "house" a few weeks before.

The chapter meeting was secret. Melmoth was not
present. There was an atmosphere of spooky solemnity.

One of the officers of the fraternity made a speech.
He said he was sure we noticed the absence of Melmoth and there was a reason for it and the reason was
such a shocking thing that it was hard for him to mention it.

He said slowly, with a ferocious glare into space,

"It has been discovered that Melmoth is a cock-sucker."

An awed silence.

Then another brother, God bless him, spoke up.

"That isn't so," he said. "I've been his roommate all year and I know what cock-suckers are and he isn't."

The boy who spoke up was a very, very handsome black Irishman. Logically, I should think Melmoth would have attempted to seduce him. But Melmoth was a cool one.

The officer said, "I'm sorry, but we happen to be very certain that it's true."

He then told how Melmoth had gotten very drunk one night and had put the make on some boys at another house, and how, having failed with them, he had gone up to the dormitory and made advances to one of our own "brothers."

Well, it was decided that Melmoth must not only leave the fraternity at once, but also his job and the town. Within a week, he had gone from the scene and I don't think I've ever heard of his subsequent fate.

More about Smitty, now.

About once a month I would hitchhike home to St. Louis—I mean to University City and to the apartment on Enright. It so happened that my sister Rose's room was available to Smitty and me one weekend, for Rose had gone to Barnes Hospital for a checkup. Her long period of mysterious indigestion—preceding her mental crack-up—had set in.

He and I shared her ivory bed, which was double. And all that night we lay sleepless; he embraced me tightly while pretending to be sleeping and I—the trembling, teeth-chattering bit.

Is a lifetime long enough to hold the regret that I have for that fantastically aborted but crazily sweet love-affair?

I decided yesterday that once again, as I did a few days ago and before then, I would take a role in *Small Craft Warnings*, the part of Doc, as a way to draw

people to the play. After the performance, I escorted
Candy Darling to a nearby bistro named P. J. Clarke's.
The party grew to about eight. And during our supper,
there, I got a bit high on wine and I said, "You know,
I only sleep alone nowadays. You see, I'm such a light
sleeper that anyone else in the room would keep me
awake . . ."

"I'm like that, too," said Candy. We exchanged com-
miserating glances.

I said a lot of other stuff, mostly about my faith in
God and in prayer, but my paradoxical disbelief in an
after-existence. I also said that I believed in angels
more than I did in God and the reason was that I had
never known God—true or false?—but that I had
known several angels in my life.

What?

"Oh, I mean human angels," I explained. And that is
true for sure . . .

My return to "the boards" as Doc last evening was a
distinct letdown. I am no longer the capacity draw
that I was during my first stint at the New Theatre,
when I followed my performances with the "symposi-
ums." At the first return performance, Tuesday evening, we did have a full house, and a certain
exhilaration at being back in action as actor carried
me through the evening, despite a few fluffs, with a
degree of bravura.

Yesterday evening, though, I was immediately de-
flated, upon entering the men's dressing room, by Brad
Sullivan, who plays the pathetically boastful stud, Bill.
Sullivan has always had a tendency to put me down,
at least so it seems to me, and I don't understand why.
I've always treated him with an easy and amiable in-
formality, a manner of behavior toward the cast that
I've tried to establish since the start of rehearsals. I
must acknowledge that most of the others have responded in kind, that is, most of the time. Actually I
was closest, both in age and in spirit, to that fine actor,
David Hooks, whom I have replaced in Doc's part.

Now my return to the role has been a matter of box-office exigency. During those very hot summer weeks, business had dropped rather badly. Billy Barnes, my present agent, asked me if I would go back in the part since I had proved such a draw that single week when I appeared earlier in the summer.

But the bloom has worn off a bit. The house, last night, had noticeably shrunken in size and perhaps it was apparent to the actors that I was not going to be the draw I'd been before. At intervals, Gene Fanning, who plays Monk, complained about my opening monologue saying that it was not "conversational" enough. This was not quite fair in my opinion, and I was much disenchanted with Gene, who had always been so helpful to me in previous performances. After all, I was laboring under double jeopardy. I had been continually told that I did not project sufficiently and must always "cheat" toward the front of the house. However, I would always relate to Gene by quick glances at him. The stage manager also gave me a bad time. He said that I had left out some important bits. It was true that I had made a couple of one- or two-line cuts in my expanded role, but the cuts were not important and, without Gene's assistance, I believe that I covered them up and possibly the talky play was improved by these deletions.

Bill Hickey was my only male defender now, though Patrick Bedford was, as always, very friendly to me. But I was—probably out of wounded ego—quite annoyed after the performance and I said, with only a surface jocularity, that from now on I would use the ladies' dressing room or the separate room devised for Candy Darling—who, being a transvestite, had been given special quarters. She is, by the way, becoming my closest friend in the cast.

I left the theatre in costume, going to Candy's room before leaving and asking her to go with me to Joe Allen's restaurant, a night spot for theatre people on West Forty-sixth, which she had mentioned favorably the night before. She dressed up in a glamorous fifties style, with her very becoming blond wig, on which she placed a black velvet cloche hat with brilliants over her forehead.

We must have made quite an entrance at Joe Allen's, since Candy is over six feet tall and I only five foot six. And I had on my "planter's hat," a thirty-dollar Stetson with wide upswept brims which I had bought to wear in the play.

We were cordially received by the manager and we had a nice talk. Candy recited a poem she'd written called "Stardust" and it was very touching. We talked about our private lives, the loneliness of them, our difficulties "with men." Then I took her home—her duplex apartment next to the Christian Science church (from which she says she gets good vibes) —and when I took her to the entrance of the apartment, she invited me to come up but I declined. I was tired and didn't want another drink.

My third year at the University of Missouri was relatively colorless. My adored Smitty did not return to school at all, and the roommate I had was of no interest to me. In the spring of that year, I had a poignant and innocent little affair with a very charming girl named Anna Jean. My feeling for her was romantic. She was very pretty, she lived just across the street at the Alpha Chi Omega sorority and she had a delightful sense of humor. I wrote a little poem about her, well, I think several. Here's one:

> Can I forget
> the night you waited
> beside your door—
> could it have been more
> plainly stated?—
> for something more.

You spoke a rhyme
about young love
while we stood
breathing the rain-sweet
fragrance
of the wood.

I was a fool, not
knowing what
you waited for.
And then you smiled
and quietly
shut the door.

This was to be my final year at this first of three
universities. My grades were good in English and one
or two other subjects, but I flunked out of ROTC and
got poor grades in several other courses.

When I came home, Dad announced that he could
no longer afford to keep me in college and that he was
getting me a job in a branch of the International Shoe
Company.

This job was to last for three years, from 1931 to
1934. I received the wage of sixty-five dollars a month
—it was the depression.

Well, truly, I would take nothing for those three
years because I learned, during them, just how disgraceful, to the corporations, is the fate of the white-
collar worker.

I got the job because Dad had procured for the top
boss his position at the Continental Shoemakers
branch. (This was still before the poker game and the
decline and fall of "Big Daddy.") Of course the bosses
were anxious to find an excuse to get me out. They
put me to the most tedious and arduous jobs. I had to
dust off hundreds of shoes in the sample rooms every
morning; then I had to spend several hours typing out
factory orders. Digits, nothing but digits! About four in

the afternoon, I was dispatched to the establishment of our main client, J. C. Penney, with great packing cases of shoes for their acceptance or rejection. The cases were so heavy that it was a strain to lift them: I could carry them only half a block before having to set them down to catch my breath.

Still, I learned a lot there about the comradeship between co-workers at minimal salary, and I made some very good friends, especially a Polish fellow named Eddie, who sort of took me under his wing, and a girl named Doretta, with whom Eddie was infatuated. Then there was the spinster at the desk next to mine, little plump Nora. While we worked we carried on whispered conversations about the good movies and stage shows in town and the radio shows such as "Amos and Andy."

My first year there I came of age and I registered and I cast my first and last political vote. It was for Norman Thomas: I had already turned Socialist, and for reasons already made clear.

Hazel was still in school in Wisconsin. She was singing on the radio with considerable success. I continued to see her mother, Miss Florence, at least once a week.

I started writing at night. I would write and complete one story a week and mail it, as soon as I finished, to the distinguished story magazine called *Story*. It was the time when the young Saroyan had made a sensation in that magazine with "The Daring Young Man on the Flying Trapeze." At first the editors encouraged me with little personal notes of criticism. But soon I began to receive those dreadful "form" rejections.

I had Saturday afternoons off from my job at Continental. I had an unvarying regime for those lovely times of release. I would go to the Mercantile Library, far downtown in St. Louis, and read voraciously there; I would have a thirty-five-cent lunch at a pleasant little restaurant. And I would go home in a "service car"—to concentrate upon the week's short story. Of course all of Sunday was devoted to the story's completion.

During the weekdays I would work on verse: quite undistinguished, I fear, and upon one occasion I knocked out what is probably the most awful sonnet ever composed. It strikes me, now, as comical enough to be quoted in full.

I see them lying sheeted in their graves,
All of the women poets of this land,
Each in her own inscrutable small cave,
Song reft from lip and pen purloined from hand.
And no more vocal, now, than any stone,
Less aureate, in fact, now, than winter weed,
This thing of withered flesh and bleached bone
That patterned once beauty's immortal creed.
Rudely death seized and broke proud Sappho's lyre,
Barrett and Wylie went their songless way.
He does not care what hecatomb of fire
Is spilt when shattering the urn of clay.
Yet, Death, I'll pardon all you took away
While still you spare me glorious Millay.

My work in the short-story form, then confined to weekends and spurred by strong coffee, was considerably better, and most of these stories are preserved in the archives of the University of Texas.

The onset of my cardiovascular condition occurred in the spring of 1934, and it is a condition which has remained with me ever since, in greatly varying degrees, sometimes not enough to draw my attention but other times sufficient to become an obsession.

The first dramatic onset of this condition, in the spring of 1934, was triggered by two things. First, the quite unexpected marriage of Hazel to a young man named Terrence McCabe, whom she had been dating at the University of Wisconsin. I felt as though the sky had fallen on me, and my reaction was to start working every evening on short stories, overcoming fatigue with black coffee.

One evening I was at work on a story titled "The Accent of a Coming Foot," perhaps the most mature short story that I undertook in that period. I had arrived at a climactic scene when I suddenly became aware that my heart was palpitating and skipping beats.

Having no means of sedation, not even a glass of wine, I did a crazy thing: I jumped up from the typewriter and rushed out onto the streets of University City. I walked faster and faster as though by this means I could outdistance the attack. I walked all the way from University City to Union Boulevard in St. Louis, expecting to drop dead at each step. It was an instinctual, an animalistic reaction, comparable to the crazed dash of a cat or dog struck by an automobile, racing round and round until it collapses, or to the awful wing-flopping run of a decapitated chicken.

This was in the middle of March. The trees along the streets were just beginning to bud, and somehow, looking up at those bits of springtime green as I dashed along, had a gradually calming effect—and I turned toward home again with the palpitations subsiding.

I did not mention this experience to any member of the family but the following Monday I consulted a doctor who informed me that I had high blood-pressure and a heart defect of unspecified nature.

Still I said nothing to the family and I continued to work each day at the shoe company.

That weekend my sister and I went downtown to see a movie, *The Scarlet Pimpernel,* with Leslie Howard. I was too tense to pay much attention to the film. Afterwards, we took a service car home, a phenomenon of city transportation in the depression era. It cost fifteen cents a passenger from downtown St. Louis to suburban University City.

As we progressed along Delmar Boulevard toward University City, my tension steadily increased and a very alarming symptom occurred. I lost sensation in my hands, the fingers stiffened and my heart pounded.

When we were approaching St. Vincent's Hospital, I leaned forward and said to the driver, "Please take me to the hospital entrance, I am having a heart attack or a stroke."

I stayed in the heart ward for a week or ten days. It was when I returned home that Rose had her first mental disturbance of an obvious nature . . .

I remember her wandering into my small room and saying, "Let's all die together."

The suggestion did not appeal to me in the least.

Within a week, I had submitted my resignation to Dad's friend, Mr. Fletcher of Continental Shoemakers, and had received a politely phrased acknowledgment of it: "Best wishes for an early return to health. We have all appreciated your *many sterling qualities*" (my own italics). I do wish I had that letter to frame it in silver . . .

It was decided by the folks that I should spend a summer recuperating with Grand and Grandfather at their little home in Memphis.

And so, as a twenty-fourth birthday gift, I received a permanent release from the wholesale shoe business in St. Louis, and my first full opportunity to approach maturity in my "sullen art and craft," as Dylan Thomas described the vocation of writing. In my own case, it was oftentimes a desperate commitment, but I have never found anything very sullen about it. Even the best of poets can sometimes put a thing rather badly, as did Stephen Spender when he spoke of "the evening's grave demand for love." What's grave about the genital itch? No matter how romantic one is, the urge to "lay knife aboard" can hardly be regarded as a thing of gravity, confined to the evening hours, as though it were Evensong in a high Episcopal church. *Chacun, chacun,* perhaps some poets confuse it with kneeling in prayer before the high altar: maybe a practical position, at times, but hardly the right place.

And so I'm a clown today. I fear it results from reading over my funny melodrama *Kingdom of Earth,* which Michael Kahn has promised to revive at Princeton to which he will transfer his fine directorial gifts from The American Shakespeare and Hot Cat Theatre at Stratford, Connecticut.

Everything is next season, next season, and I feel as if next week were all but impossibly remote!

I wish to God I had the spirit of Bricktop. She was the surprise guest at Chuck Bowden's dinner party night before last. It was her eightieth birthday: she entered the apartment singing *"Quiéreme Mucho,"* the song which I always requested her to sing at her club on the Via Veneto of Rome. Then she sang many other favorites of mine and her voice, her enunciation of words and her phrasing are as lovely as ever.

Michael Moriarty also sang to his own accompaniment on the piano and I still consider him our most promising young dramatic actor . . .

Jim Dale of *Scapino* sang and played a song of his own composition, *molto con brio.*

My first play was produced when I was 24 years old and staying in my grandparents' home in Memphis the summer of 1934. This play (*Cairo, Shanghai, Bombay!*) was successfully produced by The Rose Arbor Players, a little-theatre group, in Memphis. Grand and Grandfather Dakin had a pleasant little house on Snowden Avenue. It was a block or two from Southwestern University and less than that distance from the residence of Knolle Rhodes and his wife and mother and cat. Professor Rhodes and his little family were great friends of ours. They were Virginians of the first rank. Later on Professor Rhodes became the president of the university: in the summer of 1934 he was, I believe, head of the English Department. He got me access to the library of the university and I spent most of those summer afternoons reading there, or at the downtown library on Main Street.

That summer I fell in love with the writing of Anton Chekhov, at least with his many short stories. They introduced me to a literary sensibility to which I felt a very close affinity at that time. Now I find that he holds too much in reserve. I still am in love with the delicate poetry of his writing and *The Sea Gull* is still, I think, the greatest of modern plays, with the possible exception of Brecht's *Mother Courage*.

It has often been said that Lawrence was my major literary influence. Well, Lawrence was, indeed, a highly *simpatico* figure in my literary upbringing, but Chekhov takes precedence as an influence—that is, if there has been any particular influence beside my own solitary bent—toward what I am not yet sure and probably never will be . . .

Last night Donald Madden reminded me of my promise to do a new adaptation of *The Sea Gull* (both of us feel it has never been let out of the confines of the translation straitjacket, not even by Stark Young) and of my longing to direct it, sometime, with Madden in the role of Trigorin, Anne Meacham as Nina or Mme. Arcadina—

But last night I shook my head a little at this reminder of that ambitious project: I said—no self-pity —I don't think I have time, now, to undertake anything of a writing nature but this "thing," my memoirs, and possibly the final version of *Milk Train* for Michael York and Angela Lansbury . . .

In that summer of 1934, when I first became a playwright, there lived next door to my grandparents in Memphis a family of Jews with a very warmhearted and actively disposed daughter named Bernice Dorothy Shapiro. She was a member of a little dramatic club in Memphis. Their productions took place on the

great sloping back lawn of a lady named Mrs. Rosebrough, which accounts for the "Rose Arbor" name of
that cry of players. Dorothy wanted me to collaborate
with her on a play for the group—she knew that I
was a writer and she wasn't. I wrote a play called
*Cairo, Shanghai, Bombay!*—a farcical but rather
touching little comedy about two sailors on a date
with a couple of "light ladies." Bernice Dorothy
Shapiro wrote a quite unnecessary and, I must confess,
undistinguished prologue to the play. Thank God the
prologue was short: that's all I can remember in its
favor.

The play was produced late that summer. It was not
long, either, but it was a great success for the group.
On the program I was identified as the collaborator
and was given second billing to Dorothy. Still, the
laughter, genuine and loud, at the comedy I had written enchanted me.

Then and there the theatre and I found each other
for better and for worse.

I know it's the only thing that's saved my life.


During that same summer of 1934 in Memphis,
when I started to realize fully an attraction I had
long suspected, to writing for the theatre, I also began
to realize more fully an attraction, also suspected for
some time, to young men. And, the delicacy of my
physical nature.

One afternoon I went out with two young university
students who had become friends of Grandfather.
They were exceptionally handsome: one was dark,
the other a shining blond.

In retrospect, I realize that they must have been
lovers. They took me out to a lake near Memphis
where there was a swimming-beach—and, well, the
love-bug bit me in the form of erotic longings for the
blond. I believe the interest was reciprocal, for one
evening he invited me to have dinner with him at the
Peabody Hotel restaurant. We had beers; I doubt that

the beer was the true cause of the palpitations that suddenly began to occur in my excitable heart. I went into panic and so did the blond. A doctor was summoned. The doctor was a lady, and an extremely bad doctor. She gave me a sedative tablet of some kind but informed me, gloomily, that my symptoms were, indeed, of a serious nature.

"You must do everything carefully and slowly," said this gloom-pot. She told me that with the exercise of care and a slow pace I would live to be forty!

"Oh, I'm so glad you told me that," said the poor blond, "he walks much too fast on the street for someone with a cardiac condition."

This incident resulted in a return of the cardiac neurosis which had begun to subside late that summer.

My first and last and only consummated sexual affair with a woman occurred after that, when I had returned for a year of college, in the Drama Department at the University of Iowa, the fall of 1937. The girl was, I suppose, a genuine nympho, and I'll call her Sally. She was not only a nympho but an alcoholic and she came on with me all of a sudden and like gangbusters, a little before my second long (semiprofessional) play, *Fugitive Kind,* was performed by the Mummers of St. Louis. That I was having a play performed in St. Louis gave me a certain panache that fall season at Iowa. Sally found me interesting for that reason, I suspect, although, also, I was not a badlooking young man. I had developed a slim swimmer's physique and the cataract in my left eye had not yet appeared. Sally had a sort of Etruscan profile, I mean the forehead and nose were on a straight line, the mouth full and sensual and her breath always pleasantly scented with tobacco and beer. She had a terrific build, especially her breasts, which were about the most prominent on the campus.

One evening that early fall she borrowed an apartment from a friend, for the purpose of my seduction. I

remember how all the right oldies came over the radio, like "Kiss Me Again," "Embraceable You," "Oh
Promise Me," and so forth, as if we'd requested them,
and we were soon on the sofa, naked, and I couldn't
get it up, no way, no way, and all of a sudden I felt
nauseated from the liquor consumed and from the
nervous strain and embarrassment. I rushed into the
bathroom and puked, came out with a towel around
me, hangdog with shame over my failed test of virility.

"Tom, you've touched the deepest chord in my nature, the maternal chord," she said.

The next night I took her home to the rooming-
house she lived in. She was wearing crimson ski-pants
and a white sweater with those great boobs standing
out. She turned out the light in the rooming-house
parlor and motioned me to the sofa.

Her caresses were wildly successful. She unzipped
the front of her ski pants and I fucked her with my
overcoat on. We were interrupted once or twice by
other roomers returning. She would zip up her pants
and I would button my coat but no one was much
fooled and no one cared, for it was a raffish house.
The roomers would go upstairs at once and we would
at once return to our wild break-through of my virginal
status.

I took to it like a duck to water. She changed posi-
tions with me, she got on top of me and rode my cock
like a hobbyhorse and then she came and I'd never
imagined such a thing, all that hot wet stuff exploding
inside her and about my member and her gasping
hushed outcries.

I was not yet in love with Sally but terribly impressed with myself. I got home long after midnight. I
went straight to the men's room at the ATO house.
Another brother was peeing as I peed, and I said, "I
fucked a girl tonight."

"Yeh, yeh, how was it?"

"Oh, it was like fucking the Suez Canal," I said,
and grinned and felt a man full grown.

Then it was every night for about two and a half or three months before the start of the Christmas holidays. We repeated the same scene with more and more satisfaction on both sides, I believe. I learned how to hold back my orgasm. But in those days I could have one and still keep it up.

There was the weekend interval of my play's opening, put on by the Mummers, a semi-pro theatre I worked with in St. Louis.

Then I got my first taste of blood drawn by critics.

It was a much better and more promising play than the first long play, *Candles to the Sun,* but the critics put it down. Afterward there was a desperately drunk party in someone's downtown hotel room. I made a sudden dash for a window but was tackled and I cannot say reliably whether or not it was my intention to jump.

The point is that I already knew that writing was my life, and its failure would be my death . . .

I had wonderful friends in those days and I think I deserved them because I responded so warmly to any warmth that was offered. Sally consoled me, showing not the least disappointment in the flop of *Fugitive Kind.* Things went on as before between us.

One night she said to me, in a whisper on that living-room sofa, "Tom, I want to show you something."

She started to go down but I was shocked and wouldn't let her.

Then the last night before vacation for Christmas, we took a room in a shady hotel in town and spent our first night naked in bed together. Somehow it was a bit of a comedown from our nights on her rooming-house sofa. She had her beer under the bed and kept drinking between love-making and her breath turned a little sour.

When we'd slept a while and woke up and I tried to kiss her, she said, "No, no, baby, I've got a mouth full of old chicken feathers."

When I returned from the holidays she wouldn't see me. She said something had happened and she'd tell me later. It was several days later when we met again that she told me she was pregnant.

I didn't believe her. I suspected she was dating a new boy and I was right.

It was a short affair, but a very deep one we'd had and I think that she had loved me as long as I'd satisfied her but now she was with a real stud and she was letting me out.

I had, during all that time I was involved with Sally and for months afterward, no interest in a member of my own sex.

After she had irrevocably dismissed me in favor of the new stud, I tried to date other girls.

Somehow I didn't manage.

There were two very beautiful young men who acted in a play at the University Theatre, a dramatization of a Jane Austen novel. One was the actor Walter Fleishman, as he was called then, who actually, some years later, made a screen debut in the film based on the life of Valentino. He had a fantastically perfect body. The other beautiful young actor in the Jane Austen play, based on *Pride and Prejudice*, asked me to have dinner with him one night—he was troubled over something, he said, and he didn't know how to tell me what it was. But after a few beers he did.

"Y'know, I went in Fleishman's bedroom last night and he was in there naked and I—well, I—I don't know how to tell you but I felt something like I wanted to touch him like a man does a woman, y'know."

He kept his long-lashed eyes on the table. His face was beautifully flushed.

I had an ideal opening and I suspect he had intended to give me one.

When I finally spoke, I said to him, "There's nothing about it to be upset over."

"It isn't a natural thing," he whispered.

"Yes, it is," I said. "It's a perfectly natural thing and you're just being silly."

I walked him home to his dormitory and we shook hands good night.

It was to secure a private place in which Sally and I could make love that I had elected to share an apartment with an outrageous young Middle Eastern student, whom I'll call "Abdul."

"Abdul" was a notorious girl-chaser and he had gotten in bad with the local police because of his intemperate tactics.

However, when I was looking around for an apartment, he had one which he wanted to share. He was a scrawny, dark young man and the apartment was not attractive, naturally, and it was always filled with the odor of his cooking, a strong, sweetish odor.

He was a good enough companion except that he would sometimes come home all liquored up and inform me that when he was drunk he'd just as soon fuck a girl or a boy or a goat: he once tried to enter my bed and encountered savage resistance which persuaded him that I was no willing substitute for girls and goats.

One night he was arrested and he called the apartment and begged me to come to the lockup and obtain his release. Fortunately he had the money for the fine. I went to the jailhouse and he was in the tank with a bleary-eyed bewhiskered old alcoholic and Abdul was trying to communicate with him. He kept shouting at him, "You pees, too? You pees, too?"

It seemed that on this occasion Abdul had been arrested for pissing in an alley behind a bar.

My efforts to entice Sally to the apartment were only once successful and she came with her new boyfriend, which seemed a bit like rubbing Siberian salt in my wounds as she could not keep her hands off him during the dinner prepared by Abdul.

She did allow me a few minutes of private talk in an alcove.

"I love you, Tom, and I don't want to hurt you, sweetheart, but I'm just no good, I'm not pregnant, I made that story up, in fact I've lost one ovary from an operation, but the point is I'm a sex-fiend, I want it from one after another and I'd fuck up your life."

She let me kiss her and hold her for a moment, then she returned to her new young man. I was desolate, for a while. But then I became a close friend of a young man named Lomax and his Negro girl-friend; they were marvelous companions and were also in the school of drama.

I had been cast as a page boy in *Richard of Bordeaux* and they said they'd make me up for it. They painted my cheeks, rouged my lips and tousled my hair into curls. Then Lomax put me into my page-boy outfit and brought me in for the black girl's inspection.

"See what I mean?" he asked her. I wasn't sure what he meant. Then I looked in the mirror and I knew. I looked like a young girl . . .

In the page boy's part I had only one line. I had not recovered from my dreadful shyness. Throughout the scene in which I appeared I had to sit on the fore-stage, polishing a helmet, all the while my throat getting tighter and tighter with apprehension at delivering that one line. I simply had to say that somebody had arrived at the gates. But when my cue came, the sound that issued from my constricted throat was quite unintelligible and would always bring down the house —it was like a mouse's squeak. They said it was effective, however. I suspect, though, that I was merely on the stage because I looked so well in the make-up applied by Lomax.

I recall having one other part on the stage of the great theatre at the University of Iowa. It was in a play about the Penitentes and I was drafted into a scene of flagellation among the young monks. I'll never forget one line from the show, home-written on the campus. An actor was floundering bare-shouldered about the stage, lashing himself with his whip and he cried out loudly, "Tonight there will be much glory in the Morada" (the Morada being the subterranean chamber in which these flagellations were practiced).

The Christ figure, the one who performed as victim with the ritual crucifixion, was Fleishman, the leading young actor that year. He was elevated nearly naked upon the cross—and it was his virile young beauty that drew me back toward my more predominant sexual inclination.

Sally began to fade out of my libido.

Others of my own gender began to fade in.

Once during the rehearsals for *Richard of Bordeaux,* Lemuel Ayers, who was a postgraduate student at Iowa and who had, like myself, fallen into the displeasure of E. C. Mabie, head of the Drama Department, was walking around the men's locker room quite naked before a performance. He was like a young saint out of Italian renaissance painting—darkly gleaming curls, and a perfectly formed body.

Once we had met at dusk in a tiny zoo on a hill. No one was around. There was, just at the moment we saw each other, a great flutter of wings.

"What's that?"

"Guinea hens roosting," he answered.

We lingered a while, which I would have liked to prolong, but Lem, I suspect, was accustomed to more aggressive types, and he smiled and he drifted away.

It was a lonely spring. So much of my money had gone into the apartment with Abdul that I had, for a month, to live almost entirely on eggs, of which there was a surplus that season, which made them very cheap. I still like eggs, though now they're forbidden me because of my high cholesterol count, but they do get unpalatable after a while when you have to eat them exclusively.

Then I met this marvelously lively young Irish companion and he used to take me on long canoe rides upon the river Iowa; then he would bring us to a secluded nook where we would sing Irish ballads. And there was a carnival in town and he took me there, too.

I'd lost interest in studies and so I failed that term and had to stay over for the summer term to get my degree. The summer term I was almost continually with Lomax and his lovely black girl-friend.

I felt no interest in getting a degree, I didn't want to get out of college. We were in the depression.

Two dreadful things occurred: Rose was submitted to a lobotomy, one of the first performed in the States, and my Aunt Belle died in Knoxville, the result of an infected wisdom tooth the poison of which had permeated her system.

Aunt Ella wrote, "Your poor Aunt Belle was surrounded by a solid wall of prayer but Death got through."

I was just beginning to write well in an individual style. I remember writing there the story "The Malediction" and a number of nice little poems.

When the summer term ended and I had my diploma, Lomax and his black girl-friend invited me to go to Chicago with them, saying that I could get on the WPA writers' project up there. What we did was meet some fantastic black fags who were entertaining in a wild night club. I remember one particularly exuberant one who remarked, "You know, I take the sheets every trip"—meaning he loved playing the passive role in sodomy. I tried to get on that WPA project and I was rejected because I could not say my family was destitute. I had only about ten dollars to carry me through the time there, and so I had to wire home for money to get me back to the house in St. Louis County.

Clark Mills McBurney was home in St. Louis, from Paris, and we picked up our friendship; it was a lively summer. There were other friends, and picnics along the Meramec River and almost continual diversions. Dad allowed me to take out the family Studebaker a good many times: he was still trying to overcome my dreadful shyness of him. I was important to Dad because I was the namesake of his own father, Thomas Lanier Williams II.

While I'm fairly close to the subject of Iowa University, let me tell you about old E. C. Mabie, who headed the Drama Department there. For a good many years Mabie had suffered from an inoperable brain tumor that was said to be benign but that affected his behavior at times in a very erratic fashion.

He was dedicated to that great new theatre plant he'd had built on the Iowa campus and he would always attend the final rehearsal of an impending show.

One night the show about to open was in such deplorable shape that Mabie was enraged. He took off his glasses and hurled them at the actors and then he kept them rehearsing all night until the production had been revamped to suit him.

Mabie was prejudiced against me and against Lemuel Ayers. He used to hint that Ayers, who'd come as a postgraduate from Princeton, was a fag—which indeed I suspect he could have been, but a very talented and very nice fag and quite undeserving of Mabie's persecution.

(This is parenthetical, but one night—years later, in 1943—while I was staying on the West Coast working for MGM, not working for them but receiving the salary they were legally obliged to pay me each week —Lem Ayers invited me to spend the night at his charming little house in Beverly Hills. When I woke in the morning it was to the enchanting vision of Lem, quite naked, wandering along the upstairs hall. He greeted me cordially. Of course I had my cue right in mind: "Come on in, Lem, I've seen you naked before." But shyness prevented me and that last golden chance escaped me for *toujours* . . .

Lem really was about as beautiful a young man with an available disposition as I've ever laid eyes on, without attempting seduction—with the possible exception of . . . no, a bit of discretion's in order.

How can I honestly say, *"Je ne regrette rien"*—in the words of the "Little Sparrow" of Montmartre . . . ?)

That single summer at Iowa, I was still lonely, and I took to wandering aimlessly about the streets at night to escape the stifling heat of my room. There were many great trees and the town had an old-fashioned charm. At night it almost seemed Southern. I was lonely and frightened, I didn't know the next step. I was finally fully persuaded that I was "queer," but had no idea what to do about it.

I didn't even know how to accept a boy on the rare occasions when one would offer himself to me.

Yesterday, Saturday, I did a most remarkable thing for me, and one that was really delightful. In the company of a young friend, I spent about five hours strolling about Central Park, which we entered at the "gay" corner of Seventy-second and Central Park West. We bought lemon and cherry ices and we strolled out upon the area across the lake that is all but exclusively pre-empted by the homos. And they're quite a nice and personable lot in the daytime. They have cast off, I noticed, most of the swish and camp that made them, when assembled in such numbers, unattractive to me. I enjoyed the company of the "camps" at one time when I was young and lived at the "Y." But my closest friends, though as capable of camp as I was, then, were not the "obvious" types.

I did know some very obvious types in New Orleans, however, when I first "came out." There was, for instance, one whom I'll call Antoine who walked about the streets of the French Quarter with a tiny cut-glass bottle of smelling salts in liquid form and at the approach of a woman or girl, would stop and lean against a wall with the stricken whisper of *"Poisson"*—and sniff his counteractive vial until the lady had passed;

and even then he would affect a somewhat shattered condition . . .

I found him hilarious, but Antoine had a serious and gifted side to him, like most of our kind. He was not a brilliant painter but he had a distinctive and highly effective flair which later made him a successful designer in New York.

I remember an evening when Antoine, who had a charmingly decorated apartment on Toulouse, presented his production of *Four Saints in Three Acts*—the cast all homosexuals—and they did not camp it but presented it with true style and it was the best evening of Stein I've yet experienced.

I also remember, when I returned to New Orleans after my first exposure to the more discreetly organized gay world of New York, proselytizing my "gay" friends in the Quarter to conduct themselves in a fashion that was not just a travesty of the other sex. I told them, those who would listen, that that type of behavior simply made them distasteful, sexually, to anyone interested in sex . . . and that it was "dated," as well.

Of course, "swish" and "camp" are products of self-mockery, imposed upon homosexuals by our society. The obnoxious forms of it will rapidly disappear as Gay Lib begins to succeed in its serious crusade to assert, for its genuinely misunderstood and persecuted minority, a free position in society which will permit them to respect themselves, at least to the extent that, individually, they deserve respect—and I think that degree is likely to be much higher than commonly supposed.

There is no doubt in my mind that there is more sensibility—which is equivalent to more talent—among the "gays" of both sexes than among the "norms" . . .

(Why? They must compensate for so much.)

Continuing along this happy mood of self-congratulation, I find that I've established or am in the process of establishing, a sort of personal following in New York. For instance, yesterday I stopped with a friend at a small and expensive men's shop. I found a beautiful copper-colored cotton-and-polyester suit that fit me with little alterations to be made. When I produced my charge-card the proprietor made a great fuss over me and, to prove its sincerity, he made me a gift of a thirty-dollar silk tie that went perfectly with the suit. I shall have on both at my appearance on the "Midday" talk show this coming Wednesday with Candy Darling, to promote *Small Craft Warnings*.

Despite my totally exhausted state after the night-owl show, at 10 P.M., of *Small Craft Warnings*, I went out with our star, Helena Carroll, to meet Donald Madden, the only actor beside Brando—no, that's not true, Michael York has now joined the select, making it a trio—for whom I have "written plays," or at least parts in plays, more than once. You see, I was still capable of falling in love in the sixties, and during the rehearsals of *In the Bar of a Tokyo Hotel*—despite my condition, which was verging on mental and physical collapse—I was "mad about the boy," Madden, but refrained from declaring it as he was involved in my work.

My feeling toward Madden has now settled sensibly into a platonic one based upon my very deep regard for him as an actor. I think there's no better actor in the States . . . (Perhaps Michael Moriarty will challenge that pre-eminence someday.)

# 4

I want to tell you about another pivotal love in my life, after Hazel and Sally, the first great male one. In the early summer of 1940 my friend Paul Bigelow put me on a train to Boston, whence I was to go to Provincetown, a place I'd barely heard of. I had finally managed to arbitrate from the Theatre Guild a regular Dramatists Guild contract for *Battle of Angels* in place of the half-rate "understanding" which they'd offered in the beginning: which means my preproduction stipend was now a hundred dollars a month instead of fifty. And I felt quite affluent. But Bigelow thought I'd best get out of town. In those days people were always putting me on trains or buses like I was a pawn in a chess game. Well, I must have wanted it that way. And that's the way I got it. How very kind they were to me, in those long ago days! That I do *mean*, you know . . .

From Boston I took the daily boat to P-town and there, the first few days, I stayed in a rooming-house, a charmingly casual old frame building with a swing on the verandah. The house was tenanted by equally charming and casual young people. There was a blond youth who succumbed to my precipitate courtship the first evening.

Yes, you see, now I had finally come thoroughly out of the closet; I was not a young man who would turn many heads on the street, this being before the vogue of blue jeans and T-shirts, which would have been to my advantage, since I had a good swimmer's physique. The pupil of my left eye had turned gray with that remarkably early cataract. And I was still very shy except when drunk. Oh, I was quite the opposite when I had a couple of drinks under the belt.

(In those days I used to cruise Times Square with another young writer who would prefer to remain unmentioned by name in this context, and he would dispatch me to street corners where sailors or GIs were grouped, to make very abrupt and candid overtures, phrased so bluntly that it's a wonder they didn't slaughter me on the spot. I would just go up to them and say, [Deleted by author]—sometimes they mistook me for a pimp soliciting for female prostitutes and would respond, "Sure, where's the girls?"—and I would have to explain that they were my cruising partner and myself. Then, for some reason, they would stare at me for a moment in astonishment, burst into laughter, huddle for a brief conference, and, as often as not, would accept the solicitation, going to my partner's Village pad or to my room at the "Y.")

Surely this adequately covers, to say the least, the deviant satyriasis with which I was happily afflicted in those early Manhattan years of my life. Sexuality is an emanation, as much in the human being as the animal. Animals have seasons for it. But for me it was a round-the-calendar thing.

I wonder, sometimes, how much of the cruising was for the pleasure of my cruising partner's companionship and for the sport of pursuit and how much was actually for the pretty repetitive and superficial satisfactions of the act itself. I know that I had yet to experience in the "gay world" the emotion of love, which transfigures the act to something beyond it. I have known many gays who live just for the act, that "rebellious hell" persisting into middle life and later, and it is graven in their faces and even refracted from their wolfish eyes. I think what saved me from that was my first commitment being always to work. Yes, even when love did come, work was still the primary concern.

During the summer of 1940, the first month of it, in Provincetown, at the frolicsome tip of the Cape, I had encountered the blond kid on the verandah of a frame rooming-house. There is a magic about a frame rooming-house with a verandah and a porch swing, whether it be North or South. And it is *l'heure bleue,* so flattering to blonds.

I have seated myself beside the blond kid on the front porch swing. The dusk obscures my opaque iris of the left eye, and I don't think it took me more than ten minutes to convince him, despite his protestations of being "straight," that his life would not be complete until he'd passed an evening in my embrace.

(There's a line in *Streetcar* which belongs to Blanche. Mitch has told her he'd thought that she was "straight," and she has replied, "What is straight? A line can be straight, or a street, but the human heart, oh, no, it's curved like a road through mountains!")

Lechery possessed me, still under thirty, that summer of 1940. And it was approaching a climax.

The blond kid was just a one-night lay, an evanescent bit of trivial music.

However . . .

It must have been only two or three days later that I encountered Kip on Captain Jack's Wharf in P-town.

Some casual acquaintance took me to the wharf one noonday, clear and blue. At the stove of a little two-story shack on this wharf built on stilts over the incoming, outgoing tides was the youth to whom I dedicated my first collection of short stories. He had his back to me, as I entered, since he was facing the stove, up-stage, preparing clam chowder, New England style, the dish on which he and his young (platonic) friend Joe were subsisting that summer through economic need. He was wearing dungarees, skin-tight, and my good eye was hooked like a fish. He was too preoccupied by the chowder-cooking to more than glance over his shoulder and say "hello." The other tenant of the shack was a youth named Joe who was into Oriental dancing. Kip was into modern dancing. And when he turned from the stove, I might have thought, had I been but a little bit crazier, that I was looking at the young Nijinsky. Later he was to tell me, with a charmingly Narcissan pride, that he had almost the same bodily dimensions of Nijinsky, as well as a phenomenal facial resemblance. He had slightly slanted lettuce-green eyes, high cheekbones, and a lovely mouth. But I will never forget the first look I had at him, standing with his back to me at the two-burner stove, the wide and powerful shoulders and the callipygian ass such as I'd never seen before! He didn't talk much. I think he felt my vibes and was intimidated by their intensity.

It was only a few days later that Joe and Kip invited me to share their two-story shack on Captain Jack's Wharf in P-town. A cot was provided for me downstairs, alongside Joe's.

The wharf was fully occupied. A few doors away was an attractive girl in her late twenties who invited us to dinner one evening. Her radio played "Sweet Leilani." It blew my mind. I remember that cornily seductive Hawaiian song—and a bit later Kip and I were alone in the downstairs of the two-story shack and I, with crazed eloquence, was declaring to him my desire. He was silent a few moments and then said, "Tom, let's go up to my bedroom."

The bedroom was a small loft with a great window that held in it all one half of the night sky.

No light was turned on or off as Kip removed his clothes. Dimly, he stood there naked with his back to me.

After that, we slept together each night on the double bed up there, and so incontinent was my desire for the boy that I would wake him repeatedly during the night for more love-making. You see, I had no sense in those days—and nights—of how passion can wear out even a passive partner.

And just at this time my old habit of blushing when looking into the eyes of another person came back and it was a torment that made the days difficult but was exorcised by the fog-dimmed nights in the bedroom-loft.

I remember that the first day after the first night, when we were crossing the dunes to the ocean-side cabin of a dance critic, Kip and I lingered behind the others in the party and Kip said to me, "Last night you made me know what is meant by beautiful pain."

In that loft I wrote my only verse play, "The Purification"—I had set up a little writing-table, a wooden box with my portable on it, and in that play I found a release, in words, of the ecstasy of the affair. And also a premonition of its doom.

All at once Kip turned oddly moody. We would go places together and he would suddenly not be there, and when he came to bed, after an absence of some hours, he'd explain gently, "I had a headache, Tenn."

I had a wire that called me back to Manhattan for a week in July. I resumed the tenancy of a little apartment shared with Donald Windham and Fred Melton, for that week, and I wrote poem after poem for Kip. When the business matters were concluded at the end of that week, I returned straight away to P-town.

It seems to me now, in retrospect, that Kip had shyly discussed with me the difficulty of supporting himself in America, being a Canadian draft-dodger with no identity that he dared reveal to any employer except a sympathetic sculptor who used him as a model for his classes. And it seems that I had mistakenly assured him that I might be—in the fall—in an economic position to relieve him of all anxieties on that score. That was very likely the understanding between us.

I know Kip loved me, after his bewildered fashion. And I also know it couldn't have been very easy to be waked up four or five times a night for repeated service of my desire.

This is not a way to write a love-story, I know.

Toward the end of August, a girl entered the scene. I did not regard her as a threat. And then one day I was on the dunes with a group that included the yet-unknown, or uncelebrated abstract painter, Jackson Pollock. Later on he was to become a "dark" man, outside his work, but that summer I remember him for his boisterous, just slightly drunk behavior. He was a sturdy, well-built young man, then, just a little bit heavier from beer-drinking than was attractive to me, and he used to carry me out into the water on his shoulders and to sport about innocently.

Oh, it was a golden time, that summer, everyone seemed lighthearted despite the war being on!

Well, one afternoon late that summer I was on the dunes with the group, when Kip appeared, looking very solemn.

"Tenn, I have to talk to you."

He rode me into P-town on the handle-bars of a bike, and on the way in, with great care and gentleness, he told me that the girl who had intruded upon the scene had warned him that I was in the process of turning him homosexual and that he had seen enough of that world to know that he had to resist it, that it violated his being in a way that was unacceptable to him.

It was no longer tenable, the two-story shack—now that Kip wouldn't share the loft with me. So we moved into a larger two-story habitation which was not furnished except with three cots and a table and a few chairs.

I was in a state of shock. Kip observed a law of silence and of troubled remoteness.

I determined upon a course of action, flight to Mexico. In those days there was an advertised service by which someone desiring transportation by car to some other city—in this case, another country—could contact a driver going that way and arrange to share the expenses of the journey. I applied to that service, when I'd returned to Manhattan in my state of shock, and was quite speedily introduced to a young Mexican who had come to New York by car to see the 1940 World's Fair and who had married a prostitute in Manhattan and now was taking her home to meet his wealthy family in Mexico City. There was a total language barrier between this young lady and her Mexican bridegroom. She was a voluptuous piece and he was voluptuous, too, and when you say a man, a bridegroom, is voluptuous it's not a compliment to him.

We had a fantastic ride south. There were three other male Mexicans in the party and they took turns at the wheel. Sometimes a road map was produced but they couldn't follow it. We kept making involuntary detours from our route, some that took us hundreds of miles out of the way. I had come down with a terrible cough and was spitting up blood now and then but was quite unconcerned with that normally disconcerting symptom, could think only of whether or not a letter would be waiting for me from Kip at Wells Fargo in Mexico City.

As we gradually approached the Texas border, the prostitute-bride became increasingly nervous at the prospect of entering her husband's household and I soon got the impression that things were not working out very propitiously between the pair in the sack. She looked gloomier and more separate from her new spouse and his bachelor friends each day and she began to give me nervous glances and whisper to me hints of apprehension.

(I have never been frightened of Mexicans but my mother has a terror of them. Once when she was staying with me at a hotel in La Jolla, California, an old friend and I decided to take her across the border at

Tijuana. I didn't mention this intention until the car arrived at the International Customs. She then observed that she was entering, or about to enter, Mexico and she made a great disturbance. "Oh, no, oh, no, oh, *never!*" as if being assaulted, the heroine of an old-time melodrama, but we just ignored these protestations and drove on down. When we got her out of the car in Tijuana, she would flatten herself against the wall whenever an adult Mexican approached her, and we had to take her into the nearest restaurant and return Stateside immediately after dinner.)

Back from *that* little excursion to the situation on the honeymoon trip to Mexico, August 1940. We had checked into a motel in Monterey. I had settled down in a small, hot bedroom with a book on a bed enclosed by mosquito netting when there came a rap at the door: it was the bride.

She was near hysteria. "Honey, I don't know what I've got myself into. You know what I mean?"

I told her that I could imagine.

She then admitted that the marriage had yet to be consummated and other admissions and wails of trepidation continued for an hour. She had perched herself in an attitude of more and more permanency on my bed and at last I thought it best to inform her that I was quite ineligible as a surrogate for her bridegroom. And I told her why. She nodded sadly and there was a little respite of silence, during which perhaps the germ for *Kingdom of Earth* was first fecundated in my dramatic storehouse. At last she sighed and got up.

"I guess you're lucky, honey. Female hygiene's a lot more complicated than men's . . ."

When we arrived in Mexico City, the party deposited me at the YMCA. Such was my indifference to material matters that I left a lot of my clothes in the trunk of the car. And I think it must have been five or six years later that they were returned to me by the bride with a sweet note accompanying the package, mailed from Mexico City, expressing her happy recollections of the trip we'd enjoyed together.

There are so many gratuities of kindness in my life that I've never properly acknowledged.

I passed a lonely week, that August of 1940, at the Mexican "Y." Only one incident during the week returns to memory. I was once descending the stairs when I encountered an elderly American queen wearing make-up. She greeted me like a close friend of long standing and she soon invited me to visit her room and look at her album of souvenir photos. (The kind of photo collection called a fag's album.) There was one picture that I remember distinctly, it was a photograph of Glenway Wescott in the bloom of his youth, skinny-dipping in a mountain lake of very clear water.

After the week in the capital city, I went on to Taxco by bus. There I joined a group of American students who drove me to Acapulco. We arrived at dusk at a seaside resort called Todd's Place, charmingly primitive, and with a very rough surf. We went swimming that night with the surf roaring in. I contrived to be washed repeatedly against and over the most attractive one in the group. I think he got the general notion but could not be separated from his companions.

Later I was at the Hotel Costa Verde over the rainforest and the still-water beach which were the offstage background for *Night of the Iguana*. That summer much of Mexico was overrun by Nazi Germans. A party of them arrived at the Costa Verde, jubilant over the fire-bombing of London which was then in progress. There was an attractive girl in the party and I said "hello" to her one morning. She glared at me and growled, "Sorry, I don't speak Yiddish." Apparently she assumed that all Yankees were Jewish.

It was there in Acapulco that summer that I first met Jane and Paul Bowles. They were staying at a pension in town and Paul was, as ever, upset about the diet

and his stomach. The one evening that we spent together that summer was given over almost entirely to
the question of what he could eat in Acapulco that he
could digest, and poor little Janie kept saying, "Oh,
Bubbles, if you'd just stick to cornflakes and fresh
fruit!" and so on and so on. None of her suggestions
relieved his dyspeptic humor.

I thought them a very odd and charming couple.

That summer between swims I worked on the first
draft of a play called *Stairs to the Roof,* and enjoyed
long conversations with another young writer who had
just been forced to relinquish his residence in Tahiti
due to wartime conditions. We lay in adjoining ham-
mocks along the sleeping-verandah, drinking rum-
cocos and talking until the numbered cubicles were
cool enough to enter for sleep.

And some Mexican boys did catch an iguana and tie
it up under the verandah, to be fattened for eating—
but nobody cut it loose.

The check (advance royalties) from the Theatre
Guild was mysteriously delayed and delayed in the
mails. I think the proprietress of the Costa Verde was
about to bounce me when the check arrived without a
word of comment. It was not until I was on a bus back
across the border that I noticed in a theatre column of
the New York *Times* that Miss Miriam Hopkins had
been cast in *Battle of Angels* and that rehearsals were
about to begin.

Kip died at the age of twenty-six. It was just after I
had completed my professionally abortive connection
with MGM, and I had come through St. Louis and witnessed the death of Grand on the Feast of the
Epiphany, and had just arrived back in New York.

The phone rang one day and an hysterical lady
said, "Kip has ten days to live." A year before I had
been told that Kip had been successfully operated on
for a benign brain-tumor, and so I accepted her report
with shocked credence.

He was at the Polyclinic Hospital near Times Square.

You know how love bursts back into your heart when you hear of the loved one's dying.

Donald Windham accompanied me to the hospital for my visit, I was afraid to go alone. As I entered Kip's room he was being spoon-fed by a nurse: a dessert of sugary apricots. He had never looked more beautiful, although the sugar syrup dripped from his mouth. His wife was there, too. They were calmly discussing taking a trip to the West Coast in a train compartment.

Kip's mind seemed as clear as his Slavic blue eyes.

But his vision was limited.

"Tenn, sit there in the corner so I can see you."

(The range of vision is always very limited in terminal brain cancer cases, I believe.)

I sat there and he inquired about my life on the coast.

I longed to leap up from my corner and embrace him, but I observed the ritual of sprightly dissimulation.

"It seems that when I had that tumor cut out last year they left some sutures in my brain, and that's why I've had this setback."

"That's right," said the wife, as if confirming the statement of an infant.

"I'll be all right when they get the sutures out," said Kip.

But his eyes kept saying things to me that controverted the undignified prattle.

"Nothing went wrong till I started to stumble on the street."

"You won't anymore," said Wifie.

"Kip is tired," said the nurse.

I rose and reached for his hand and he couldn't find mine, I had to find his.

When Donnie and I left, we went straight to the nearest bar.

After several drinks, I went to a Japanese shop and bought Kip a lovely cream-colored Shantung robe and the next day I brought it to him.

"No visitors," it said on his door. Inside, it was deathly still.

"May I leave this for him?"

The wife, also excluded from the death room, nodded and took the parcel.

Kip's brother sent me, from Canada, snapshots of Kip posing for a sculptor and they remained in my wallet twenty-some years. They disappeared mysteriously in the sixties.

Well, Kip, you live in my leftover heart. How gentle and kind you were when you drove out to the beach at P-town, and told me to sit on the handle-bars and let you drive me home and on the way, how gently and honestly gently, you told me that our love-affair was finished, now, since it was turning you homo.

Have I told you how, when the girl who was Elaine (Tynan) Dundy's sister arrived to pick up Kip that summer in P-town, while I was on the balcony packing my gear to move out, I heaved one of my riding boots down at the lady: missed her, but not intentionally ... ?

I first met Tallulah Bankhead that same summer in Provincetown, before my flight to Mexico. She was the first actress I had thought of in connection with *Battle*, which I was then hoping might be produced, and she was playing in a Pinero play, I believe, at the Dennisport Playhouse. I rode a bicycle down from Provincetown to see her in the play and she was fabulous in it, very beautiful, and I was more than ever convinced that she should play the female lead in *Battle*. I went backstage and was introduced to her. She was all charm and said she would be delighted to read the play. However, I heard no more after that from Tallulah about the play. I'm glad, for Tallulah's sake, that she didn't land in *Battle*, but I'm sorry for poor Miriam Hopkins' sake because Miriam did. It was a disaster, of course, and poor Miriam had to bear the brunt of it, as did I.

When I knew her later, Tallulah always impressed me by her honesty and her gallantry and her lack of shame. It is a quality I have discovered in Southern ladies of a certain kind. There are certain kinds of Southern ladies who could be called tramps, if you want to use abusive language toward ladies. I suppose you could say Tallulah was a tramp, in the elegant sense. I remember she never wanted to interrupt a conversation for bodily functions, and if she was carrying on an animated conversation with me and had to pay a call of nature, she would ask me to accompany her into the bathroom and sit on the edge of the tub while she completed her story and the call of nature. This didn't shock me, in fact it delighted me by its forthrightness and lack of embarrassment. This is a quality that Anna Magnani also had. I guess you could say that Anna was also a Southern lady, although a Southern Italian lady. Well, I don't like ladies of excessive propriety, with the exceptions of my mother and sister. They were both victims of excessive propriety but naturally I find it easier to get along with ladies who not only tolerated but seemed to get along best with a very free way of life, excepting, of course, my sister.

Nobody has ever known Tallulah Bankhead. At least, they have never written about her in a way that showed any real comprehension of her nature. Tallulah was not a sexual animal. I think that sex was not a matter of any particular importance to her. She was a Narcissan, and one of the great humorists of our time, she was always one of the wittiest people I have ever known.

I will now tell you about the closing of a Broadway-bound play in Boston and the munificence of a firm of New York producers which was, at that time, the most prosperous in the American theatre and the most prestigious . . . oh, why be diffident about it, the surviving members of that firm couldn't care less now. It was the Theatre Guild, the play was, of course, *Battle of Angels,* and the time was around Christmas of 1940.

The play was pretty far out for its time and included, among other tactical errors, a mixture of super religiosity and hysterical sexuality coexisting in a central character. The critics and police censors seemed to regard this play as a theatrical counterpart of the bubonic plague surfacing in their city.

I was summoned to a suite at the Ritz-Carlton on Boston Common. All the big brass of the Guild was present, except their playreader, John Gassner, who had persuaded them to produce my play and was understandably absent. Among those present were the director, Miss Margaret Webster of the United Kingdom, dainty little Miss Theresa Helburn, of the light lavender hair, who was co-administrator of the Theatre Guild with Mr. Lawrence Langner, who founded it.

"We're closing the play," I was coolly informed.

"Oh, but you can't do that!" I cried out. "Why, I put my heart in this play!"

There was a slightly embarrassed pause before Miss Webster spoke up quite eloquently with this one-liner: "You must not wear your heart on your sleeve for daws to peck at."

Miss Helburn said, "At least you're not out of pocket."

Whereupon my agent, Audrey Wood, inquired, cannily, "What about money?"

The pause after that one-liner was less embarrassed than calculating.

I continued to gaze, I hope not piteously, at either Miss Helburn or Mr. Langner, and for the first time they gazed, or probably just glanced, at the unabashed face of my agent.

"Well, now," said Mr. Langner, "we'll give him a hundred dollars to go away somewhere and rewrite the play, and if it's submitted again in the spring, we will consider the rewrite for next season."

Financially, the situation was like this. I had run out of my thousand-dollar grant from the Rockefeller Foundation, my two-week Boston royalties did not quite cover those paid in advance, and I had just about train fare back to New York and my room at the "Y."

The hundred dollars looked big in this situation, since a dollar was worth a dollar in those days, and that hundred took me to Key West, Florida, where I met Marion Vaccaro and lived in a cabin behind her mother's boardinghouse, and worked like hell's hammers on the rewrite of *Battle*.

In the course of this thing I will deal with some of the humorous events in my long friendship with Marion Vaccaro; at one point though she was perhaps my most devoted friend and also the definition of a Southern lady. Her family came from Georgia. She was the daughter of an Episcopalian minister, Reverend George Black, who, I understand, was somewhat given to drink, and they had a rather itinerant life on that account. His stay in one parish was somewhat limited, let us say; they moved from parish to parish. Well, everyone knows how little money ministers earn. My grandfather Dakin, who was an Episcopal minister, earned a salary of one hundred dollars a month. Marion's father probably earned about the same, so she grew up under straitened circumstances. She received a scholarship to Smith College; she was a well-educated woman with fine taste in literature. Moreover, she was a very talented poet.

But she was so humble about her poetry that she made no provisions for its publication. George, her brother, who survives in Coconut Grove, had promised to send me her poetry and I was going to see that

it was published; but he didn't until just this year,
when he sent me a small portion of her earlier work.
Previously he gave me a wonderful portrait of Marion,
which hangs in my bedroom in Key West, and which
shows how she looked when I first met her in 1941.
Very lovely, with a piquant face. She was not a classic
beauty but she had great charm and animation. In
1941 her mother was running a very genteel boardinghouse in one of the great mansions of Key West, a
place called the Tradewinds. I met the Blacks and
Marion in January of that year when I went to Key
West for the first time, after the disaster of *Battle of
Angels* in Boston. I chose Key West, in fact, because
swimming was practically a way of life with me, and
since Key West was the southernmost point in America, I figured I would be able to swim there while I
was rewriting *Battle*. Well, I had a very good friend,
Jim Parrott, the kid who was with me on the squab
ranch in Laguna and who in 1941 was living in Miami. He was a lovely guy, not a homosexual. I might
say that it would be incorrect if, whenever I mention a
man, the inference be drawn that he is a homosexual.
I assure you that I have known and liked many men
who weren't. Anyway, I saw Jim in Miami first and he
drove me down to Key West, and we pulled up at this
very, very handsome frame house—it was made of
solid mahogany—and it had verandahs on all four
sides, downstairs and upstairs, and it had what I think
they called a captain's walk on the roof. A fabulously
beautiful building. Unfortunately it fell victim to an
arsonist after the Blacks gave it up. But in 1941, Mrs.
Black received us there very cordially, and when I
mentioned that I was the grandson of a minister, she
decided that naturally I was a gentleman, a rather
sudden and premature conclusion. She took me in. She
took Jim and me in first and gave us a bedroom downstairs. Then the following morning Jim had to go back
to Miami—he was working there—and I was very reluctant to leave this beautiful house and Mrs. Cora

Black, who had so much charm. She saw how I felt, and she said, "Tom, there's a little shack in back of here. I don't know what you'll make of it, but it's big enough for you." She showed it to me and I said, "This is ideal, Mrs. Black, I don't like living in large places," which is true. So she fixed it up very charmingly for me. She installed a shower, and she charged me only seven dollars and fifty cents a week rent and it was there that I rewrote *Battle*. I used to ride a rented bike down to a Cuban restaurant and wake up on very strong black Cuban coffee, which was certainly not what the doctor would have prescribed for a man with a heart condition. Then I would ride the bike back to my cabin and I would knock out page after page of all kinds of things—not just *Battle*, but poetry and short stories. This Cuban coffee really was dynamite. It wasn't doing my heart any good but I have a funny heart. Sometimes it seems to thrive on punishment.

In those days in Key West there was a wonderful colony of artists. There was Arnold Blanch, and there was his lady friend, Doris Lee. Then there was the wife of the Japanese artist Kuniyoshi. And Grant Wood, the man who painted *American Gothic*, was there. It was the last year of his life. He was a rather dumpy little man with a white shock of hair and very, very friendly. Quite flushed in the face all the time, and not from embarrassment either. Well, we all used to forgather in the evenings at Hemingway's old resort called Sloppy Joe's. Hemingway had already left but his ex-wife, Pauline Pfeiffer Hemingway, was still here, living in that lovely old Spanish colonial house on Whitehead Street. And they had a dance band at Sloppy Joe's, a really good black dance band that played wonderful dance music. Key West had in those days a very authentic frontier atmosphere which was delightful. Even the weather seemed better. Sloppy Joe's was far more colorful than it is today. It had a long front-to-rear bar; now it has a horseshoe-shaped bar. Hemingway's old cronies were still hanging out there in 1941, and Marion and I used to go there in the evenings and dance.

Now Marion had a husband who was the worst alcoholic I have ever known in my life. He was a likable guy, but he was giving Marion and Mrs. Black quite a good deal of trouble. When he wasn't on alcohol, he was on ether. He had to be on one or the other, either alcohol or ether, that was how bad he drank, and he took a liking to me and he was continually coming back into my cabin while I was trying to work. And I have a horror of the smell of ether. As a child, I had my adenoids and tonsils removed and was circumcised at the same time under ether, and I received anesthesia shock, which has lasted ever since.

This man would come in there exhaling these fumes of ether and glaring at me with his glass eye. I must have been much better natured in those days because I never threw him out. Of course, I probably couldn't have thrown him out as he was physically powerful. Well, he was part of the local color at the time, but he was giving Marion a really hard time which she bore with great fortitude. He was one of the principal heirs of the Standard Fruit Company fortune. Marion must have married him in her middle or late twenties. I think she was rather late in marrying because she had had to earn her own living after she graduated from Smith and she was employed by Flo Ziegfeld as a tutor for his children. She worked with those children for quite a long while; Marion was very loyal in her friendships and up until the very end she was a close friend of Mr. Ziegfeld's widow, Billie Burke.

Occasionally during that winter, Jim Parrott would visit me for a weekend at the Blacks'. Once his visit coincided with a domestic crisis at the Tradewinds. Jim and I had been invited to dinner and during the course of it, for no apparent reason, Mr. Vaccaro removed his glass eye and hurled it at his mother-in-law. It landed in her soup bowl. Only a truly great lady could have handled this incident with such composure. Miss Clara, without a change of expression or intonation, simply fished the glass eye out of her soup, passed it to Marion on her soupspoon with the casual remark, "Sister, I think Regis has lost this."

Later on that evening he ran afoul of some gangsters who ran a gambling joint in the town. They threatened his life. It was decided that he must be removed immediately from the Keys. The only vehicle that was available for this purpose was Jim Parrott's old Ford jalopy.

The fugitive party consisted of Miss Clara, Marion, Jim, and myself, with Regis under a blanket, unconscious on the floor of the back seat.

The Ford had developed a leak in the radiator. At frequent intervals we would have to stop and fill the steaming thing with sea-water that we scooped up along the way.

Later I was to renew my friendship with Marion in New Orleans in 1946. She was a great enthusiast for all kinds of betting, and I often accompanied her and her mother to the New Orleans race-track. In New Orleans they lived in a lovely apartment of the Pontalba buildings alongside Jackson Square. When the touring company of *Menagerie* came to town, Marion and Miss Clara threw a lavish party for them, whole turkeys and hams, unlimited liquor, the whole bit.

A few years later Marion and Miss Clara purchased a charming home in Coconut Grove. (Regis had now passed away.) Marion and Miss Clara had a keen interest in real estate and an instinct for it. At this time I entertained the notion of bringing Miss Rose and an attendant nurse to Florida. Marion thought this a good idea, too, and she found a residence, bay-side in the Grove, with that project in mind. It was furnished nicely when I bought it and it was a real bargain at forty thousand dollars. The house itself was not too attractive. It was stucco, U-shaped, Spanish mission style, with a steeple containing a mission-bell on the roof. The grounds, however, were enchanting. They faced the bay and they were regally populated by very tall royal palm trees.

I regret to say that the idea of establishing my sister in Florida had to be abandoned and so I rented out the property. I rented it to a man who worked for the magazine *Life*. Not long after he and his family took residence in it, the bay was struck by a hurricane and all the furnishings were scattered far and wide, but the house remained and, remarkably, so did the royal palms.

In the years since then property on this location has greatly increased in value. The latest offer for the house and ground is $150,000, but I have turned it down, expecting that its value will further increase.

I am lucky at real estate, lucky at cards: also sometimes at love.

Then why should I regard myself as a wasted dude? Possibly because my adventures in theatre have failed more often than not.

Before Castro took over Cuba, Marion and I used to have riotous weekends in Havana. Marion just as much enjoyed the frolicsome night life of Havana as I did and we would go to the same places to enjoy it. We even went back after Castro came in. The first time I went back to Havana after Castro's triumph, I was introduced to him by Ernest Hemingway, whom I met through the British theatre critic Kenneth Tynan. Tynan called me—I was staying at the Hotel Nacional in Havana—and he said, "Would you like to meet Ernest Hemingway?" and I said, "I don't think that's advisable, do you? I understand that he can be very unpleasant to people of my particular temperament." And Tynan said, "Well, I will be there to lend you what support I can. I think you ought to meet him because he is one of the great writers of your time and mine." I said, "Okay, I'll take a chance on it." So we went down to the Floradita, which was Hemingway's nighttime and daytime hangout, when he wasn't at sea, and he couldn't have been more charming. He was exactly the opposite of what I'd expected. I had expected a very manly, super-macho sort of guy, very bullying and coarse spoken. On the contrary, Hemingway struck me as a gentleman who seemed to have a very touchingly shy quality about him.

Tynan has reported this first encounter humorously but not accurately. I was naturally awkward and I said some *gauche* things, for instance I mentioned to him that I was so distressed that his ex-wife, Pauline, had recently died, and then I inquired, "What did she die of?" Hemingway didn't seem to take it amiss, but he said (sort of a struggle), "Well, she died and she's dead," and went on drinking. We started talking about bullfighting. I was not an *aficionado* of bullfighting, not somebody who knew the fine technique, the fine points of bullfighting, but one who enjoyed the spectacle of it and I had become, the previous summer, a good friend of Antonio Ordóñez, who was, you might almost say, an idol of Ernest Hemingway's. I mentioned to Hemingway that I knew Antonio Ordóñez. Hemingway was pleased, I thought, and he was also pleased that I shared his interest in bullfighting.

Hemingway said, "You know that this revolution in Cuba is a good revolution." Well, I knew that it was a good revolution, because I had been to Cuba when Batista was in power and he had the charming habit of torturing young students. He would make them sit in chairs that were electric—or that had electric attachments that would burn them horribly. He would sometimes emasculate them. He was a horrifying sadist. The United States, in my opinion, made a drastic error. If only they had appreciated the possibility of a détente. Castro was, after all, a gentleman, and well educated. It would have been quite possible for Cuba to have been drawn amiably into our orbit where Cuba naturally belongs, but our State Department chose instead to try to oust Mr. Castro. Consequently, we made an enemy of Cuba and Cuba turned toward Russia for support. This had not yet happened when I met Hemingway.

Anyhow, Hemingway wrote me a letter of introduction to Castro. Kenneth Tynan and I went to the palace. Castro was having a cabinet session at the time. His cabinet session lasted quite long. We waited it out, sitting on the steps outside the room in which the session was being held. After about a three-hour wait, the door was thrown open and we were ushered in. Castro greeted us both very warmly. When Kenneth Tynan introduced me, the Generalissimo said, "Oh, that cat," meaning *Cat on a Hot Tin Roof*, which surprised me—delighted me, of course. I couldn't imagine the generalissimo knowing anything about a play of mine. Then he proceeded to introduce us to all of his cabinet ministers. We were given coffee and liqueurs and it was a lovely occasion, well worth the three-hour wait.

Now, back to Marion. I loved her very deeply, though perhaps not as generously as she did me. Some of my very closest friends have been women and she was one. Marion was lovely and she drank quite excessively. We traveled a lot together.

Once when she and I were at the Hotel Nacional, we were playing gin rummy in our cabana by the pool one afternoon and we saw Jean-Paul Sartre and Simone de Beauvoir sitting in another cabana and I said, "Marion, I think we ought to meet them." She didn't object so I went to introduce myself to Mr. Sartre. He was quite pleasant and I said, "Won't you come and have a drink with us, sir." He and Miss de Beauvoir came over and joined us. Miss de Beauvoir was rather an icy lady, but Jean-Paul Sartre was very warm and charming. We had quite a long conversation; I mentioned that Marion wrote poetry. She had showed me some particularly lovely poems the evening before. He said, "Oh, I would love to see them!" I said, "Marion, do you mind if I let Mr. Sartre see your poetry?" She said, "Oh, Tom, please don't. I just scribble. I just amuse myself at night, scribbling these things." I said, "Yes, but, Marion, they are lovely poems in my opinion." Mr. Sartre said, "Oh, just go up and get them." So I just went up and fetched them down. Well, Sartre was very, very impressed. I must say that Miss de Beauvoir continued to be icy. I think that's just her demeanor. At one point in Paris, I had expected Sartre to come to a party of mine, but he hadn't, and that's why it surprised me so that he was cordial on this later occasion.

So back to the spring of 1941, when I was first in Key West. With spring came a lovely five-hundred-dollar bonus from my friends the Rockefellers. On it I returned with my rewritten *Battle* to Manhattan, submitted it to the Guild, and after some weeks of reflection Mr. Langner phoned me. (I mean *he* answered when I phoned *him*.)

"About this rewrite, Tennessee. You have gone like the Leaping Frog of Calaveras County, you know, that Mark Twain story, I mean you rewrote it too much like the frog jumped out of the county."

And that was that.

After he'd hung up, I thought ruefully of my first meeting with Mr. Langner, whom I still like and remember fondly. He had a desk the size of a President's and it had been covered that day with more playscripts than I had imagined to exist in the world. In one great gesture, he swept the desk clean of all scripts but mine and said, "I have no interest in anything but *genius*, so please sit down."

(Since that day, when people have spoken to me of "genius," I have felt an inside pocket to make sure my wallet's still there.)

Running elevators in Manhattan: My most colorful term of employment of this type was on the night shift at the old San Jacinto Hotel, a building now demolished, on Madison Avenue in the Fifties. This hotel was really a sort of retirement home for dowagers of high degree but diminished fortune who would spend their last dime on a good address. Not all of these dowagers got along well together. In fact there were two of them, an old girl who bore the stately name of Auchincloss and went into a manic seizure whenever she inadvertently found herself in the elevator with another old girl who bore an equally prestigious surname.

There was a young poet on the night shift with me. He was the phone operator and he had warned me that I must never, not even if the San Jacinto caught fire, permit these two dowagers to occupy the elevator at the same time.

Well, it happened: they did. And the scene in that elevator was like the climax of a cockfight. And (wouldn't you know) the elevator stuck between floors! I tried to get it back up to the Auchincloss floor, and the other dowager shrieked, "Not back up, down, down!" I swung the crank and the elevator stalled between floors nine and ten and the disturbance must have wakened everyone in the building that midnight. (I am now convinced that old ladies are immune to strokes, despite many reports to the contrary.)

I remember that the hotel also contained a marvelous old character actress named Cora Witherspoon. I believe it is safe for me to say that this delightful lady, now gone from us, was addicted to morphine and that the poet and I had to fill her prescriptions for her at an all-night pharmacy.

Morphine is supposed to be a "downer" but it always gave Miss Witherspoon a "high."

She used to rap with the poet and me till nearly daybreak in the San Jacinto lobby. Her "fix" would never wear itself out till the first cock's crow. Then the poet and I would sort of lift her into the lift, the poet would open her bedroom door and I would get her to the edge of her bed and let her drop on it.

"What will I do without you boys?" she'd murmur, with that sweet, sad wisdom of the old who know that "all will pass."

(Has anyone ever understood the irresistible gallantry and charm of old ladies, in and out of the theatre, so well as Giraudoux in *The Madwoman of Chaillot*? Kate Hepburn was just not quite old or mad enough to suggest the charisma of their lunacy.)

Toward the end of 1941 I was companion to an abstract painter in the warehouse district of the West Village. This friend was, nervously speaking, a basket case: I mean he was a real freak-out before it was fashionable to be one.

During that period I was very briefly employed at a bistro called The Beggar's Bar, owned by a fantastic refugee from Nazi Germany named Valesca Gert.

She was a dance-mime, and that is by no means all. I was working only for tips. She was licensed to serve just beer but she stretched the license a bit to include setups. There was food in the nature of knackwurst and sauerkraut. There was a singer who was either a male or female transvestite, I've never known which, and there was always and forever the incomparable Valesca.

At times I supplemented my tips as a waiter by giving recitals of my light verse.

The verse was pretty raw for those days and I became something of a draw. And tips were sizable.

One night the Madam called the waiters together and announced a change of policy.

She said that the waiters (there were three of us) had to pool their tips and then split them with the management, meaning herself.

On this particular evening I had a number of close friends and acquaintances in the bar, among them the abstract painter. He was present when Valesca announced her new policy, just after closing time, in the kitchen of The Beggar's Bar.

I told the lady that I had absolutely no intention whatsoever of pooling my tips with the other waiters and having it split with the management. The abstract painter was attracted to the kitchen by this noisy confrontation. Near the kitchen entrance there was a crate of quart soda bottles and as soon as he entered he began to hurl these bottles at the celebrated dance-mime. At least a dozen bottles were hurled at the lady before one of them struck her. The paddy wagon and an ambulance were summoned, the lady received several stitches in her scalp, and, needless to say, I was out of a job at that particular night spot.

Not long after on a bitterly cold Friday which was not Good, with the new year, 1942, just begun, I was unexpectedly evicted from my fickle friend's apartment. My friend, the abstract painter, had taken to his bed with some malaise of nervous origin but he still desired company, and each evening he would dispatch me out upon the streets of Greenwich Village to fetch home carefully specified kinds of visitors. I was willing to oblige and so was another friend, whom we called "the pilot fish"; the nervous young painter was kept agreeably diverted most evenings of that season. But one night "the pilot fish" and I fetched home some guests of a roguish nature, and the following morning the painter found several prized articles missing. After making an inventory, he sadly decided to dispense with my company and services: I was kicked out, and I had the ticket but not the cash to pick up my laundry at "the Chinaman's," and barely a subway fare.

Two desperate days later, for the first and last time in my life, I made a direct and personal appeal for economic assistance: a phone call to the dramatists' branch of a union devoted to the care and feeding of writers. I was lent, yes, *lent* the sum of *precisely ten dollars* to keep me off the slippery streets until the spring thaw set in, a season later ...

In my own addled fashion I am a rather ingenious, as well as ingenuous, creature, and in those days I had a sort of pathetic appeal to certain individuals; and when the ten dollars was exhausted I dropped in for dinner at the Madison Avenue penthouse of ,a very successful composer of "pop" music, and I not only stayed for dinner but for the next four months, till spring arrived.

After that, it was summer and I had another friend, much less prosperous but equally goodhearted. Knowing the problems of my situation in Manhattan, he wrote me from Macon, Georgia, inviting me to spend the summer with him.

I arrived in that deep Southern town and found that he was occupying a room in an attic and I was to be billeted in the other half of it.

It was the middle of summer and it was the middle of Georgia. My room in the attic had two windows the size and shape of transoms. Let's say it was a very wet summer despite the fact that there was practically no rainfall.

My friend had a revolving electric fan and was unable to sleep without it, due to a painful infection of the jawbone. I had no cooling electric appliance and I spent long hours at night glaring across the breathless hall between these attic rooms at my friend lying in bed with that revolving Westinghouse ruffling his hair as he chuckled over cartoons in *The New Yorker,* an excellent magazine at the mere sight of which I still break out in a deathly sweat.

In the dog days of August another tenant arrived in this Georgia attic, a somewhat retarded youth who worked at the A & P. This tenant sweated enough to die of dehydration, but he never, literally never, bathed or changed his socks and I mean to tell you that the odor which emanated from this nice country kid began to permeate the attic like Eugene O'Neill's sense of doom. And if I wanted to elaborate fancifully on this item I would add that late in August a polecat moved into the attic one night and moved out before daybreak to escape that odor of doom.

I think it was about this time, still in the early forties, that I experienced a brief term of employment at a Southern branch of the U. S. Corps of Engineers. Some of you may remember the awful shortage of manpower in those days, those war years, and even I impressed the personnel manager as an employable person. He put me on the graveyard shift, which are those hours between 11 P.M. and 7 A.M., and on this shift there were just two of us in the office, a massive young man who had been prematurely discharged from an asylum and myself who had not, at that time, been committed to one. Our job was to receive and to acknowledge coded messages which would now and then come in late at night on the teletype apparatus. My co-worker was a silent, withdrawn type who glanced at me now and then with homicidally suspicious eyes. This didn't alarm me at all. I've always felt at home with people like that. There was a lot of free time and I spent it writing short plays and I came and went on a bicycle, I lived at the "Y" and I had an adolescent roommate employed as bellhop at a leading hotel. We would arrive back at the "Y" room at about the same hour, and each morning he would turn his pockets inside out, littering the floor with paper money he'd received as tips, fives, tens, twenties—wartime economy seemed to work well in those days, especially for bellhops in hotels that attracted conventions.

But at the U. S. Engineers things were deteriorating on the graveyard shift. My co-worker and I were sinking into separate dreamworlds. Our boss kept begging us not to force him to fire us, and this continued for three months till one night some really important message came over the teletype and we blew it sky high, and then our boss thought it best to let me go and retain the services of the certified loony.

Now about those eye operations which I had off and on from the ages of twenty-nine to thirty-four. I had no Blue Shield and no Medicare but there was a reputable ophthalmologist in New York who was willing to perform these cataract operations on credit. The cost on the books was one hundred dollars per operation, but this good doctor did not press me for payment till I hit the jackpot in the year 1945.

It is peculiar to have a cataract—it was on my left eye and I paid little attention to it till someone in a bar addressed me as "White Eye"—I was only in my twenties! But rare and peculiar things have happened to me all my life, no less in youth than in approaching "age."

The operations for cataracts in those days were performed with a needle under local anesthesia, with the head and the whole body securely strapped to the table, and the great hazard was that you would vomit convulsively during this surgery, and thus joggle the needle as it penetrated the iris and got into the lens, which is a liquid substance in a healthy eye but solidifies with the advance of a cataract. This progressive induration is what causes the lens of the eye to take on a grayish and finally whitish cast of color, and unfortunately, in my case, my eyes had always been considered my most compelling feature.

The ophthamologist said I must have received some childhood injury to my left eye, which was now reacting with this cataract, and I had, indeed, received such an injury in a childhood game of considerable violence. This was in Mississippi and we were playing Indians and early white settlers. The early white settlers were in a shack that was being besieged by the redskins. I was an aggressive kid and I led the charge out of the shack and was hit in the left eye by an

"Indian" with a stick and he fetched a considerable
clout. I had a swollen eye for several days, but no
sign of lasting eye damage till my late twenties.

In my case, rare and special, of course, it took three
needling operations to remove the lens of the left eye
and I vomited each time during the operation and
nearly choked on the vomit, which I had no choice
but to swallow. The worst of these operations was
performed completely free of charge in a medical college. They charged me nothing at all because I consented to have it performed before a class of student
ophthalmologists, seated all about the operating
table, while the surgeon-teacher delivered a lecture
on what he was doing, the whole theatrical procedure.

"The patient is now in position, apply the straps.
Tighter, tighter, he has a history of vomiting during
the surgery. Eyelids secured against blinking, pupil
anesthetized now. The needle is now about to penetrate the iris. It is now into the iris. It has now penetrated the lens. Oh, oh, vomiting, nurse, choking, tube
in esophagus. My God, what a patient. I mean very
good, of course, but an unusual case." (Of course I
am not quoting verbatim, but you get the idea if you
wish to.)

Young, gifted, and destitute, with a cataract in the
left eye and an impressionable stomach. Oh, well, my
eyes are still a compelling feature ...

The other night I was feeling lively, so we took to
the streets, here in New Orleans. I whispered to my
companion that I was "in heat," so we went again to
that delightfully scandalous night spot on Bourbon
Street which features the topless and bottomless go-
go boys—all of whom are hustlers and some of whom
are very pretty indeed. The one I found most attractive was serving our table—the go-go boys double as
waiters as well as hustlers. I immediately asked his
name. It was Lyle. He looked a bit underfed—but

had lovely proportions, a clear, sweet face and a smooth, nicely curved behind. The boys wear G-strings only—so you can be pretty sure what you're getting. I would recommend, however, that penetration be avoided, as they are most probably all infected with clap in the ass. And I'd also recommend that you get them to bathe as their hours are long and sweaty. And that you have a pubic pesticide such as A-200.

This young Lyle made a date with me for 5 A.M. and he arrived below the verandah just before I started work at four-thirty. He buzzed and was let in the gate, but I came out on the verandah and called down to him that I had just woke up and would he please return in about three hours as I had work to do. I asked him if he needed money and he replied no and went amiably off into the penumbra of pre-dawn on Dumaine, promising to return about 8 A.M.

He has a softly nubile look and a soft Southern voice—and I contemplate no intimacy beyond the tactile—I mean the relatively chaste knowledge of his skin surface with my fingers. This restriction is particularly prudent since I am allergic to penicillin and the last thing I need is a clap.

A friend was employed in 1943 at the old Strand Theatre on Broadway as an usher, and, knowing that I was between profitable engagements, he told me that the Strand was in need of a new usher and that I might get the job provided I fitted the uniform of my predecessor. Luckily it happened that this former usher was about my height and of similar build. I was put on the job. The attraction at the Strand was that World War II classic, *Casablanca*, which was an early starring vehicle for Ingrid Bergman and Humphrey Bogart, both hot as blazes; the cast also included that fabulously charismatic "Fat Man," Sydney Greenstreet, and Peter Lorre and Paul Henreid, and there was Dooley Wilson playing and singing that immortal oldie, "As Time Goes By." In those days, with an attraction like that, the movie-houses of Broadway were literally mobbed and the aisles had to be roped off by the ushers to restrain the patrons till they could be seated. It was my job, at first, to guard the entrance to one of these aisles, and at an evening performance an enormously fat lady broke through the velvet rope and started to charge down the aisle, evidently intending to occupy a seat on the screen, and when I attempted to restrain her, she struck me over the head with a handbag that seemed to contain gold bricks. The next thing I remember I was still employed at the Strand but I was now situated near the entrance, in a spot of light, and directing traffic with white-gloved hands. "This way, ladies and gentlemen, this way, please," and "There will be a short wait for all seats." And somehow, during the several months' run of *Casablanca*, I was always able to catch Dooley Wilson and "As Time Goes By."

The pay was seventeen dollars a week, which covered my room at the "Y" and left me seven dollars for meals. And I loved it . . .

Then one day Miss Wood summoned me to her office and informed me that I had been sold to MGM. It was a package deal and in this human package were Lemuel Ayers and a young male dancer, Eugene Loring; he was the first to create the balletic role of Billy the Kid.

Audrey said, "You are going to get two fifty."

"Two fifty a month!" I exclaimed, bug-eyed at the prospect, and she said, "No, two hundred and fifty a week." And then I knew that there was a gimmick, and I was right; there were several gimmicks. I was set to work writing a screenplay based on a dreadful novel to be transmogrified into a starring vehicle for a young lady who couldn't act her way out of her form-fitting cashmeres but was an intimate friend of the producer who had engaged me and I was soon told that my dialogue was beyond the young lady's com-

prehension although I had avoided any language that
was at all eclectic or multisyllabic: and then I was
asked to write a starring vehicle for a female child
and I threw in the sponge.

Then, to my total disbelief—although it was quite
true—I learned that I had six months' option whether
I was on assignment or not.

I bought a secondhand motor scooter over the anxious protests of my new friend, Christopher Isherwood. I had met Chris a little after I arrived in
Hollywood; I had a letter of introduction to him given
to me by one of my first advocates, Lincoln Kirstein. I
discovered that Christopher was staying in a monas-
tery in Hollywood. I went there and knocked at the
door and the door was opened and I said, "I want to
see Christopher Isherwood." And somebody put his
finger to his lips and made a sign to wait and Christopher came out and said, "We're having our meditation." He said, "Come on in and meditate with us." So
I went on in and sat down. I didn't find myself meditating, but I sat there. I thought this was a very
unfortunate meeting for a man I admired so much.
He phoned me, subsequently, and we became great
friends. We used to go out on the pier at Santa
Monica for fish dinners. This was during World War
II when everything was blacked out. There was an
almost sentimental attachment between us but it didn't
come to romance: instead, it turned into a great
friendship, one of the continuing friendships in my
life, and one of the most important ones.

Shortly after I arrived in California to start employment in the movie-mill at MGM, I found what
were to be ideal living-quarters in Santa Monica. It
was a two-room apartment on Ocean Boulevard in a
large frame building called The Palisades. It was
managed by a fantastic woman, half gypsy, matri-
monially shackled to an unpleasant little man who was
withering with cancer. Her description, and her angry

little husband's, are contained in one of my better short stories, "The Mattress by the Tomato Patch," and as for that summer, it was as golden as the later summers in Rome.

As I have mentioned elsewhere, I was soon released from employment on unsuitable projects at MGM but remained on the payroll for the whole six months' option.

My little apartment was very close to the Palisades of Santa Monica, that high promontory over the Pacific beach which was studded with the palatial homes of such movie stars as Marion Davies.

By this time the motor scooter had been sensibly replaced by a bicycle, and each evening after dinner I would ride my bike out on the Palisades. It was a park planted with royal palm trees and fronted by a long, curving balustrade of stone: at intervals along this route were little arbors and bosky retreats. And that summer the California coast was blacked out at night, for seven miles inland, in fear of Japanese air attack. The Palisades were full of young servicemen, positively infested with them, I'd say, and when I'd driven by one who appealed to my lascivious glance, I would turn the bike about and draw up alongside him to join him in his spurious enchantment with the view.

Presently I would strike a match for a cigarette. If the match-light confirmed my first impression of his charms, I would mention that I had a pad only a few blocks away, and he would often accept the invitation. If the first one or two were not to my satisfaction, I would go out for a third. There were memorable ones, particularly a gay marine. I wouldn't believe it if it were not recorded in my journal of that summer, but I screwed him seven times that night.

Several nights a week I would go into Hollywood to see a movie. I would return by bus, and before the interior lights were turned off, I would spot someone on the bus with an empty seat beside him: when the

lights were extinguished in observance of the black-
out, I would then seat myself in the previously unoccupied seat beside him. After a few moments, my
right knee would permit itself to be jolted against his
left knee. If the contact were permitted to continue, I
would know that it would not be necessary, when I
got off at Santa Monica, to resort to the Palisades.

The gypsy proprietress was totally complacent
about these adventures of mine, in fact she jested
about them with great good humor. After all, she had
replaced her sour little husband in the sack with a
young boxer, and sexual morality was the last thing
she'd be concerned with.

Early each morning I would prepare myself very
strong black coffee in the combo dining room-kitchen
which adjoined the sanctified bedroom. The proprietress would join me at coffee. She subscribed to *The
Daily Worker* and would read me items from it while
babbling hilariously about *La Vie horizontale*, hers
and my own. Fortunately I have never been attracted
to Communism so that aspect of her ample nature
did not impress me. As soon as I'd had my second
cup of coffee, I would dismiss her and turn like a
blast furnace to the morning's work. In those days a
six- or eight-hour stint was not unusual: at its conclusion, I would have a fish dinner on the pier, inspect
the boys at Muscle Beach and ride my bike to a club
I'd joined, halfway to Venice, which contained a big
swimming-pool.

It would be hard to devise a summer more to my
satisfaction, especially with friends such as Isherwood,
Lem Ayres and Eugene Loring. And later Margo
Jones arrived to produce *You Touched Me!* at the
Pasadena Playhouse. I would often spend the night
at her Pasadena cottage. It contained only two beds,
and when a certain personable young poetry publisher arrived, he was given the sofa to sleep on one
night.

When lights were extinguished, I came to the living-room door and invited him to take or to share my bed: he declined the honor quite gently.

I wasn't always rejected in such a gentlemanly fashion, and I remember being in a Hollywood bar one night. I kept staring at an attractive young sailor until he could no longer ignore the implication. He downed his beer and barged up to me and said, "The way I feel tonight I could fuck a snake."

I am proud to say that I told him to go snake-hunting . . .

I shall set down a few remarks about last evening, while I wait upon time past to bring to the surface of my "savaged wits" some material of more importance to my life.

I had been invited by an off-Broadway producer to join him on Fire Island for dinner. He makes the best pasta I've eaten in the States. And he assured me of other entertainments, including a big dance of boys with boys, and I have delighted in dancing with boys since that long-ago summer of 1945 in Mexico City when I learned to follow and was, for that reason, the belle of the balls at the weekend *tequila-dansants*—more about those later.

However, as I prepared for the one-night revelries at Fire Island, a phone call reminded me that I was to hear two extraordinarily gifted young actors, one male and the other a girl, both winners of Clarence Derwent awards, in the opulent quarters of Peter Glenville.

This was one reading too many of *Out Cry*, despite the fact that the young actress was quite gifted. Both Bill Barnes, my agent, and I came finally to realize that this play will never go on Broadway nor in the West End of London without "stars" playing Felice and Clare, for no matter how well it may be read by the young and gifted who lack the presence of stars, the play does not hold. Beautiful in parts, yes, but still doesn't go the full course. Why? Partly because

TENNESSEE WILLIAMS: MEMOIRS

there are only the two actors for the considerable length of the work, and as Clare observes to her brother Felice: "This is an exercise in performance for two star performers."—You see, I cannot help, at times, being totally honest about my work, even now that the years have made this honesty painful.

Still I do not despair about the play. Glenville has restored a lot of material that I excised with remarkable cunning during the Chicago gig. Now I must cut it out once again whether Peter approves or not.

# 5

I don't think the leaves knew they were turning to flame for that reason nor did anyone else involved in the rehearsals in Chicago of *The Glass Menagerie*. As a matter of fact, everybody but Julie Haydon, who has never been in any mental or spiritual state short of ecstasy, at least none apparent to me.

The play was being directed by Eddie Dowling, who played Tom in it, too, and he was assisted by the late Margo Jones. The play was backed by a mysterious character named Louis J. Singer, who owned a chain of lucrative fleabag hotels. He hadn't really taken his investment in the play very seriously—it wasn't a very large investment compared to his investment in the chain of fleabag hotels—but when he came to rehearsals, which he did just once, he nearly died of apoplexy when he saw what he saw and heard what he did in that rehearsal hall.

Laurette Taylor did not seem to know her lines as Amanda Wingfield, hardly a fraction of them, and those she did seem to know she was still delivering in a Southern accent which she had acquired from some long-ago black domestic. Her bright-eyed attentiveness to the other performances seemed a symptom of lunacy, and so did the rapturous manner of dear Julie, who played Laura.

I was sitting in a corner wondering what menial occupation was next in store for me when I heard someone suddenly cry out. It was the mysterious Mr. Singer.
"Eddie, Eddie, how could you do this to me!"

It seems that he felt the whole project was a practical joke that Eddie Dowling was perpetrating upon
him.

Of course this desperate cry put a temporary halt
to rehearsals. It did not dismay Laurette the least bit,
nor did it surprise me much. ·

Laurette and Margo and I went out to an early
lunch somewhere nearby and Margo and I were as-
tonished by the gaiety of Laurette. She had never
seemed to be in a better humor, although I've no
recollection of her indulging herself in sorrow, however appropriate it might seem to the occasion. You
see, Laurette knew she didn't have to give her lines
until the play opened, and so she was watching the
others, observing, waiting. But at the time we didn't
know that, I thought she didn't know her lines, and so
did everybody else. (Dowling said, "Oh, poor thing.
Poor lady. Wet brain. Can't remember her lines.")

Well, Julie was quite fond of the late George Jean
Nathan and so Mr. Nathan, appreciating her devotion,
took a certain interest in *Menagerie,* and that night
he got together with Eddie and between the two of
them they composed a drunk scene for Eddie which
they thought was the only possible salvation for the
play. This scene involved such things as a red, white,
and blue flask, a song for Eddie—"My Melancholy
Baby"—and other unmentionables.

This "drunk scene," obviously composed in a state
that corresponded, was given me as a *fait accompli*
the next day, when I crept into rehearsals.

I said to myself, "This is the living and dying end."

I went into a huddle with Margo. She shared my
opinion of the drunk scene. And more than that, she
said she was going to confront the no longer myste-

rious Mr. Singer and poor Eddie with a protest of the kind that had earned her the sobriquet of "The Texas Tornado."

As usual, in such cases, a compromise was reached. I said they would have their drunk scene but that I would accept no collaboration on it.

I wrote it and it is still in the script and I honestly think that it does the play little harm.

A day or two later we had the cast playing in *Winged Victory* come to see a preview, and that's when we discovered what Laurette had been up to. This lady knew every line—and then some. She put lines in the play that had to be cut out, just because they were pure Laurette. She was a great, great person. They don't come that way anymore. Maureen Stapleton is very close, and Anna Magnani was. There was a great performance in Europe of *Sweet Bird* by Edwige Feuillère, the great French actress who had trained with the Comédie Française, and she was even better than Geraldine Page.

Feuillère, Anna Magnani, and Laurette Taylor are three of the great female performers in my plays. Of the male performers, Marlon Brando is outstanding. I think he is probably the greatest living actor; I think he is greater than Olivier. I saw *Last Tango in Paris* reluctantly, because I heard it was pornographic. It was not pornographic, and I think Brando gave in it his best performance that I have seen. Paul Newman is also terribly good. He works up to a part slowly, but when he finally gets to it he's marvelous.

Now obviously this "thing" has dealt so far mostly with the vicissitudes of my lean and green years as a writer. I hope it doesn't seem characteristic of me to have omitted so much of a happier nature. I am not really a misanthrope or a gloom-pot. In fact, I am much more of a clown, an almost compulsive comedian in my social behavior. The humor sometimes may be black, but it is still humor. This fact has been exploited (whether to my advantage or disadvantage I am not quite certain) by various interviewers in the last dozen years. Perhaps I should not have used the word "exploited" to cover all instances. I suspect it has always been an instinctive thing with me, when being interviewed, to ham it up and be fairly outrageous in order to provide "good copy." The reason? I guess a need to convince the world that I do indeed still exist and to make this fact a matter of public interest and amusement.

Once I met a stately professor at Harvard whose last name was Lanier. When I mentioned that I was also a descendant of the first Lanier in the States, from whom all Laniers here are presumably descended, he looked at me icily and gave me this beautiful put-down: "The ramifications of the Lanier family are wonderful and terrible."

I don't mind being put down when it's done as cleverly as that.

I had finished *Menagerie* in the law-school dormitory of Harvard, in the rooms of a wild boy I'd met in Provincetown the summer of 1944. That boy was one of the aboriginal "beats"—I mean he was beat before there were "beats"; he was a beautiful gangling kid with dark hair and light eyes and a stammer. The boy appeared in P-town and was said to be straight. However, I got him into my cabin one night and—he didn't exactly twist into a circle but he proved to have a warm sort of puppy-dog playfulness of nature. It was near the end of summer and I was not yet quite through with my last draft of *Menagerie* and I was not yet quite ready to return to Manhattan with it. This boy, Bill, had a group of friends at Harvard and they were all sort of freaked out, in varying degrees. One had attempted to slash his wrists a few days before—I remember how this attempt on his life had made him a celebrity in the group and the shy pride he took in exhibiting the scars when the wrists were unbandaged.

Bill was a peeping Tom—that was his sex hangup, or practice if you prefer—at the time I knew him. It was a funny thing. He had a map of the town of Cambridge with X's marked to indicate the location of window shades that were likely to expose an exciting peep show. He would start out precisely at midnight upon the carefully mapped-out tour and he'd return, rocks off, about 2 A.M.—sometimes with rapturous reports on intimacies he had witnessed through those lucky windows.

I think it was a year or two later that Bill began to visit me in various New York hotel suites, before I had a Manhattan apartment with Frankie Merlo and maybe after—and by that time Bill was way out of his closet and he was always drunk but a good drunk, I mean a wildly exuberant drunk, and he was a good lay.

He died in a shocking way. He was leaning out of a subway train in New York, very far out and very drunk, shouting good-by to friends on the platform, when the subway train rushed forward.

And he was decapitated by a column in the subway.

On the Broadway opening night of *Menagerie*, the performers took bow after bow, and finally they tried to get me up on the stage. I was sitting in the fourth row, and somebody extended a hand to me and I went up on the stage. And I felt embarrassed; I don't think I felt any great sense of triumph. I think writing is continually a pursuit of a very evasive quarry, and you never quite catch it.

In the essay that accompanies one of the printed editions of *Cat on a Hot Tin Roof*, I talk very honestly about my goal in writing, what I want to do. That goal is just somehow to capture the constantly evanescent quality of existence. When I do that, then I have accomplished something, but I have done it, I think, relatively few times compared to the times I have attempted it. I don't have any sense of being a fulfilled artist. And when I was writing *Menagerie*, I did not know that I was capturing it, and I agree with Brooks Atkinson that the narrations are not up to the play. I didn't feel they were at the time, either. Thank God, in the 1973 television version of it, they cut the narrations down. There was too much of them. And the play itself holds without much narration.

Maybe I am a machine, a typist. A compulsive typist and a compulsive writer. But that's my life, and what is in these memoirs is mostly the barest periphery of that which is my intense life, for my intense life is my work.

Mother came up to Chicago for the opening there of *Menagerie* in the late December of 1944. I don't recall her precise reaction to the play but it was probably favorable, for Mother was very concerned with my long-delayed success. I do recall her coming backstage after the performance which she attended and paying her respects to Laurette.

"Well, Mrs. Williams," said Laurette, briefly scrutinizing Edwina Williams in her dressing-room mirror, "how did you like yourself?"

"Myself?" said Mother innocently.

Laurette was as kind a person as I have known in a theatre mostly inhabited by jungle beasts, but even she, being Irish, was not one to pass by an opportunity to be mischievous.

"You notice these bangs I wear? I have to wear them playing this part because it's the part of a fool and I have a high, intellectual forehead."

Miss Edwina did not pick up on this either. She let it go by her without a sign of offense. She was probably bedazzled by Laurette's somewhat supernatural quality on a stage.

Through the course of this thing I may talk a lot about Miss Edwina. But right now I'll only say that she was a lady and that she still is a lady at the age of eighty-nine or ninety. My dear friend, Marion Vaccaro, once said to me, speaking of my sister, "Miss Rose is a lady but your mother just misses." I never quite knew what she meant about Miss Edwina. I think perhaps she sensed that Miss Edwina had not been quite so perceptive about Miss Rose as she might have been, but I feel that Mother always did what she thought was right and that she has always given herself due credit for it even though what she sometimes did was all but fatally wrong.

In Chicago the first night, no one knew how to take *Menagerie,* it was something of an innovation in the theatre and even though Laurette gave an incredibly luminous, electrifying performance, and people observed it. But people are people, and most of them went home afterward to take at least equal pleasure in their usual entertainments. It took that lovely lady, Claudia Cassidy, the drama critic of the Chicago *Tribune,* a lot of time to sell it to them, to tell them it was special.

She said Laurette ranked with Duse.

Eventually, though, *Menagerie* was a startling success, which success I attribute in large part to Laurette. She was, as I have said many times, a gallant performer; I still consider her the greatest artist of her profession that I have known. I wrote a tribute to her, on her death, in which I said that it is our immeasurable loss that Laurette's performances were not preserved on the modern screen. The same is true of Duse and Bernhardt, with whom Laurette's name belongs.

I also wrote that there are sometimes hints, during our lives, of something that lies outside the flesh and its mortality. I suppose these intuitions come to many people in their religious vocations, but I have sensed them equally clearly in the work of artists and most clearly of all in the art of Laurette. There was a radiance about her art which I can compare only to the greatest lines of poetry, and which gave me the same shock of revelation as if the air about us had been momentarily broken through by light from some clear space beyond us.

I have always been awkward and diffident around actors so that it has made a barrier between us almost all but insuperable. In the case of Laurette Taylor, I cannot say that I ever got over the awkwardness and the awe which originally were present, but she would not allow it to stand between us. The great warmth of her heart burned through and we became close friends. I am afraid it is one of the few close friendships I have ever had with a player. I said, when she died, that a whole career of writing for the theatre is rewarded enough by having created one good part for a great actress. Having created the part of Amanda Wingfield for Laurette Taylor is sufficient reward for all the effort that went before and a lot that has come after. (Not that I'll settle for it!)

Almost directly after *Menagerie* went into rehearsals I started upon a play whose first title was *Blanche's Chair in the Moon*. But I did only a single scene for it that winter of 1944–45 in Chicago. In that scene Blanche was in some steaming hot Southern town, sitting alone in a chair with the moonlight coming through a window on her, waiting for a beau who didn't show up. I stopped working on it because I became mysteriously depressed and debilitated and you know how hard it is to work in that condition. I decided not to drink black coffee and not to work for several months and I really did stick to that self-promise. I had a strong will in those days, which are now past. However it was a happy time, there in Chicago.

I had a lot of fun with Tony Ross, now dead, who played the Gentleman Caller in *Menagerie*. Laurette was very fond of us both and she used to call us the Big Bum and the Little Bum. He and I went out together every night almost, after the curtain came down in Chicago. We went out cruising together. I had more luck than Tony for the reason that Tony would get drunk, and drunks are not likely to cruise well in Chicago or anywhere. He was an amiable drunk, but something in Tony was broken and the fine performances that he gave every night were an extraordinary accomplishment for a man who had so much torment in him.

It was about this time that I began to look about for more permanent, I mean relatively permanent, relations with young men. I hoped to have one with a young Irishman who was appearing in a small part in *Winged Victory*, which was then playing Chicago and in the same building as *Menagerie*. I shall not give his name, of course, but he was remarkably handsome and remarkably gifted off-stage. I was staying in the Loop of Chicago, at the Hotel Sherman, and this young Irishman spent the nights with me in my single room and the nightingales sang and sang. I remember one morning we dropped in on Tony, who was recovering from one of his epic hangovers, and it was a mistake for us to do that, since Tony, much as he liked me, was quite obviously overwhelmed at the sight of my young companion. Tony's hands always shook and he always sweated copiously but that morning, observing my companion, he almost fell to pieces.

Then *Winged Victory* left town and so did the Irishman, and I took up with a student at the University of Illinois, a tall blond who swam with me at the Chicago "Y" and spent the night with me in my single room at that hotel, the Sherman, and the nightingales continued to sing their hearts out.

I am sorry that so much of this "thing" must be devoted to my amatory activities, but I was late coming out, and when I did it was with one hell of a bang.

It was sometime late last winter when Barbara Baxley, a friend and brilliant performer in two of my plays, called me to tell me that William Inge, with whom she had once had a tender "romance," with whom he was probably closer than almost anyone else outside his family, had fallen into a desperate situation.

Her feeling for him remained as tenderly concerned as ever.

"He's going to pieces," she told me in that inimitable voice of hers. "He keeps himself under sedation all day and night, getting up only to drink and then back under sedation."

"Oh, then he is on a suicide course: something has to be done."

"But what? He commits himself voluntarily for two days and then has himself released."

"Isn't his sister with him?"

"Yes, Helen's with him and she's desperate."

"Tell her to commit him herself so he can't get right back out till he has gotten through the present crisis."

"You call her, Tenn."

"I don't know her, Barbara."

"Introduce yourself to her on the phone and give her that advice before it's too late. I've tried but she seems immobilized with panic."

Barbara gave me the California telephone number. Before calling, I phoned Maureen Stapleton to confer with her on the advisability of the suggested call to Bill's sister.

Maureen was equally disturbed. Being a survivor of nervous crises herself, she could empathize with Bill's and his sister's dilemma.

I then called the number in Hollywood and Bill's sister, Mrs. Helen Connell, answered the phone. I introduced myself to her and she lowered her voice to a whisper, saying she never knew whether Bill was listening to calls. She gave me further details of the predicament. He had, she told me, entered the falling-down stage and a few nights ago had fallen down in the shower and suffered deep scalp cuts and she'd had to assist him back to bed. Under his mattress, she told me, he kept strong sedative pills, seven of them a night, and she confirmed Barbara's report that he only got up now to make a drink and that his pattern was to commit himself to a sanitarium and release himself in two days.

Knowing certain things about Bill, from our long association, I was aware of the fact that he was the type of alcoholic who can't tolerate a single drink, that he had put up a very brave and successful struggle to abstain completely, was a member of Alcoholics Anonymous, and that he suffered from extreme claustrophobia, a fact that explained his inability to accept hospital confinement for more than two days.

I suggested to Mrs. Connell that, being his nearest relative, she commit him herself to the best sort of psychiatric hospital, such as Menninger's in his home state of Kansas, make sure that he had an attractive and spacious room there, and see that he remained till he was back on his feet.

She suddenly cut the phone conversation short, whispering that she heard him stirring about the house and that he was paranoiac about phone calls. Then she assured me that she would follow my advice.

I was in rehearsals with the most difficult play I have written and made no further call and heard no further from Bill's sister.

Two days ago I opened the Rome *Daily American* and saw a photograph of his anguished face: then the caption declaring that he had committed suicide.

I met Bill Inge in December 1944 when I returned home briefly to St. Louis. At that time he was writing for the (defunct) *Star-Times*, doing dramatic criticism and interviews and I think also serving as music critic.

This was during the Chicago break-in of *Menagerie* and Bill came to our suburban home to interview me. He was embarrassingly "impressed" by my burgeoning career as a playwright. It's always lonely at home

now: my friends have all dispersed. I mentioned this
to Bill and he cordially invited me to his apartment
near the river. We had a gala night among his friends.
Later we attended the St. Louis Symphony together.
He made my homecoming an exceptional pleasure.

When I returned to *Menagerie* in Chicago, Bill
shortly arrived to attend and cover the play, and I
believe he was sincerely overwhelmed by the play
and fabulous Laurette, giving her last and greatest
performance.

A year or two later I was back in St. Louis and we
met again. He had now retired as journalist and was
teaching English at Washington University, not far
from our home, and was living in the sort of neo-
Victorian white frame house that must have reminded him of his native Kansas. There, one evening,
he shyly produced a play that he had written, *Come
Back, Little Sheba*. He read it to me in his beautifully
quiet and expressive voice; I was deeply moved by
the play and I immediately wired Audrey Wood
about it and urged him to submit it to her.

She was equally impressed and Bill became her
client almost at once.

It was during the rehearsals of that play, starring
Shirley Booth and the late Sidney Blackmer, that Bill
had his first nervous crisis. The tension was too much
for him, he assuaged it copiously with liquor. The
legendary Paul Bigelow took him under charge and
had him hospitalized and I don't think Bill even attended his opening night.

Bill and his work were suffused with the light of
humanity at its best. In each play there would be one
dark scene and it was always the most powerful scene
in the play: but he loved his characters, he wrote of
them with a perfect ear for their homely speech, he
saw them through their difficulties with the tender-
ness of a parent for suffering children: and they
usually came out well.

Bill was a mystery as a person, and he remained

one. Ever since he came to New York, probably even before, he found it difficult to open himself up to people, especially at social gatherings. He was inclined to silent moodiness: his face was prematurely etched with hidden sufferings: he would remain at a party rarely longer than half an hour: then he would say quietly, "I think I'd better go now."

Because others were drinking and he couldn't? Or because a shyness, a loneliness beyond comprehension except to a few such as Barbara Baxley, Elia Kazan and Miss Wood, was inextricably rooted in his being, despite the many years of analysis and the deserved fame and success?

His shyness was never awkward: he had true dignity and impeccable taste, rarely associated with "Middle America": his apartment on the East River contained lovely paintings by "name" painters but reflecting his own taste. Interviews with him contained no touch of vulgarity: impersonal, perhaps, but impressively thoughtful and modest.

*Menagerie* played till the middle of March in Chicago and by the time it got to New York many theatre people had stopped off to see Laurette in it and it had become a legend in New York before it arrived.

There was really little question that it would be well reviewed by everyone but my nemesis, the critic George Jean Nathan, who said that it hardly mattered except for Laurette, and I am not sure that his feeling for Laurette was sincere, since he sent her a bottle of booze as a present on opening night in New York.

Laurette may or may not have been drinking, I never cared about that, but she wrote a thank-you note to Nathan: "Thanks for the vote of confidence."

Thank God she was happy that spring and apparently unaware that she was dying.

"I am kicking around the clouds," she said in an interview.

She stayed with the play for a year and a half, sacrificing much of her personal comfort and health; she remained in the part that long because of a heroic perseverance I find as magnificent as her art itself. She died in December of 1946.

I was in Dick Orme's house on St. Peter Street in New Orleans, the second-floor apartment. While I was at work one morning, he shouted up the air shaft, "Tennessee, it's just come over the radio that Laurette Taylor is dead."

I couldn't respond.

After a few moments he then shouted this appalling one-liner: "I knew you'd be *disappointed.*"

# 6

After the success of *Menagerie*, as I've said before, I felt a great depression, probably because I never believed that anything would continue, would hold. I never thought my advance would maintain its ground. I always thought there would be a collapse immediately after the advance. Also, I had spent so much of my energy on the climb to success, that when I had "made it" and my play was "the hottest ticket in town," I felt almost no satisfaction.

I remember one night I was in my room at the Algonquin. Audrey Wood, Bill Liebling, and Mother were there and I felt so tired that I stretched out on a sofa. Then suddenly I felt nauseated and I rushed to the bathroom to vomit.

Mother said, "Tom, you need a rest, come home for a while."

But home was not where my heart was. I decided to go to Mexico, which I had enjoyed so much that summer of 1940. I went there by way of Dallas, where my dear friend Margo Jones, also the "late," was putting on an early draft of *Summer and Smoke* in her arena theatre. Well, I thought the production was awful but I loved Margo and I pretended to like it. Soon afterward I took off for Mexico City on a train, passing through the Sierra Madre mountains, which were so lovely in those days, and taking up

residence in Mexico City at an annex of the great Hotel Reforma.

I was lonely at first. But soon I met Leonard Bernstein, who was quite friendly to me. And then I met a
rich man who gave strictly male parties in his apartment every Saturday night. And then I was lonely no
more. The parties were really dances and at these
Saturday night dances I learned how to "follow." You
see, the Mexicans always had that *macho* complex
and I was also a rather short young man to be leading other young men, so I learned to follow quite
well. It was a happy time, there, but I have never
been a polygamous person when I could be otherwise,
and I was happy to meet a young student, part Indian and extremely well formed in body and spirit, on
a boulevard in the capital city. I was walking along
when I heard these footsteps behind me, maintaining
a close distance, so presently I looked back and I saw
this darkly handsome boy and there were stone
benches along El Paseo de la Reforma, so I sat down
on one of those benches and the kid stopped and sat
down beside me. I knew no Spanish and he knew
little English but we spent that night in my room at
the annex of the Reforma, a little hotel called the
Lincoln, which didn't mind a guest bringing in a guest.

The altitude of Mexico City gave me a sort of false
animation and I wrote a great deal, including the
short story "One Arm" and perhaps a bit more about
Blanche, and I was very happy with the student. I
have never liked hairy bodies, and, being half Indian,
he was very smooth skinned and if I hadn't been restless—who knows?

But then life is full of transient loves when you are
young, even though you may long for the comfort of a
lasting companion.

I remember taking a bus to Cuernavaca and stop-
ping at a big hotel there which had a swimming pool,
but after a swim, I walked about the town a bit and
took a curious dislike to it which was so intense that,

when I got back to my hotel, I inquired when the next bus would leave for Mexico City. Being told that none would go there until the next morning, I committed the first great extravagance of my life, I hired a taxi to drive me back. I remember how deliciously cool and fragrant with pine wood the air was through the open window of the taxi, how fast it drove and how I longed to resume my intimacy with the half-Indian student and the Saturday night dances.

I still believe that the open country of Mexico is the most beautiful I have seen in the world, and I have seen a great deal of the world.

A little anecdote of not much consequence:

One day Leonard Bernstein and I were both invited to lunch by a pair of very effete American queens. Bernstein was very hard on them and I was embarrassed by the way he insulted them.

"When the revolution comes," he declared, "you will be stood up against a wall and shot."

Bernstein has since been accused of something called "radical chic." But looking back on that luncheon, I wonder if he is not as true a revolutionary as I am, the difference being I am not interested in shooting piss-elegant queens or anyone else, I am only interested in the discovery of a new social system—certainly not Communist, but an enlightened form of socialism, I would suppose.

That summer past me, I returned to New York, where rehearsals were about to begin on my collaborative effort with Donald Windham, a play called *You Touched Me!* based upon the short story by that title, written by one of my idols, D. H. Lawrence, whose widow had given us the rights to dramatize it some years before.

I feel a bit tired now and I'm going back to bed, here on Dumaine Street in the French Quarter of New Orleans.

I am working against time, and there is no reason to evade that issue, I mean to ignore the matter of time running out so rapidly.

I could, at this point, assume some sort of heroic posture but it would only be for self-satisfaction of a kind I despise, attributable to self-pity, a quality I find particularly abhorrent. My attitude toward myself has never been one of pity, thank God. I've got, to quote Leona Dawson in *Small Craft Warnings,* this terrible pride in my nature: if a person, whether a lovesick beautician like Leona or not, has pride in his nature, he is not about to indulge in the demeaning exercise of self-pity.

Speaking of demeaning exercises, this morning another one of those television companies, complete with commentator and crew, arrived at my place on Dumaine and set up in the patio for an interview with me. This time it was German television. The commentator was from Hamburg, one of my favorite resorts during the restless fifties. The crew was led with Wagnerian intensity by a very tall German lady named Ingrid. The commentator sat beneath a spreading banana tree which protected him from the rain while I had to sit out in the open getting drenched and answering all of those innocuous questions and pretending total ignorance of their reason for having come down here, which is, of course, the fact that they want to get some footage on the notorious American playwright, the queer one, whose decease will soon give him a moment of prominence in the media. Do you know how people are about things like that? Well, if you don't, I can tell you. They love it. It quickens their blood. It makes them feel immortal.

Well, that is human, but I don't think I am going to continue to perform for these visiting TV folks unless they come up with more interesting questions.

Now only a few weeks back, when I was at my home in New Orleans, the Canadian Broadcasting

Company sent a commentator and a crew down there. Basically, it was for the same reason, to get some footage on the notorious playwright, addicted to dope and all that. The commentator was Harry Rasky and Harry and I got along fine together despite the fact there was no direct allusion on his part to the object of his pilgrimage. I was not feeling much better, then, than I am feeling today, and it was just as hot then as it is now and we had to walk about the streets of the Quarter while Harry interviewed me and I was drenched on that occasion with sweat instead of rain. But so was Harry. He did not sit under a sheltering banana tree.

Then there was the Austrian company last spring in Key West. They were very nice, indeed, and I did not have to leave the vicinity of my pool and patio. Viola Veidt was there. She speaks perfect German, being the daughter of the late Conrad Veidt. They wanted me to say something in German (since I am one-quarter Hun) but I know very little of that language besides *auf Wiedersehen* and it was not yet time to say good-by, so Viola whispered to me, "Say *Ficken ist gesund.*" That means, "Fucking is healthy." Well, I said it to them and they were very amused, it was the sort of remark that I was expected to make. They said it would not be used by the Austrian stations, but if they released the show in Germany, the remark would be left in.

Yesterday's commentator from Hamburg was obviously disconcerted when I cut through the prepared questions to talk about the atrocity of the American involvement in Vietnam, about Nixon's total lack of honesty and of a moral sense, and of the devotion I had to the cause of Senator McGovern.

On the subject of television shows, I was living, at a point in the sixties, in a high-rise apartment building adjoining the Dakota Apartments on West Seventy-second Street, in New York City. I was at that time under drugs, rather deeply, and did not know, when I got up one morning, that I had previously acquiesced, perhaps involuntarily, to a request by the TV commentator Mike Wallace to interview me in my apartment that morning.

Out I came stumbling in a pair of shorts from my bedroom with the twin beds, one never occupied. I entered the blaze of television cameras in the big front room of the thirty-third-story apartment. A full TV crew had been set up and there was Mike Wallace, an old friend of mine, staring at me with a blend of dismay and chagrin and God knows what else. I fell down flat on my face. I had a habit of doing that in the sixties. They picked me up. Somebody put a robe on me. Then Mike Wallace began asking me things. I don't remember what. I simply remember that I sat there in a blank silence and that after about fifteen minutes Mike turned sadly to the crew and said, "Pack up, we're not going to get anything."

The early autumn of 1946, the production of *You Touched Me!*, put on by Guthrie McClintic and a fine cast of players, went not too well. In the cast was the young Monty Clift and he was at the time the most promising young actor on Broadway, this being a couple of years before the astonishing advent of Brando, which I suspect had much to do with the long and dreadful crack-up of dear Monty. I haven't seen or read *You Touched Me!* since 1946 and as far as I know it has never been produced anywhere again, which is unfortunate for it had some very funny and, also, some very touching scenes in it. That wonderful old character actor with the bulldog face, Edmund Gwenn, told a very funny story, in the play, about his affair with a female porpoise. Also in the cast was an Irish actor of the same vintage, Neil Fitzgerald, playing a parson and there was a hilarious scene in which he proposed marriage to the spinster proprietress of the pottery.

At the back of the house, when the opening night curtain had dropped to unenthusiastic applause, stood little Audrey Wood Liebling. As I filed out of the theatre with crestfallen Windham, my collaborator, she said in a sort of crooked-mouth whisper, "Mixed notices, dear." And right she was, the notices were very mixed.

In those days, however, a play could run for several months on mixed notices, and it seems to me that *You Touched Me!* played through the fall season.

I had been introduced to two lovers in 1939 by Harold Vinal, editor of *Voices*. He was living at the Hotel Winslow on Madison, he had a tiny room with a double-decker bunk and he had invited me over, having published a sequence of my lyrics.

He invited me to meet a pair of "delightful Georgia boys" who were living on Fifty-second Street in conditions close to starvation.

The prospect pleased me so off we went to West Fifty-second, the block of it known in those days as "Tin Pan Alley." The street floor din was frightful but "the boys" had a sparsely furnished room on the second floor, it was a walk-up.

I had no sooner seen one of these boys, with his great dreamy eyes and willowy figure, than I thought, Baby, this one's for you.

We all started dancing to a band that was playing directly below their room and I no sooner had him in my arms for the ostensible motive of dancing than I began to kiss him and paste my pelvis to his.

His companion sat down gloomily and menacingly in a corner. A young man of Cherokee or Choctaw extraction broke in on my partner and me and he took me as his partner; he told me that I must relinquish my amorous advances on "Dreamy Eyes" at once, as his companion was extremely, dangerously jealous.

I had not yet dug the turnabout nature of homosexual attachments. I was an honorable young queer so I turned my attentions immediately upon the Indian.

The party broke up and the Indian offered to see me home to the "Y."

"Oh, thanks," I said, "I am new in town and can't get about alone."

I sublimated my attraction to Dreamy Eyes and we became close buddies. We soon were cruising together, mostly about Times Square. One night we were approached by two sailors outside the Crossroads Inn after midnight. It so happened that my friend had booked a room at the Claridge Hotel because the painter with whom he stayed had an overnight guest.

Well! It was a night to remember but not for romantic reasons. I was somewhat suspicious and not very intrigued when the sailors insisted that we enter separately, my friend and I going straight up to the room and the sailors following later.

I was far from enchanted by the brutal sex-bit. When it was completed, the sailors abruptly ripped the telephone cord from the wall. Then they stood me against the wall while they beat up my friend, knocking out a few teeth. Then they stood *him* against the wall with a switch-blade knife while they beat me up.

My upper teeth cut through my lower lip.

The violence, the terror, deprived me of my senses. My friend got me back to the "Y," but I was in a state of fantasy, totally out of my skull.

At the "Y," a sympathetic young doctor stitched my lip.

Thus ended for quite awhile our Times Square cruising together. I wonder if its chief attraction was not our companionship, our being together?

I shall never retract my statement of my sublimated love for this friend, and why should I? Time doesn't take away from true friendship, nor does separation.

I recall a "truth game" at Tallulah's mansion in Coconut Grove, in the 1950's, where her assault upon the part of Blanche was in preparation. During this truth game, when it came the turn of a friend of my old friend Dreamy Eyes to demand truth about the circle of players, he asked me why I had stopped caring for that boy.

I said to him, "Baby, both of us found lovers. He found you and I found Frankie—and we were both so absorbed in our loves that we neglected our friendship."

About the time that *You Touched Me!* opened on Broadway in 1946 I began to feel as if I were going into a physical decline, as indeed I was, it turned out. Nevertheless I was having a good time, socially and sexually. I had a suite on the eighteenth floor of the Hotel Shelton. My room overlooked the East River and there was a good swimming pool and a steam room downstairs and so I had my favorite exercise, swimming, and I also had access to a lot of attractive chance acquaintances whose acquaintanceship I struck up mostly in the steam room. Being surrounded by moist vapor, a cloud of it, used to be a sexual excitant to me. Now I find it obnoxious but in those days, well, I was still presentable with my clothes off and many other patrons of the Shelton pool and steam room were quite lovely. Entertainments were continual, afternoon and evening. At this time an old friend of mine was in New York and his successful activities in the steam room were quite phenomenal. After almost every session in that retreat of moist vapor he would come up to my suite with a congenial young man and it got so that the house dick would follow him up to the suite to see where he was going, and make continual notes upon it.

I eventually noticed that I had begun to receive sour and disparaging looks from the management of the hotel, but this did not disturb me much for I had never gotten along well with managements or land-ladies, I mean not during my emancipated years.

So things went gaily along until sometime in early December when it was no longer mistakable that my health was failing. And so I gave up my suite at the Shelton and I went down to New Orleans before the Christmas season, to live a quiet life, as the doctor advised. I was still, at this time, relatively affluent and I put up in a rather plush hotel, the Pontchartrain, on the edge of the Garden District. I remember writing one of my favorite one-act plays there: it was called *The Unsatisfactory Supper* and I don't know why it is so seldom produced for it is very funny.

But I was alone there and lonely and I began to look at advertisements for furnished apartments in Vieux Carré, where I had lived on previous stays in New Orleans. I was so fortunate as to discover a lovely furnished apartment on Orleans Street half a block from the rear of St. Louis cathedral. It had a lovely gallery and sitting out there on that gallery I could see in the garden behind the cathedral the great stone statue of Christ, his arms outstretched as if to invite the suffering world to come to Him.

That season in New Orleans I did not live alone but with a friend. (Due to the uncompromisingly honest nature of these memoirs, which may be their principal virtue, a number of friends prefer not to have their names linked to mine in this story of my life. I understand and respect this preference. I could invent them as characters the way one might in a piece of fiction, making them different from themselves, but that would violate the first premise of this book; and so I'd rather omit them completely, however regrettable a gap that makes in a work which is a stage for all the *dramatis personae* of my past life who were of importance to me. It may be that some of them will be contented with the omission of certain details that I found endearingly colorful but that offend their present sensibilities. In any case, I'll omit the name of the friend about whom I'll now write.)

As to this particular friend who occupied the center of my life from the late fall of 1946 till at least half a year later, and who continues to be among the closest of my friends, let me only say, now, that he relieved me, during that period, of my greatest affliction, which is perhaps the major theme of my writings, the affliction of loneliness that follows me like my shadow, a very ponderous shadow too heavy to drag after me all of my days and nights . . .

At first I lived a very reclusive life for a resident of New Orleans, that gregarious city. I reduced my activities mostly to that of writing. At first it was difficult, the work didn't seem to have the old impetus to it. I felt as if I had in my organic system some debilitating poison. I had to conserve my energy.

Eventually that season I was entertained a good deal by the elite New Orleans society which in those days resided mainly, if not entirely, on the far side of Canal Street, in what is called the Garden District.

One evening I decided that I felt well enough to give my socially elite friends a party in my little apartment on Orleans Street. Probably some of the young debutantes had never before entered an apartment in the Vieux Carré unless it were in the Pontalba buildings that were on Jackson Square, the only "respectable" dwellings in the Quarter. I mean recognized as such by the Garden District mothers.

My party was a curious occasion.

I remember a young debutante inquiring if she could see my bedroom.

"Why not? It's very nice."

"He's going to show us his bedroom!" exclaimed the young lady.

The whole party trooped in.

They seemed to like the bedroom. Who wouldn't? A bedroom is either the loveliest room of a place of residence or the most abhorrent: this one belonged to the first category.

Then somebody turned to my apartment mate.

"Now show us yours."

"Oh, I—"

He probably knew that a scandal was brewing and would have wished to avoid it but I found it perfectly natural to say, "We share this room."

I thought the silence that followed my statement was not natural at all.

You see, the bed was somewhere between single and double . . .

Debutantes began to whisper to their escorts, there were little secretive colloquies among them and presently they began to thank us for an unusual and delightful evening and to take their leave as though a storm were impending.

I suppose it was better that way. My place in society, then and possibly always since then, has been in Bohemia. I love to visit the other side now and then, but on my social passport Bohemia is indelibly stamped, without regret on my part.

I neglected to mention an extraordinary incident which occurred just following the somewhat precipitate dissolution of the party.

About half an hour after the escorted debutantes had taken to their heels and my friend and I were about to retire, there came a short, nervous rap at the door. I threw on my dressing gown and opened the door upon the handsomest of the young men who had attended our party. He wore only a raincoat and immediately after the door was opened for him, he flung his coat off, rushed into the bedroom and fell sobbing drunkenly on the bed.

"At last a little truth and they couldn't take it," he kept saying, until we put him to sleep.

In the morning he explained that for some reason, obscure to him and certainly to us, he had undressed downstairs in his car and returned to our apartment with just the waterproof coat buckled about him.

*Such are the flowers called immortelles:*
*They are meant to be kept under crystal bells.*

The physical lethargy which had begun to trouble me that season increasingly affected my writing, the work didn't seem to go with its usual *élan vital.* I suffered a strange lassitude. I would get up in the morning and drink my strong black coffee as before but my energy did not respond. All that I distinctly remember writing that time in the French Quarter was a strange little play called *Ten Blocks on the Camino Real.* I sent it to Audrey Wood and I waited several weeks before I got from her an acknowledgment that she had received it. The acknowledgment was of a peculiar nature. I was having dinner in a restaurant when I was called to the phone. It was Audrey calling me from New York.

"About that play you sent me," she said stridently, "put it away, don't let anybody see it."

I don't think Audrey ever realized how subject I was to depression about my work or surely she would not have acknowledged the play in that particular fashion. But agents live in a different world from the artists they represent. They are often very good at making deals but they are sometimes very obtuse in their recognition of an original and striking piece of work in its early stages. I am afraid that her phone call may have prevented me from making a very, very beautiful play out of *Camino Real* instead of the striking but flawed piece which it finally turned into several years later.

Please remember at this point that I am quite capable of being unfair. I am not unfair by intention. But my work—I don't think anyone has ever known, with the exception of Elia Kazan, how desperately much it meant to me and accordingly treated it—or should I say its writer—with the necessary sympathy of feeling.

In the spring of 1946, a great deal happened to me of a most upsetting nature, which I will deal with directly and simply.

It was becoming oppressively warm in New Orleans in early May. I began to think of the cool plateau of New Mexico where I had met Frieda Lawrence and Dorothy Brett and Spuds Johnston and Witter Bynner, and where I'd begun a play about Lawrence, while reading his collected letters, edited by Aldous Huxley. I think those letters are the greatest of Lawrence's work and I'll never forget the last one. It was a one-liner and it referred to the sanitarium in which he died: "This place no good." He was too weak to write anymore. And I remember Frieda's account of his death in her beautiful, unsentimental memoir of her life with him. As he lay dying, he finally said, "I think it's time for morphine."

I decided to go back to Taos and see those Lawrence people again and to breathe the fine mountain air. But, alas, I decided to return there by car while my friend preceded me by train. I went to a second-hand car lot and some shifty-eyed salesman, perhaps a relative of a recent President, sold me a lemon. It was a newly painted black Packard convertible. It looked great. But I was only halfway up the Mississippi Delta, intending to pass through St. Louis for a brief visit with my family, when it broke down for the first time. The water boiled out of the radiator and it stalled on the highway. I got the radiator repaired and continued on to St. Louis. I remember that Dad came out to look at my sporty vehicle and he shook his head dubiously. "It doesn't look to me like a solid piece of goods," he remarked. And right he was.

But what happened in St. Louis was that late one night, after an attack of diarrhea, I felt a stabbing pain in my abdomen.

I was really in an alarming condition, but I had made up my mind to continue my trip to Taos the next morning, so I made no mention of the severe pain but hit the road after breakfast.

The pain continued, with varying degrees of ferocity, all the next day and night. Then, when I was just outside of a town in Oklahoma, something under the hood of the car began to rattle more and more loudly and the car came to a slow halt and refused to start up again.

I hitched a ride into town and went to a garage where I directed a mechanic to pick up the car and haul it in for repair.

Then I checked into one of the hotels. My pains were now not only severe but peculiarly located. Whenever I took a step, I had a shooting stab of pain down the urethra and it was by far the most severe pain I had ever experienced. I got hold of a local doctor who said that I probably had acute appendicitis and that the appendix was probably in an unusual position so that it caused the pain to shoot down my penis. He said that I ought to go at once to a hospital in Wichita, Kansas.

Next morning I followed his advice, I went to Wichita in a day coach and checked into a hospital where I was subjected to quite an ordeal. They diagnosed appendicitis, too, but kept me in the hospital for several days, subjecting me to X-ray examinations. I noticed the doctors whispering together. They would shut up when I came near them in my hospital gown, waiting for the next examination. They said I probably had a chronically irritated appendix. After about three days they released me. I went back to the town in Oklahoma, where the car was now permanently installed in the garage. The owner—who was the meanest son of a bitch I've known in my life, during

which I've known quite a few mean red neck sons of
bitches—told me that the bearings had burnt out and
that he couldn't say when he'd be able to get it repaired.

So the next morning I set out for Taos by train.

I got there and the pain got there with me. In fact
it was now much worse. My friend had taken a house
for us but I couldn't sleep and I had no pain-killing
drug or sedative tablets.

The next day I went to a little hospital which had
been established in Taos by Mabel Dodge Luhan and
which was run by a pair of handsome young doctors.
The nurses were Catholic nuns. It was a charming
little hospital in some respects. The doctors were wise
enough to give me a blood count. They were shocked
by my quantity of white blood cells, and said that I
must have a perforated appendix to account for this
and that I must have immediate surgery if I expected
to live.

That was evening. My friend sat in the hospital
with me and I made out my last will and testament
while the young doctors shaved my groin for surgery.
I had nothing to leave but the playscript of *Battle of
Angels* and I left it to my friend. He took the will and
tore it to pieces. (He always had moments of great
style and this was one of them.) I was carted to the
operating room. As I went under ether, I had a sensation of death. I went out trying to tear the ether mask
off my face and shouting, "I'm dying, I'm dying."

When I came to I was back in my hospital room. A
nun who was the hospital pathologist was cheerily
bustling about the room. She told me that I had been
on the operating table for seven hours.

"You'll probably be all right for a while," she informed me. "Of course we all have to die of something sooner or later."

When the young doctors came to my room later
that day, I told them what the pathologist had said to
me, that I thought I must be dying. There was a great

disturbance. They were furious at the pathologist and gave her a great dressing down. Soon she rushed into my room and said, "I don't care what you've got, it's nothing to me."

The doctors informed me that they had removed what they called a *"Maecles Diverticulum"* of the small intestine (a medical rarity), which had contained pancreatic tissue and that it had been at the point of bursting and that had accounted for the great number of white blood cells.

In a few days I was out of the hospital, free of pain, and in contact with Frieda Lawrence.

She wanted to take me up to the Lawrence ranch in the mountains, and off we went. For some reason, the altitude, I guess, I became wildly exhilarated. We had stopped at a cantina along the road and purchased a big jug of wine and we drank and laughed as we went up the mountain and then all at once I found myself breathless. "Please stop the car, I can't breathe!" I got out and stood under a pine tree but the breathlessness continued. We must have been about eight thousand feet up in the mountains and we commenced a wild race down. It was like something out of a chase scene in the movies. Frieda drove that car like a firetruck and I kept drinking wine and struggling to breathe. We went straight back to the hospital. One of the doctors said, "Of course you couldn't go up eight thousand feet with your heart after a seven-hour operation."

I have never talked much about that experience in the spring of '46. It marked the beginning of about three years in which I thought I was a dying man. I was so convinced that I was dying that, when Bill Liebling told me, in New York, to buy a new suit, I was reluctant to buy one as I didn't think I was going to live long enough to justify its purchase.

When I first returned to Manhattan that late spring, my dear friend Professor Oliver Evans arranged for me to stay with an elderly lady who lived alone in a two-floor apartment. The elderly lady with whom I stayed was of high social position and wealth but she was ill and lonely, companioned only by servants. She had an odd diversion, or hobby, which was clipping from newspapers and periodicals everything she could find about the newsworthy Senator Joseph McCarthy, whom she regarded as a saintly crusader against the Bolshevik terror in the States. Her other diversions were dancing after dinner in her living room and lunching or dining at an exclusive club. We loved dining and lunching with her but were somewhat embarrassed by her postprandial suggestion: "Shall we dahnce?" She was so very ill and so very thin, it was like dancing with a skeleton in silk. She insisted that her doctors could find nothing wrong with her but "a few little adhesions after her operation." She was very touchingly quaint.

About this time I found a new companion, one whom I encountered after the one who prefers to be unmentioned by any name in this book left me.

The new companion was serenely accepted by our hostess. He danced with her gladly. He served as model for her technically accomplished but conventional portraits.

One day the charmingly eccentric old lady said to me: "I want to give you a party. Pick out some friends from this book."

The book she handed me was the *Social Register* of New York and the only friend, a distant relation, whom I could find in it was a Mrs. Inman, née Coffin, a lady of high degree but afflicted with periods of deep melancholia. Some months before she had returned from Europe with half a million dollars in Belgian lace. Then deep melancholia struck her, the lace was left out of whatever fine lace should be kept in for moth protection, and the moths ate it up. Oh, well. *Tant pis*. She was nevertheless on the upgrade from her psychic syndrome and she came to the party, very silent but benignly present. I'd had to confess to

my hostess that this relative was the only acquaintance
I could find in the register.

The lady appeared to be about to drop dead at this
information, but she recovered from it gracefully after
a while.

"Oh, you artists!" she said.

And then she permitted me to invite the friends I
had from my own social echelon in New York. And I
am happy to say that she had a lovely time at the
party.

Now I must invent, much as I dislike invention in
these memoirs, a name for my new companion I met
in New York. He was sort of an off-beat Saint and so
I'll call him Santo. The dark side of his nature (since
overcome) was a drinking habit that made him, at
times, disturbingly unpredictable and startling in his
behavior.

He didn't understand that I had a number of young
platonic friends in New York; he suspected that I had
nothing but business associates and lovers, often combined. This was certainly not at all the case.

One afternoon in Manhattan I was sitting in the
lobby of the Hotel Algonquin having a pleasant chat
with an old friend and his boy-friend, when into the
Algonquin lobby, crowded with suburbanite types,
much like the matrons out of *New Yorker* cartoons, in
rushed Santo. In a tempest of rage he shouted at my
decorous young guests, "You two are the two biggest
whores on Broadway."

The lobby was evacuated by all of the suburbanite
ladies in a flash as Santo went on with his invectives.
At last he turned on me. "Go over to the Royalton
and see what I've done!"

(We were staying at the Royalton Hotel, directly
across Forty-fourth Street from the Algonquin.)

Well, I went over there and I discovered that he
had literally ripped to shreds all of my clothes, that he
had demolished my typewriter and suitcase. But, for

some reason, he had left my manuscripts undamaged.

Of course I should have parted company with Santo right away, but he was pitiably contrite. I had made plans to go to the island of Nantucket, on which the Coffin side of my family had once flourished, and I didn't want to go alone, so I permitted Santo to go along with me. On Nantucket we rented a gray frame house a bit outside of town and for some reason I remember its address clearly: 31 Pine Street.

Now about this time I had written a letter to Carson McCullers, a writer I didn't know, full of very sincere praise of her new novel, *The Member of the Wedding*. And in the letter I told her I was very anxious to meet her.

It must have been a persuasive letter for it was just a few days later that she came to Nantucket. She got off the ferry looking very tall and wearing slacks and a baseball cap and grinning her delightful crooked-toothed grin.

After our affectionate greetings, I said that I wanted to go to the beach for a swim. She said that suited her fine and we went to the beach, Santo very drunk but coming along.

At the beach a scene occurred which seems rather funny in retrospect. Carson and I had changed into bathing suits but Santo was still in the bathhouse and all at once a great disturbance began inside there. Then Santo came dashing onto the front gallery. Along this front gallery was a long row of rocking-chairs and in each chair was seated an old lady. For some reason Santo did not like the way they looked and he turned his rage upon them.

At the top of his voice, addressing these very proper old ladies, he shouted, "What are you looking at? You're nothing but a bunch of old cock-suckers!"

Well, I don't suppose this would create such a tremendous sensation today, but I am surprised that back then, in 1946, the old ladies didn't all fall out of their rockers in a swoon.

Carson was delighted. "Tennessee honey," she said, "that boy is wonderful, you are lucky to have him with you!"

I was by no means convinced of this, but we went home and we set up housekeeping at 31 Pine Street. This was before Carson was ill. She was a good cook and she put the house in order while she prepared good meals. It was all quite nice for a time. She had the downstairs guest room and Santo and I slept upstairs. Santo was temporarily subdued. Carson played the piano and created an atmosphere of harmony about the place.

One night there was a great thunderstorm and all the windows broke on one side of the house and they were never repaired.

A pregnant cat climbed in one of the windows and had a large number of kittens on Carson's bed. Santo served as midwife. With the tender side of his nature, and a certain animal intuition which he possessed, he gave the cat, during her time of delivery, teaspoons of whiskey to keep her energy up. This is the only time that I have seen an animal drink whiskey but it worked and the mother cat provided us with eight or nine kittens. The cat had a bad habit, though, of bringing old fish-heads into the house, through the broken windows. This did not bother Carson; in fact she put up with anything and everything. That summer we sat at opposite ends of a table and worked together, she on her dramatization of *The Member of the Wedding* and I on *Summer and Smoke*, and in the evenings we read aloud to each other our day's work.

Later on that summer her husband, Reeves McCullers, came to join us. He was an ex-marine and I didn't particularly like him at that time. He was not good company. He seemed morose and introverted and so was I and he interrupted my happy companionship with Carson.

I was still not well, in fact I got so that I could not

keep down food, I would vomit almost everything I ate, and so the summer ended with my returning to New York and entering a hospital again. I stayed there a week. They gave me various medications and soon I was able to return to New Orleans.

After that summer Carson and I remained friends, and over the years the memories accumulate. I think of three important times in my life when Carson was there, all of them exits in which Carson and I took part: three of the longest, the most agonizing exits that I can remember.

One was from the birthday party given for Dylan Thomas by my publishers, who were also his. When I was introduced to him, all that he said by way of acknowledgment was this put-down: "How does it feel to make all that Hollywood money?"

In retrospect it was thoroughly understandable and excusable, but then it stung me badly. Carson he simply ignored. After a few moments, she said, "Tenn, honey, take me out of here!" —This was after her stroke, and as I led her out of the birthday celebration, she trembled in my supporting arm and the exit seemed to be everlasting.

Another exit was more painful.

Carson had made the mistake of attending the opening night party of her play, *The Square Root of Wonderful* and the greater mistake of remaining there till the reviews came out.

They were simply awful.

Carson again said to me, "Tenn, help me out of here." And it was an even longer and more agonizing exit.

The third exit we made together was also from an opening night party: the opening in New York in 1948 of the Margo Jones production of *Summer and Smoke*. On this occasion it was I who said to Carson: "Let's get out of here." It was also a long and agonizing exit, everyone staring at us, the notices out . . . And those notices were not very good. I was living then in a Tony Smith designed apartment on East Fifty-eighth Street. When I woke in the morning, it was to a record of Mozart. Carson had already arrived in the apartment and put the record on to comfort my waking moments.

Well, I was not in the mood for comfort or for pity, which is really not comforting, much . . . so I told Frank Merlo (who will appear later in this book; I lived with him for a long, long time) to cut the Mozart off and to see Carson to a cab before I got out of bed.

I wanted to get back to work: alone, and right away.

In New Orleans, in the autumn of 1947, I obtained one of the loveliest apartments I've ever occupied. It was on the second floor of Dick Orme's residence near the corner of St. Peter and Royal, and since Dick worked in an antique store and had exquisite taste, the apartment was beautifully furnished. What I liked most about it was a long refectory table under a skylight which provided me with ideal conditions for working in the mornings. I know of no city where it is better to have a skylight than New Orleans. You know, New Orleans is slightly below sea level and maybe that's why the clouds and the sky seem so close. In New Orleans the clouds always seem just overhead. I suppose they are really vapor off the Mississippi more than genuine clouds and through that skylight they seemed so close that if the skylight were not glass, you could touch them. They were fleecy and in continual motion. I was alone all day. Consistent with my habit, which I still follow today, I would rise early, have my black coffee and go straight to work.

I was going on with the writing then of *Summer and Smoke*, but the play was a tough nut to crack. Miss Alma Winemiller may very well be the best female portrait I have drawn in a play. She simply seemed to exist somewhere in my being and it was no effort to put her on paper. However, the boy she was in love with all her youth, Johnny Buchanan, never seemed real to me but always a cardboard figure and I knew it and it distressed me but I kept at the play for a couple of months, I wrote several drafts of it. Then one evening, when I thought it completed, I read it aloud to a young man who was friendly to me. He kept yawning as I read and so I read badly and when I finished, he made this devastating remark: "How could the author of *The Glass Menagerie* write such a bad play as this?"

I was crushed for a few days, but then I took up where I'd left off with *Streetcar,* which I was then calling *The Poker Night.* I wrote furiously on it. For despite the fact that I thought I was dying, or maybe because of it, I had a great passion for work. I would work from early morning until early afternoon, and then, spent from the rigors of creation, I would go around the corner to a bar called Victor's and revive myself with a marvelous drink called a Brandy Alexander, which was a specialty of the bar. I would always play the Ink Spots' rendition of "If I Didn't Care" on the jukebox while I drank the Alexander. Then I'd eat a sandwich and then I'd go to the Athletic Club on North Rampart Street. It had a pool that was fed by an underground spring of artesian water and it was cool from the underground and it would pick me up.

I continued to think I was dying of pancreatic cancer. But then my grandfather, the Reverend Walter Edwin Dakin, came to live with us. He had cataracts on both eyes and was nearly deaf. Grand and Grandfather had together been the source of the greatest support and kindnesses to me all my life. By then Grand had died, but I remember her great dignity, especially during the summer after I had received my diploma from the University of Iowa, and Grand and Grandfather were living with us in St. Louis. Grand had entered the terminal state of her malignancy and she had been forced to give up the little house in Memphis.

Grandfather was even then almost totally deaf and he had to crouch before the radio to get the news, which was all he cared about in the broadcasts. Grand would stand terribly thin and tall and stork-like just behind the front window curtains, and when Dad's Studebaker came charging up the drive, she would turn in a panic to my grandfather and cry out, "Walter, Walter, Cornelius is coming, will you hurry upstairs, don't let him see you down here!"

But poor Grandfather, it took him forever to mount those stairs and he was always overtaken in his escape effort by the slam-door entrance of C.C.

"Oh, there's the ole hound-dawg," Dad would mutter. But he would always turn to Grand and say, "Good evening, Mrs. Dakin," and she would say to him, "Good evening, Cornelius."

And then, instinctively she would cross over to the piano and play a soothing étude by Chopin to smooth over the abrasive incident as best she could.

Dinner would be served almost immediately after Dad's return to the house from the office, via his favorite bar. He would not show any physical sign of inebriation except the fiery red of his little piercing blue eyes.

All that is not the worst of me surely comes from Grand, except my Williams anger and endurance, if those be virtues. Whatever I have of gentleness in my nature, and I do have much in response to gentle treatment, comes from the heart of Grand, as does the ineluctable grace and purity of heart that belong to the other Rose in my life, my sister.

Later in 1946, Margo Jones and her friend Joanna Albus arrived in New Orleans, where Grandfather and I were living, and I read them the first draft of *Streetcar*, aloud. I think they were shocked by it. And so was I. Blanche seemed too far out. You might say out of sight. But when Margo and Joanna left, I de-

cided to drive down to Key West with Grandfather.
It was a lovely drive, the Pontiac behaving well. We
crossed the Suwannee River and we cut across from
the west coast of Florida to the east. Grandfather was
a wonderful traveling companion. Everything pleased
him. He pretended to see clearly despite his cataracts
and in those days you could shout to him and he'd
hear you. All his life he had been in love with life, and
just being with him revived my own pleasure in the
fact of existence.

We arrived in Key West and occupied a two-room
suite on the top of the Hotel La Concha and it was
there that I really began to get *Streetcar* into shape.
It went like a house on fire, due to my happiness with
Grandfather.

Every afternoon when I was through work we
would drive out to South Beach. It was still nice in
those days, before the advent of the motels and the
parking lots. I would swim and swim and Grandfather
would sit at the edge of the water and let the waves
wash over him.

Several hospitable and interesting people were
there. Pauline Pfeiffer Hemingway was occupying
the Spanish colonial home where Ernest had left her
when he split to Cuba and Pauline entertained
Grandfather and me. Then Miriam Hopkins arrived
on the scene and enlivened it still more with her extravagant wit and charm.

I finished *Streetcar* and mailed it to Audrey Wood
and this time I received from that little lady a much
more positive and encouraging reaction.

Then I first encountered Irene Selznick. My meeting
with her was arranged by Audrey with the atmosphere
of high-level espionage. I was wired to come directly to Charleston, South Carolina, to the best hotel
there, where I was to have a rendezvous with Irene
and Audrey. I went there posthaste. Irene flung open
the door of her suite with her eyes ablaze and it was
settled that very evening that she would produce

*Streetcar*. The atmosphere of mystery continued. Irene wired the office she had set up in New York: it was a coded message to her assistant and the message read: "Blanche is coming to stay with us." This was all very exciting for me. I left Charleston to rejoin Grandfather in Key West, where Mrs. Hemingway and other friends had been looking out for him.

Mardi Gras was now approaching in New Orleans and Grandfather was determined not to miss it, so he went ahead by plane while I drove the snow-white secondhand Pontiac convertible up the east coast of Florida. All went well until I came near the town of Jacksonville. I had picked up a redheaded youth, hitchhiking, and we were beginning to discuss the matter of checking into a roadside motel for the rest of the night, when suddenly a highway patrol car came screaming up to us and ordered us onto the shoulder of the road. The highway patrolman said I had no taillights on my car and then he demanded to see my registration papers and my driver's license, of which I had neither. I was not at all bright about the exigencies of driving, or was I merely indifferent to them? Anyway the fiendish highway patrolman handcuffed my right wrist to my left ankle and told me to get out of the car. I asked him how it was possible for me to get out of the car with my right wrist handcuffed to my left ankle and he yanked me out and told me to crawl to his patrol car. Well, I managed to do it while he marched the redheaded hitchhiker to the car behind me. We were driven to the jailhouse in Jacksonville. It was about midnight. We were thrown into a bull-pen, a small barred enclosure containing drunks and addicts and homos. I had always suffered from claustrophobia and I had a hard time controlling my nerves. That night the police had raided some black whorehouses and their brutality to the poor girls was hardly to be believed. They kicked them up and down stairs and they hit them over the head with their billy-sticks. About daybreak a bondsman came to see me. He said he would represent my case, when it came up, for three hundred dollars. I happened to have some traveler's checks with me which covered that extraordinary demand.

About noon the next day I was let out of the bullpen and told that before my car would be released to me and before I would be permitted to continue my journey to New Orleans, I would have to pass a driver's license test. I was given a bunch of test papers to study and I don't think I've ever studied anything so hard. Miraculously, I managed to pass the test and was released by the law.

For some reason they wouldn't allow me to pay the bond for the young hitchhiker. I had to leave him in that Jacksonville bull-pen and heaven knows what he endured there.

With a driver's license and taillights working, I resumed my journey to New Orleans, where Grandfather was enjoying Mardi Gras, a celebration that has never appealed to me but that was great fun for Grandfather since the floats passed directly by our corner and he was thrilled by the spectacle, which he managed to see despite his growing blindness.

How much trivia there is to be set down in the record of one's life: There must be much between the lines that is more deserving of recollection but somehow that remains in a nebulous state while the mere surface history comes back clearly to mind. I mean relatively clearly . . .

# 7

Tonight I have been announced as appearing in *Small Craft Warnings* with the replacement for Helena Carroll a very gifted actress named Peg Murray, whom Bill Hickey calls one of the best in the business, despite the fact that she is not well known outside the profession.

It will be exciting to see a gifted actress, after such short preparation, take over the demanding role of Leona and to see us all up there giving her our support, covering the almost inevitable "fluffs" as best we can, and loving her as actors must love each other on such critical occasions, if there is love in this world, and I think there is. I think there is love in this world and even in the profession of acting, love that may expire backstage but that I think, in the form of co-operation, is nearly always present on-stage when the play is imperiled by the performance, the opening one, of a new star who has not been allowed enough time and rehearsals to undertake her part.

It will be exciting and it may be beautiful, too.

I recall a letter from Brooks Atkinson when he retired as drama critic for the New York *Times*.

I was on the Coast and I wrote him: "I think it is time for me to retire, not you, Brooks."

He wrote me back: "You must go on with your allusive work." I am not sure that my work was, at that time, still allusive but there is no question that it should be and that the advice was warmly given and well intended.

Yesterday two events of importance: one personal, the other political and very, very public.

The personal event was dinner with Miss Rose and her increasingly irritable and irritating companion. To complete the party, I brought along a young friend, a gifted painter, model, and sometime actor.

Miss Nameless had decided to book us a table at Lüchow's, the beautiful Bavarian-looking restaurant, half as old as time, and we were very nicely placed just under the bandstand. The band, in Bavarian or Tyrolean costume and not a one in the bunch that the costume was becoming to, started to play at 7 P.M., just fifteen minutes after our arrival.

What charmed me most was a skylight close to our table, through which I saw first dark going into a deep dusk as the dinner progressed—well, disintegrated is a better word for it, since Nameless had her Irish up and immediately started to put down my poor young friend—and how he controlled his temper with that Irish biddy, deep in her cups and mean as a rattler, I cannot comprehend. He must be at least half an angel.

Miss Nameless began to take on the "young" in general as a bunch of social parasites and leeches and degenerates.

She declared that the good old days had gone completely and there was no dignity or integrity left in the world.

My friend and I had agreed in advance that when this lady started to show her bitch-colors, we'd say, one of us to the other, that we had seen a robin today in Central Park, and wasn't that strange for a robin to be around so late in summer.

Well, I can't tell you how many times we had to make references to the late summer appearance of this robin and to other valentine aspects of Central Park in order to keep things bearably cool at the table.

But I'm afraid I lost my cool and I turned on Nameless and said, "Let's face it, you have turned into a reactionary and I am a revolutionary."

She then started talking about mongrels, meaning the young man and I. You see, she is completely Irish and she regards all persons not completely Irish as mongrels. And, alas, she has no Irish humor on this subject.

Of course, when the evening was over, I began to feel a bit sorry for Nameless. She is so tough in her loneliness, her spinsterhood, and her archaic "principles," which are as hypocritical as "principles" of her vintage could possibly be.

The story of my sister Rose's tragedy begins a few years before I commenced my three-year break from college to work for the Continental Shoemakers branch of the International Shoe Company.

I have mentioned that Rose suffered for several years from mysterious stomach trouble. She was several times hospitalized for this digestive trouble but no ulcer, no physical cause for the illness, could be determined. At last it was recommended that she have "an exploratory operation."

Luckily our family doctor, a brilliant physician, intervened at this point and told my mother, much to her dismay, that it was his (quite accurate) opinion that Rose needed psychiatric attention, the mysterious digestive upset being due, he thought, to psychic or psychosomatic reasons that could be determined only through the course of analysis.

You can imagine how this struck Miss Edwina. I am afraid that dear Mother has at times seemed to me to have been a moderately controlled hysteric all her life—and in her family tree (on both sides of it, Dakins and Ottes) have been alarming incidences of mental and nervous breakdowns.

As a matter of fact, when Miss Edwina herself landed in the bin, sometime during the early fifties, and phoned me at St. Thomas in the Virgin Islands, where I had gone for a brief much-needed vacation, she said, "Guess where I *am?*"

"Why, Mother, aren't you at home?"

"No, son. A horrible mistake has been made. I have been put in a psychiatric ward. Please come at once and get me right out of here."

I did come at once. She had a female psychiatrist on her case and I had a private consultation with this lady and this lady said, "Mr. Williams, you probably know or have suspected that your mother has been paranoiac all her life."

She then told me that Mother was "thoroughly artificial and superficial."

Well, I was rightly indignant, despite some grain of truth that might be in this callously worded diagnosis.

"Be that as it may, and I don't think you're a reliable authority on my mother's character since you say she has refused to talk to you—I want her immediate release."

I sprung Mother right away.

Well, now let's get back to Miss Rose.

In her early twenties Rose was sent to Knoxville with a few inexpensive party dresses to "make her debut." A formal debutante party had been planned by Aunt Belle (Mrs. William G. Brownlow), but the death of her husband's mother, the senior Mrs. Brownlow, intervened and the debut was "informal." A party was given at the Knoxville Country Club, for Rose's informal presentation to society. Aunt Belle had to buy Rose quite a few more dresses during this debut season: even so the debut was not exactly a howling success. I think Miss Rose fell in love with a young man who did not altogether respond in kind; and Rose was never quite the same. A shadow had fallen over her that was to deepen steadily through the next four or five years.

When Rose returned from her Knoxville debut, I said, "How was your visit, Rose?"

She said, "Aunt Ella and Aunt Belle only like charming people and I'm not charming."

An earlier summer, the summer of 1926, after we had all visited in Knoxville, we went on to the Appalachian Club, which Aunt Belle and Uncle Will belonged to. That summer I learned to swim in a clear mountain stream; it was Aunt Belle who taught me, in the pool of fabulously cool, clear water formed by the dam, which offered a sparkling waterfall over bone-white rocks. Aunt Belle tried to support me with a hand under my belly in the pool, and when I said to her, "Aunt Belle, I'd rather depend on myself," she came out with this choice endorsement: "Oh, Tom, dear Tom, when you depend on yourself you're depending on a broken reed."

Actually she was speaking of herself and of her dependence on God. She had an internal goiter which inclined her to extravagance of speech and of course to too much consideration of God.

I am as much of an hysteric as Aunt Belle, you know, and as much as Blanche; a codicil to my will provides for the disposition of my body in this way. "Sewn up in a clean white sack and dropped over board, twelve hours north of Havana, so that my bones may rest not too far from those of Hart Crane . . ."

The Appalachian Club was full that summer of boys that I couldn't keep my eyes off, as they lay sunning themselves on the rocks in the stream. And my Aunt Belle bought me my first long pants, a pair of flannels, and she bought Rose more charming frocks.

We stayed in a little cottage. My brother Dakin had contracted a serious distemper on the way, probably from bad drinking water, and Grand, who was along, made him buttermilk in a churn since buttermilk was all that "Dinky" could eat.

Rose had beaux, she was beautiful in her colorful

summer frocks, and every night we danced. It was the Charleston era. There were two sisters at the club and one of them, I remember, killed herself the next year over a disappointment in love.

I remember Rose and the two sisters and me walking along a narrow mountain road and some mountain boys went past us, chanting out, "*F U C K*."

None of us commented on the occurrence. We continued our way without a sign of hearing the obscenity.

And I remember the afternoon when we walked from the Appalachian Club to Gatlinburg, which is now the annual meeting place of the Seviers. We were with two adolescent youths, devoted to each other but attentive to us. On the way there was a great thundershower and it drenched us.

The girls retired to change in one place and I went to change with the boys. And the boys stripped naked in front of me and I stayed in my wet clothes until they undressed me. Nothing happened of a scandalous nature, but their beauty is indelible in my prurient mind, and also their kindness to me.

One final recollection. One evening that summer, that wild jazz-age summer, we young people gathered in the cabin of a middle-aged lady who was afflicted with some terminal disease. She retired early but remained awake. And we young people began to talk about sex, the great big mystery that we were beginning to explore.

Our hostess, from her bedroom, called out to us. "You are all just children . . ."

And she said it so sweetly and lovingly that we shut up and soon dispersed and the great new mystery of love in our lives, I mean of adolescent sex in our lives, went with us.

It accompanied us away from the afflicted lady.

Rose was a popular girl in high school but only for a brief while. Her beauty was mainly in her expressive green-gray eyes and in her curly auburn hair. She was too narrow-shouldered and her state of anxiety when in male company inclined her to hunch them so they looked even narrower; this made her strong-featured, very Williams head seem too large for her thin, small-breasted body. She also, when she was on a date, would talk with an almost hysterical animation which few young men knew how to take.

The first real breakdown occurred shortly after I had suffered the heart attack that ended my career as a clerk-errand boy at the shoe company.

My first night back from St. Vincent's, as I mentioned, Rose came walking like a somnambulist into my tiny bedroom and said, "We must all die together."

I can assure you that the idea did not offer to me an irresistible appeal. Being now released at last from my three years as a clerk-typist at Continental, God damn it I was in no mood to consider group suicide with the family, not even at Rose's suggestion—however appropriate the suggestion may have been.

For several days Rose was demented. One afternoon she put a kitchen knife in her purse and started to leave for her psychiatrist's office with apparent intent of murder.

The knife was noticed by Mother and snatched away.

Then a day or so later this first onset of dementia praecox passed off and Rose was, at least on the surface, her usual (now very quiet) self again.

A few days later I departed for Memphis to recuperate at my grandparents' little house on Snowden Avenue near Southwestern University in Memphis.

I think it was about this time that our wise old family doctor told Mother that Rose's physical and mental health depended upon what struck Miss Edwina as a monstrous thing—an arranged, a sort of "therapeutic" marriage. Obviously old Doc Alexander had hit upon the true seat of Rose's afflictions. She was a very normal—but highly sexed—girl who was tearing herself apart mentally and physically by those repressions imposed upon her by Miss Edwina's monolithic Puritanism.

I may have inadvertently omitted a good deal of material about the unusually close relations between Rose and me. Some perceptive critic of the theatre made the observation that the true theme of my work is "incest." My sister and I had a close relationship, quite unsullied by any carnal knowledge. As a matter of fact, we were rather shy of each other, physically, there was no casual physical intimacy of the sort that one observes among the Mediterranean people in their family relations. And yet our love was, and is, the deepest in our lives and was, perhaps, very pertinent to our withdrawal from extrafamilial attachments.

There were years when I was in the shoe company and summers when I was a student at the State University of Missouri when my sister and I spent nearly all our evenings together aside from those which I spent with Hazel.

What did we do those evenings, Rose and I? Well, we strolled about the business streets of University City. It was a sort of ritual with a pathos that I assure you was never caught in *Menagerie* nor in my story "Portrait of Girl in Glass," on which *Menagerie* was based.

I think it was Delmar—that long, long street which probably began near the Mississippi River in downtown St. Louis and continued through University City and on out into the country—that Rose and I strolled along in the evenings. There was a root-beer stand at which we always stopped. Rose was inordinately fond of root-beer, especially on warm summer evenings. And before and after our root-beer stop, we would window-shop. Rose's passion, as well as Blanche's, was clothes. And all along that part of Delmar that cut through University City were little shops with lighted windows at night in which were displayed dresses and accessories for women. Rose did not have much of a wardrobe and so her window-shopping on Delmar was like a hungry child's gazing through the window-fronts of restaurants. Her taste in clothes was excellent.

"How about *that* dress, Rose?"

"Oh no, that's tacky. But this one here's very nice."

The evening excursions lasted about an hour and a half, and although, as I've noted, we had a physical shyness of each other, never even touching hands except when dancing together in the Enright apartment, I'd usually follow her into her bedroom when we came home, to continue our warmly desultory chats. I felt most at home in that room, which was furnished with the white ivory bedroom set that had been acquired with the family's "furnished apartment" on Westminster Place when we first moved to St. Louis in 1918.

It was the only attractive room in the apartment—or did it seem so because it was my sister's?

I have mentioned our dancing together.

Rose taught me to dance to the almost aboriginal standing (non-horned) Victrola that had been acquired in Mississippi and shipped to St. Louis at the time of the disastrous family move there.

Dad had subleased our first real residence in St. Louis, a very charming two-story Georgian house in the suburb of Clayton, only a block or two from Washington University. The street was Pershing, and across from our house was the home of Virginia Moore, a strikingly handsome poet of that time; she had a brother who took an interest in Miss Rose and dated her several times. I recall having gone about Clayton distributing political leaflets during that disastrous campaign of his. He lost the election and suddenly was confined in a sanitarium for a nervous breakdown. When he was released from the sanitarium, the poor man killed himself, and Miss Rose lost a beau.

That summer I showed my juvenile poems to Virginia Moore, and how very gracious she was in giving one of them tactful praise.

In the rented house on Pershing, Miss Rose's mind again began to slip. Not violently but gradually.

I remember a drive in the county with young friends. We started, the young friends and I, to laugh at the outrageous behavior of an acquaintance who was losing his mind. Miss Rose turned very grave and stiff in the back seat of the car.

"You must never make fun of insanity," she reproved us. "It's worse than death."

And that's exactly what Mother said when informed that Miss Rose had dementia praecox. This was at a Catholic sanitarium on the outskirts of St. Louis, shortly before Rose was sent away to the State Asylum in 1937. It's not very pleasant to look back on that year and to know that Rose knew she was going mad and to know, also, that I was not too kind to my sister. You see, for the first time in my life, I had become accepted by a group of young friends and my delighted relations with them preoccupied me to such an extent that I failed to properly observe the shadow falling on Rose. Little eccentricities had begun to appear in her behavior. She was now very quiet in the house and I think she was suffering from insomnia. She had the peculiar habit of setting a pitcher of ice-water outside her door, each night when she retired.

As I drifted away from my sister, during this period, she drew close to our little Boston terrier Jiggs. She was constantly holding and hugging him and now and then Miss Edwina would say:

"Rose, put Jiggs down, he wants to run about."

Then there was the wild weekend Mother and Dad had gone to the Ozarks, I believe, and Rose and I were alone in the house on Pershing. That weekend I entertained my new group of young friends. One of them got very drunk—maybe all of them did—but this particular one got drunker than all of us put together and he went up on the landing, where the phone was, and began to make obscene phone calls to strangers.

When our parents returned from the Ozarks, Miss Rose told them of the wild party and the obscene phone calls and the drinking.

I was informed by Miss Edwina that no one of this group should ever again enter the house.

This was, for me, a crushing edict, since the group contained my first dear friend in St. Louis, the brilliantly talented and handsome poet, Clark Mills (McBurney).

After she had tattled on my wild party, during Dad's and Mother's holiday in the Ozarks, when I was told I could no longer entertain my first group of friends in the house—I went down the stairs as Rose was coming up them. We passed each other on the landing and I turned upon her like a wildcat and I hissed at her:

"I hate the sight of your ugly old face!"

Wordless, stricken, and crouching, she stood there motionless in a corner of the landing as I rushed on out of the house.

This is the cruelest thing I have done in my life, I suspect, and one for which I can never properly atone.

(How time does thread through this "thing," and such a long span of it.)

> Time is the flow, the continual show,
> Go says the bird, and on we go.

From the above you can see why I never made much of a mark for myself as a poet.

Have I told you that at Washington University we had a little poetry club? It contained only three male members. The rest were girls, pretty, with families who owned elegant homes in the county.

The three male poets were, in order of talent, Clark Mills, William Jay Smith, and the author of these memoirs.

Of the pretty girls who provided lovely refreshments and décor, I remember only the name of Betty Chapin and the first name of another, the wealthiest, Louise, who took us all out in the family limousine to a ballet performance one night.

Bill Smith was the handsomest of us three boys and he has turned out to be a "poet of prominence," now associated with the teaching of that unteachable art at Columbia University.

Clark's talent burned very bright in those early years. He published a paperback book of verse called *January Crossing*, a collection of distinction, jeweled with fine images and a cultivated taste. He was also a French scholar who was later to receive a scholarship to the Sorbonne in Paris and to write a study of the French *littérateur* Jules Romains, whose work I couldn't read in or out of French. I wish that Clark had devoted himself exclusively to his own work. Artists must be egocentric that way. But he may surely be excused for having written the best translation (in my unbiased opinion) of Rimbaud's *Bateau Ivre*. His translation of the final verse of that greatest lyric by Rimbaud went something, but not exactly, like this:

> Of Europe's waters I want now only
> the chill, muddy ditch,
> where a child full of sorrow crouches at dusk
> to release from his fingers a paper boat
> as frail as a butterfly's wing.

Only Clark paid any serious attention to my efforts at verse. His taste was impeccable but imposed very gently. When I didn't indulge in sophomoric extravagance, he'd say, "I like this, Tom," but when I wrote purple, he would say to me, "Tom, this is too facile."

At dusk in the early sixties I was about to enter my Manhattan apartment on East Sixty-fifth when Clark Mills appeared like an apparition on the walk and stopped and greeted me. It was winter and in his dark coat he looked somberly academic. Either Frankie was dying or was already dead and I was unable to respond at all naturally and freely. All I could think was: "He must know I've turned queer." The conversation was pitiably brief and embarrassed.

"Hello, Tom."

"—Is that you, Clark?"

"Yes."

"What are you doing now?"

He told me that he was connected, now, with Hunter College. He stayed there, with gentle patience, a few moments longer, but I was unable to say, "Clark, come in." So then, a ghost of our youth, he nodded in the winter dusk and continued on his way.

I'm sure he understood.

Someday, probably, he will re-emerge as a poet from what has apparently been a long hibernation.

Bill Smith's talent has matured along more or less methodical lines: I like it because I like Bill but it doesn't thrill me, alas.


Returning to St. Louis and the thirties.

Rose had a "serious" St. Louis beau. He was a junior executive at International, a young man of very personable appearance, social grace and apparently of great and unscrupulous ambition. For a few months he was quite attentive to Rose. They dated, I think, several times a week, they were almost going "steady," and Rose would tremble when the telephone rang, desperately hoping the call was for her and that it was from him.

This was while Dad's position as sales manager of Friedman-Shelby branch of International was still, if not ascendant, at least one of apparent permanence and continued promise.

But Dad was playing fast and loose with his position. He was continually alarming the "establishment" and International by his weekend habits. Significantly, he had not been elected to the "Board of Executives," despite the fact that he was the best and most popular sales manager of International, and the only one who delivered speeches. His speeches were eloquent—and pungent. He did not talk much about his success at oratory but I think it pleased him enormously. He got up there on the platform before the assembled salesmen much in the style of his political forebears running for high offices in East Tennessee.

"Now you boys and I all remember when we used to have to go around the corner and have a cigarette for breakfast . . ."

I mean like *that*—and they loved it.

But the scandal occurred—the episode at the all-night poker party at the Hotel Jefferson in which Dad lost an ear that had to be replaced by plastic surgery. This marked the beginning of the end for Dad's possible ascendancy to "the Board" at International.

It also marked the end of Rose's dates with her handsome and unscrupulously ambitious "beau," who no longer was a potential husband.

Her heart broke, then, and it was after that that the mysterious stomach trouble began.

But you don't know Miss Rose and you never will unless you come to know her through this "thing," for Laura of *Menagerie* was like Miss Rose only in her inescapable "difference," which that old female bobcat Amanda would not believe existed. And as I mentioned, you may know only a little bit more of her through "Portrait of a Girl in Glass."

Nowadays is, indeed, lit by lightning, a plague has stricken the moths, and Blanche has been "put away" . . .

One evening Dad, seated gloomily in the little "sunroom" on Enright, called out to Rose, "Sister, come here, I want to discuss something with you."

He told her that he was in danger of losing his job

at International—this was after the ear incident—and that she must prepare herself for self-support.

Somehow or other—precisely how I don't recall—she did obtain employment as receptionist at the office of some young dentists. The job lasted only one day and ended upon the most pathetic note. She had been unable to address envelopes properly, the young dentists had discharged her and she had fled weeping into the lavatory and locked herself in.

They called us at home and we had to go to the office to persuade her to leave her place of retreat.

Rose was removed in 1937 to the State Asylum in Farmington, Missouri. We went out to visit her.

"Tom, let me show you my ward."

She conducted me through it: it was too awful to believe, all those narrow little cots and hard wooden benches. Under one of the benches was crouched a young girl in a catatonic condition.

"Rose! What's wrong with her!"

(My God, what a question!)

With no apparent discomposure, Rose replied, smiling, "She's on her bad behavior today, that's all."

Years later, about 1949 or 1950, Rose was living with an elderly couple on a farm near the asylum—having been so tragically becalmed by the prefrontal lobotomy, which was performed in the late thirties.

I arranged for her to come to Key West for a visit, accompanied by the farm-lady caretaker. Grandfather was with me.

He came rapidly stumbling out of the house as the car arrived.

"Rose, here is Grandfather!"

"No, no, no!" she cried out. "He's an old imposter!"

The disastrous visit lasted for only four days and during this time she would eat nothing in the Key West house except a can of Campbell's soup and one of chili, and only when the cans had been opened by me.

At this time Miss Rose was being afflicted by what she called "crime-beasts." Whatever she touched that could be shaken, she shook to remove the "crime-beasts" from it. The house was under a terrible shadow despite the radiant weather of early spring in Key West. The adventure was abandoned: Rose and her cow-like companion returned to the Missouri farm . . .

At this time Miss Rose wrote letters almost daily.

I remember one that began with this phrase: "Today the sun came up like a five-dollar gold piece!"

She was devoted to the small children on the farm and especially to the canary and each of her childish little letters contained an account of how they were doing, such as "Chee-chee [the canary] seems happy today."

"Today we drove in town and I purchased Palmolive shampoo for my crowning glory."

Soon I had her removed to an expensive sanitarium called "Institute for Living" in Hartford, Connecticut. When I visited her there, a few months later, I was consternated and furious when I was informed that Miss Rose had been put into the violent ward. They told me that she had knocked an old lady down. I demanded to see Rose at once.

"I didn't knock her down," said Miss Rose—who never lies—"I just gave her a push and she fell. She kept coming into my room at night and I couldn't sleep."

I immediately told the administrator of this "Institute for Living" that Miss Rose was leaving.

We drove for hours and hours to Stoney Lodge in Ossining, where she now stays, a lovely retreat where she has a pleasant room to herself, with flowered wallpaper. The Lodge is on a bluff looking over the upper Hudson, and the grounds are beautifully landscaped.

This is probably the best thing I've done with my life, besides a few bits of work.

I gave Rose a parakeet, remembering her devotion to the canary at the farmhouse. It became a dear pet.

Whenever I took her back to the Lodge after an outing, she would say to me, as she got out of the car, "Tom, don't yóu want to come up and see my parakeet?"

It thrived for several years.

And then, one outing, Miss Rose seemed unusually troubled and when I got out of the car with her at the Lodge, she did not invite me to visit the little bird.

"Aren't we going to see the parakeet, Rose?"

"No, not this time," she said. "It isn't very well."

I insisted on going up to her room and the parakeet was lying dead in the bottom of the cage: the nurse in attendance at Rose's Lodge said it had been dead for days but Miss Rose would not allow it to be removed.

On several occasions after this tragic demise, I tried to persuade her to accept another parakeet and she has always refused.

Rose has never and will never openly admit that a death has occurred. And yet she once said, "It rained last night. The dead came down with the rain."

"You mean their voices?"

"Yes, of course, their voices."

Whenever my friend Maria mentions Miss Rose in her letters, she refers to her lovely, heartbreaking eyes.

And yet, now, Maria refuses to accept my phone calls. The contradictions in one's dearest friends appear to be quite limitless . . .

Or nearly.

I think the reason Maria is angry may be that my representative, Bill Barnes, rightly felt that we could no longer suspend a production of *Out Cry* until Paul Scofield found himself prepared to make a formal commitment and set a specific time for the production in England. With regret I acquiesced to this opinion, and in a short while the "property" was assigned to David Merrick. Peter Glenville was named as director.

Maria, the Lady St. Just, is a woman of intense

loyalties. She felt that our friend "Chuck" Bowden had been betrayed and, being a romanticist, she could not understand the exigencies of signed and sealed commitments in the theatre.

No one has ever been more furious at my vacillations, timidity, and weakness than myself—with the exception of Maria. She has always felt that I betray myself with them, and so betray myself as an artist.

She suddenly stopped answering my letters. Then she became "not at home" to my transatlantic phone calls to Gerald Road, London, and to Wilbury.

I needn't tell you how greatly distressed this makes me, since at this time Maria and my sister Rose and Billy are the only persons who are close and dear to my heart.

I am staying on in New York two or three more days, and then, having seen Peg Murray's opening in *Small Craft Warnings,* I will leave for the newly furnished apartment in New Orleans. That is, unless Mother's doctor tells me that her condition is terminal or critical to the point that I really will have to go to that dreaded city of St. Louis.

Whether or not I accompany Bill Barnes, at the end of August, to the Venice Film Festival depends on whether or not it will attract Maria as my guest on the Lido.

Otherwise I'll stay in New Orleans for the good, long rest so much needed before the next production, of *Out Cry,* which I must believe will start rehearsals late next month.

On its opening night in New York, I will fly to Italy and remain indefinitely among those lovely people; hopefully finding the little farm I've long dreamed of buying, on which to raise geese and goats, to employ an attractive young gardener-chauffeur, and swim and swim.

Yesterday I was alarmed by a state of confusion at the New Theatre. Honest to God, I couldn't tell the interval from the end of the first show. I mean I came out of the men's dressing room when I heard the applause for the first act curtain. My "fluffs" were alarming, too. And if the back of the house had been filled —it wasn't for either performance—I doubt that I would have been audible much of the time.

The problem seems to be breath. I let the end of a sentence fall because the breath runs out.

And yet I got good hands. I guess there is something about me that is recognizable as something about "Doc"—regardless of whether all that I say is heard.

It is imperative that the show complete the summer. It must, it will. I think the production of *Out Cry* may hinge upon my demonstration to draw again and to keep a show that received "mixed reviews" running for five months, which is, I mean would be, quite a prestigious accomplishment and a help with the big one.

# An Album
# of Memories

My paternal grandfather, Thomas Lanier Williams II, who practically exhausted the family's fortune, mostly in real estate, by running repeatedly for Governor against a popular demagogue. The crack across the face in the photograph is a touch of accidental symbolism, as it was not til this handsome but improvident descendant of the Williams-Sevier-Lanier line that things began to go wrong. Although educated in law at Heidelberg University he never rose higher in politics than State Railroad Commissioner. He was a great lady's man— I wonder if he would have tolerated me.

Isabel Coffin Williams,
my father's mother, who
died at the age of twenty-
eight from tuberculosis.
This meant that my father
grew up mostly without
the emollient influence
of a mother.

Mother at nine years,
studying the violin.
Grand tried to teach her
to play but Mother achieved
only a fairly correct
pose with the instrument.

Dad
before
the death
of his mother
and consequent
deprival of a gentle
influence on his boyhood.

The Rectory
in Columbus, Mississippi
—very southern Gothic.

Mother in
a snapshot taken
by her favorite beau,
after she had married
"C.C." Williams—hence
the wistful look.

Mother,
Grand
and Rose.

Grandfather
and me
in St. Louis.

My favorite picture of Grandfather, taken late in his life. A dignity and wisdom—the grace of age—in his face.

In the state
of innocence—
and Mississippi.

Mother and Dad,
on a vacation in the Ozarks.

My sister Rose
as a young woman.

Rose in a Catholic
sanitarium in St. Louis, just
after her nervous breakdown.

On Ozark holiday.
I'm on the left.

53 Arundel Place, Clayton, Missouri.

High School photo.

On the staff of The Eliot, the campus magazine
at Washington University, St. Louis.
I am in front row, far left.

Dakin and me
by a small country
club swimming pool.

In the first
New Orleans
apartment, 1946.

In the studio of
the East Fifty-eighth
Street apartment.

Why writers burn up.
Photo taken by Karsh in the
East Fifty-eighth Street apartment.

About to ride to Mexico
from the squab ranch in
Hawthorne, California,
during the summer of 1939.

A travel-scarred
photo of Kip.

On the Lido
with Maria.

One of the exits
Carson and I
took together—
Audrey Wood,
Carson McCullers
and me at the
party after the
Broadway
opening of *Summer
and Smoke*.

With wonderful
Tallulah, during
a rehearsal for the revival
of *Streetcar* in 1955.

With Irene Selznick and Elia Kazan during a break in the rehearsals for *Streetcar*.

Donald Windham, my collaborator on *You Touched Me!* in 1946, and an early friend in New York, whose present disaffection I much regret.

Magnani preceding tempest
at a Roman nightclub.
All hell was about to
break loose—Magnani was
in a rage at her escort.
I knew it and was amused.

Anna Magnani and me,
aboard the Andrea Doria. She was
about to star in *The Rose Tattoo*.

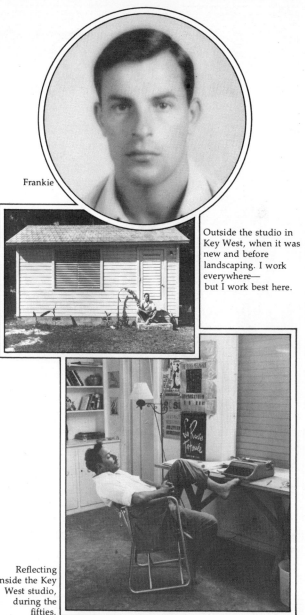

Frankie

Outside the studio in
Key West, when it was
new and before
landscaping. I work
everywhere—
but I work best here.

Reflecting
inside the Key
West studio,
during the
fifties.

Frank Merlo on the beach in Key West.

In the New York
apartment with
"Buffo" and Frankie.

Chris Isherwood
in Santa Monica.

Laurette Taylor,
with Eddie Dowling
as Tom, in *Menagerie*.

What sometimes happens
to ladies who always depend
on the kindness of strangers—
the closing scene of *Streetcar*,
the Broadway production with
Kim Hunter, Jessica Tandy,
Marlon Brando.

The awful film version of *Menagerie*—the most unfortunate film ever made of my work, mostly because of the alterations made at the end to make it "happy." With Kirk Douglas as "The Gentleman Caller," Gertrude Lawrence as the mother and Arthur Kennedy as Tom. Gertrude Lawrence deserved better, as did the play.

With Maureen Stapleton
and Frankie at a
Chicago night club
during the Chicago run
of *The Rose Tattoo*.

Viven Leigh as
Blanche, and Brando as
Stanley Kowalski—
marvelous performances
in a great movie,
only slightly marred
by Hollywood ending.

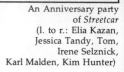

An Anniversary party
of *Streetcar*
(l. to r.: Elia Kazan,
Jessica Tandy, Tom,
Irene Selznick,
Karl Malden, Kim Hunter)

With my friend
and representative,
Mr. Bill Barnes.

Vivien Leigh and Warren Beatty in the 1950 movie based on the novel *The Roman Spring of Mrs. Stone*. This is my favorite of all the movies based on my work; it was directed by Jose Quintero, who had never shot a film before.

A scene from *Camino Real,* a version with Al Pacino as Kilroy.

Eli Wallach and Carroll Baker in *Baby Doll,* the film based on the play *27 Wagons Full of Cotton.*

The movie version of *Cat on a Hot Tin Roof*, for which I received the highest sum I ever was given for any film. Paul Newman as Brick and Elizabeth Taylor as Maggie.

The great Elizabeth Ashley in *Cat on a Hot Tin Roof*, 1974.

Kate Hepburn
stole the acting honors
in the film of
*Suddenly, Last Summer*.

Monty Clift and Liz Taylor
in *Suddenly*, a bad film that
was very profitable.

Newman and Page
brilliantly co-star again,
in the movie of *Sweet Bird*.

Bette Davis as Maxine Falk in *Iguana*.

Richard Burton
and Ava Gardner in
the film version of
*The Night of the Iguana*.

*Small Craft Warnings*, in which I made my first and last
appearance as an actor—achieving stardom without talent.

Cara Duff-MacCormich
and Michael York in
*Out Cry*, a financially
successful play that
closed precipitately
after demolition by
critics in New York.

Claire Bloom, exhausted in her dressing room after the opening of *Streetcar* in London, 1974.

# 8

Late in the spring of 1947, after returning Grandfather to his usual residence in the Hotel Gayoso in Memphis, I proceeded by car toward New York, where preparations were underway for the production of *Streetcar*.

In New York, again with Santo, and our stay at that point in New York was brief. I saw Elia Kazan's production of Arthur Miller's play, *All My Sons*, and was so impressed by his staging of that message drama, by the vitality which he managed to put into it, that I implored Audrey Wood and Irene Selznick to do everything possible to procure him as director for *Streetcar*. It was his wife, Molly Day Thacher Kazan, an old friend of mine, who first read the play. He resisted the idea of undertaking its production, but she won him over and a contract was signed.

That important business accomplished, Santo and I went up to Cape Cod. We rented a shingled bungalow directly on the water somewhere between North Truro and Provincetown. (We named it Rancho Santo and set a board with that title in front of the dwelling.) Soon we had visitors; Margo Jones and her side-kick Joanna Albus came to share the rustic bungalow with us. There were double-decker bunks on either side of the main room: the ladies shared one, Santo and I the other; and there was considerable consumption of firewater. I was not much of a drinker in those days but Margo ("The Texas Tornado") was as fond of the brew as was Santo. We had come to the Cape too early for ocean bathing, it was still icy cold. But I continued work on *Streetcar* and it was in that cabin that I thought of the exit line for Blanche, which later became somewhat historical: "I have always depended upon the kindness of strangers."

Actually it was true, I always had, and without being often disappointed. In fact, I would guess that chance acquaintances, or strangers, have usually been kinder to me than friends—which does not speak too well for me. To know me is not to love me. At best, it is to tolerate me, and of drama critics I would say that tolerance seems now to be just about worn out.

For some reason the electricity and the plumbing went kaput simultaneously. Evenings were candle lit and for calls of nature the inhabitants of the cabin had to go out into the bushes.

Well, just about this time I got a wire from Kazan, informing me that he was dispatching a young actor to the Cape who he thought was gifted; and he wanted him to read the part of Stanley for me. We waited two or three days, but the young actor, named Marlon Brando, didn't show. I had stopped expecting him when he arrived one evening with a young girl, the kind you would call a chick nowadays.

He asked why the lights weren't on and we told him the electricity had failed. He immediately fixed that for us—I think he merely inserted a penny in the light fuse.

Then he discovered our predicament with the plumbing and he fixed that, too.

He was just about the best-looking young man I've ever seen, with one or two exceptions; but I have never played around with actors, it's a point of morality with me and anyhow Brando was not the type to get a part that way.

When he had gotten the Rancho into shape by re-

pairing the lights and plumbing, he sat down in a
corner and started to read the part of Stanley. I was
cuing him. After less than ten minutes, Margo Jones
jumped up and let out a "Texas Tornado" shout.

"Get Kazan on the phone right away! This is the
greatest reading I've ever heard—in or outside of
Texas!"

Brando maybe smiled a little but didn't show any
particular elation, such as the elation we all felt.

The part of Kowalski was the first important part
he has ever performed on the stage, all the rest have
been on the screen. I think this is a pity, because
Brando had a charisma on the stage that corresponded
to the charisma of Laurette Taylor in its luminous
power.

That night we had dinner at home and we read
poetry. I mean *I* read some poetry. Then we retired
for the night. There was no bed for Brando so he
curled up in a blanket in the center of the floor.

Brando was always shy with me for some reason.
The following morning he wanted me to walk up the
beach with him, and so we did—in silence. And then
we walked back—in silence . . .

Once the part of Kowalski was cast, we then had to
find a Blanche. I was summoned back to New York
to hear Margaret Sullavan read for the part. She didn't
seem right to me, I kept picturing her with a tennis
racket in one hand and I doubted that Blanche had
ever played tennis. She read again. Margaret Sullavan
was a lovely person, an actress without ego. When she
was informed that the first reading had not been sat-
isfactory, she asked to read again. We heard her once
more, and the tennis racket, for some reason, was still
invisibly but palpably present. Irene was delegated
to tell her we were profoundly grateful but it was
no show.

Then we heard that an actress whose name was
quite unknown to me, a lady named Jessica Tandy,
was making a sensation on the Coast in a short play

of mine, *Portrait of a Madonna.* It was decided that
Irene, Audrey, Santo and I would take the Super
Chief to the Coast and catch her performance.

It was instantly apparent to me that Jessica was
Blanche.

The two most important roles cast, I told Kazan that
he should cast the rest of the parts as he wished and
I returned to Rancho Santo on the Cape. It was now
warm enough to swim, and in those days the Cape
was a lovely summer retreat. My friend's behavior
remained erratic and that is putting it mildly. Margo
and Joanna were still there and it took all our con-
certed efforts to keep him halfway under control. I
had gotten used to his fiery temperament and divided
my time that summer between mornings at the typewriter and afternoons on the sunny dunes beyond
Provincetown.

Some interesting folk began to appear in Provincetown. The lyricist John LaTouche, who had written
"Cabin in the Sky" and other songs, was among them,
and he was accompanied by a youth who was to become my closest, most long-lasting companion, a
youth of Sicilian extraction named Frank Merlo.

Frank was an inch shorter than I but designed by
Praxiteles. He had enormous brown eyes and a sort
of equine face, which led a couple of years later to his
nickname "The Little Horse."

LaTouche was going through some sort of nervous
crisis involving his mother, I think, and he suddenly
took off, leaving Frankie Merlo on the Cape.

Our first encounter was a theatrical sort of event.

Santo and I had gone to a night spot in Provincetown known as the Atlantic House. The entertainer
there was Stella Brooks, who was one of the early,
great jazzsingers, and I had a great fondness for her,
which was not pleasing to Santo. He shouted some ob-
scenities at her during her act and rushed off somewhere. Being alone in the bar when Stella's bit was
finished, I strayed out on the frame porch of the Atlan-

tic House. After a few moments, Frank Merlo also came out, alone, and he leaned smoking against the porch rail and he was wearing Levis and I looked and looked at him. My continual and intense scrutiny must have burned through his shoulders, for after a while he turned toward me and grinned.

I don't know what I said but in a couple of minutes we were in my Pontiac convertible and we were driving out to the dunes.

I don't want to overload this thing with homophile erotica, but let's say that it was a fantastic hour in the dunes for me that evening even though I have never regarded sand as an ideal or even desirable surface on which to worship the little god. However the little god was given such devout service that he must still be smiling—

After dropping off Frankie where he was staying, I parked the car and wandered dreamily about town. While I was wandering through the heavy night fog of Provincetown, Santo took my car. He first went to the home of Stella Brooks, who he thought had enticed me to her lair. Poor Stella, she knew me too well for that. Santo gave her a clout in the eye and he left her place a shambles.

Having returned to the Atlantic House during this event and having found the Pontiac gone, I started walking home. I was proceeding, very tired, up a steep hill toward North Truro when a pair of headlights on a wildly careening car appeared at the top of the hill, racing down it. With that protective instinct of mine, I somehow surmised that the driver of this car was Santo. The car seemed headed straight at me so I stepped off the road. Santo drove the car into the field of marsh grass with what seemed the intention of running me down. I did not remain there to reflect paranoically upon that possibility but took to my heels, scooting across the marshes. After me, now on foot, raced Santo, screaming invectives in English and in Spanish.

I reached the ocean without being overtaken—for it was a moonless night. I saw a wooden pier and I ran out onto it and suspended myself from its understructure, just above water level. I remained there till Santo, not being a bloodhound, had lost track of me, and had gone screaming off in some other direction. Then, quite cold and wet, I climbed onto the pier, crossed the salt marsh again—without being at all reminded of my collateral ancestor's poem, "The Marshes of Glynn."

Ultimately I got back to the Atlantic House. They rented rooms above the bar and I took one and barred the door and pushed all the furniture except the bed against it.

Then I slept.

When I woke up, I phoned Margo and Joanna at the Rancho. They said it had been a night of horror for them, too. We all agreed that Santo must be persuaded to leave.

Margo acted as go-between.

Joanna saw him off on the bus.

I returned to the little house which still had in front of it the sign "Rancho Santo." Prophetically!

The two Texas ladies and I were blithely on our way to dinner that evening when Santo rushed up to us. It seemed that he had hitchhiked back to Provincetown.

He was in the most amiable of moods—as if nothing had gone awry in our three lives.

How readily one accepts the inevitable, it would seem.

We had lobster dinners and resumed our usual lives at the Rancho. This went on until it was time for me to return to New York for the early fall rehearsals of *Streetcar*.

It took some doing to get Santo to leave. Probably this phenomenal accomplishment was handled by Irene Selznick, who has seldom found herself in a situation with which she couldn't cope, not even the situation of releasing me from Santo. Then I was alone in New York, quite gratefully so, and I took a one-room apartment with kitchenette in the Chelsea district, the first floor front of a brownstone.

Rehearsals progressed on the Amsterdam Roof. I thought the play was a certain failure and I was once again certain that I was a dying artist and not even the least bit sure that I was an artist.

Kazan understood me quite amazingly for a man whose nature was so opposite to mine. He was one of those rare directors who wanted the playwright around at all rehearsals, even those at which he was blocking out the action. Once in a while he would call me up on stage to demonstrate how I felt a certain bit should be played. I suspect he did this only to flatter me for he never had the least uncertainty in his work, once he had started upon it.

I remember his asking me to demonstrate my conception of the old Mexican woman who passed along the street selling brilliant tin flowers for graves, calling out and chanting, *"Flores para los muertos, corones para los muertos."*

I got up on the rehearsal stage and advanced to the door of the Kowalski abode bearing the tin flowers . . . Jessica opened the door and screamed at the sight of me.

"Not yet, not yet!"

"That's it, do it just like that," said Kazan.

I was still living alone in the Chelsea flat, expecting death and failure. Then while I was working, one noon, there was a great pounding on the door, which luckily was locked.

*My God, Santo was back!*

Unable to break down the door, he jumped onto the cement sills of the gable windows. I got to them just in time to lock them. A big crowd had gathered outside the brownstone by this time. Santo was on the sill, hammering at the window, until the glass split. Then a policeman intervened. He did not arrest Santo but he ordered him away. He looked back at me. His face was covered with tears. I started crying, too, a thing I very seldom do.

It was a sad occasion, and I hope that you understand my behavior.

At the advice of Audrey and Irene, I moved out of the Chelsea flat temporarily, taking refuge in an old hotel where I'd stayed years before, a fleabag called the Hotel Windsor on the West Side. I stayed there until Santo had been persuaded that I could not be induced to resume residence with him or willingly to see him again.

*Streetcar* opened in New Haven in early November of 1947, and nobody seemed to know what the notices were or to be greatly concerned. After the New Haven opening night we were invited to the quarters of Mr. Thornton Wilder, who was in residence there. It was like having a papal audience. We all sat about this academic gentleman while he put the play down as if delivering a papal bull. He said that it was based upon a fatally mistaken premise. No female who had ever been a lady (he was referring to Stella) could possibly marry a vulgarian such as Stanley.

We sat there and listened to him politely. I thought, privately, This character has never had a good lay. I got back at him years later when a bunch of theatre people were invited, during the Kennedy administration, to a banquet at the White House. All of us theatre folk were told to line up in alphabetical order in a huge room walled with glittering mirrors. We were more or less lined up. The President and Jackie and their guest of honor, André Malraux, were about to appear. And here was Thornton Wilder bustling about like a self-appointed field marshal, seeing that we were arranged in our proper alphabetical order. I was engaged in conversation with Miss Shelley Winters—both of us came under "W."

Mr. Wilder rushed up to me with the radiant smile

of a mortician and shrieked, "Mr. Williams, you're a bit out of place, you come behind me."

Well, I was just stoned enough to say to him, "If I am behind you it's the first and last time in my life."

When the long alphabetical line had nearly all shuffled past the President and First Lady and been presented to M. Malraux, it came my turn to meet him and I had actually never heard of him before. I said to him, *"Enchanté, Monsieur Maurois"*—and this made Jackie smile but did not seem to amuse M. Malraux.

One late evening while *Streetcar* was in Boston I received one more surprise visit from dear Santo. I never locked my door at the Ritz-Carlton—who would?—and suddenly into my bedroom-living room bursts this ever-valiant ex-companion. There were words of contrition, and endearment, words which I accorded no sentimental ear. Then there was a bit of breakage, a mantel vase or two. However, my room was opposite Mrs. Selznick's. She heard the disturbance and unwisely—imagine Irene doing anything unwise!—opened her door on the corridor. Santo took immediate advantage of this chance to turn his inebriate rage upon that guiltless lady. His assault upon her was entirely verbal and I believe she handled it with her usual skill and expedition.

It was years before I saw Santo again, and always since then—his conversion to Alcoholics Anonymous and the beautifully religious turn of his spirit—our meetings have been serene and pleasant. . . .

When *Streetcar* arrived in Boston we began to get good notices. Only one negative one appeared in the papers and business was excellent despite it. However, it was not until Philadelphia that it became apparent that the play would surely go.

Kazan and I were standing in the lobby of the Philadelphia theatre before curtain time and the crowd was pressing like *aficionados* of the bull ring about to see the great Ordóñez. Kazan grinned at me and said, "This smells like a hit."

I remember buying myself a very expensive tweed overcoat in Philly on the strength of the favorable notices there. Brando invited me to dine with him one evening and he took me to an obscure Greek restaurant and it was impossible to engage him in conversation and almost impossible to eat the oily food.

The New York opening was a smash.

I was called onto the stage opening night for a bow, as I had been for *Menagerie*, and I was equally awkward about it. I believe that I bowed to the actors instead of the audience.

I was still living alone in that one-room flat in the Chelsea brownstone. It was late December and a blizzard hit town. It was such a heavy snow that traffic was practically immobilized for several days. The brownstone ran out of fuel and I had to depend on the fireplace for heat. I was able to purchase some logs on the corner. And then one night during this prolonged blizzard I happened to be passing by taxi along Times Square and I noticed a youth huddled in a doorway. He was a blond adolescent, inadequately clothed for the weather, a fact which touched my heart to the extent that I shouted to the cabdriver, "Stop."

I jumped out of the cab and ran up to the kid huddling in the doorway.

"Hey, come along, you look cold."

It turned out that the kid was a young circus roustabout. I took him to the Chelsea one-room flat and we built a fire to warm things up a bit and the fire was just catching when there was a knock at the door.

After some understandable hesitation, I opened the door and there was a theatre friend and a lady friend whom I recognized but whose name I will not mention except to say that she was not his wife.

"Jesus, it's cold in here," he observed, and he and the young lady went immediately to bed—for the sole purpose of keeping warm, I suppose. The circus roustabout and I sat by the fireplace as if meditating and before long the room was filled with cries of hysterical excitement from the young lady whose name I have omitted. Afterward we all sat before the fire and had drinks and there was no embarrassment among us.

When the couple had departed, the kid and I replaced them in bed and I must say that we were much quieter though I believe that my sensations were equally ecstatic. The kid stayed with me for a couple of days and nights, then his circus left town and I was alone again.

Shortly after the blizzard I bought passage on a ship to Europe, the *America,* and it was Christmas time and I had bought and decorated a big tree in the flat and I gave a big party. The room could hardly hold the guests. Perhaps the two stars of the evening were Greta Garbo and Helen Hayes.

Garbo made a terrific impression, she was radiantly beautiful. Only a few weeks ago I happened to pass her on the street, unknowingly. My companion said, "That lady we just passed was Garbo." I spun around and rushed up to her. True, the lovely face had aged but the beauty was still there. And also the terrible shyness. She was gracious but frightened. I informed her that I was appearing that evening in my own play, *Small Craft Warnings,* and invited her to come as my guest. It was a stupid invitation to offer Garbo but she declined it with grace. "How wonderful. Thank you: I don't go out anymore."

Then she rushed on.

I believe I have had five meetings with Garbo and one occurred during that December of 1947 when *Streetcar* had just opened in New York. I happened to tell George Cukor that I had written a screenplay called *The Pink Bedroom.* Cukor was a dear friend of Garbo's and he said, "I want you to show it to Garbo. I'll arrange for her to see you."

To my surprise the fabulous lady received me alone in her apartment at the Ritz Tower.

We sat in the parlor drinking schnapps. I got a big high and I began to tell her the story of *The Pink Bedroom*. There was something about her curious and androgynous beauty that inspired me out of my characteristic timidity. I told her the story and she kept whispering, "Wonderful!" leaning toward me with a look of entrancement in her eyes. I thought to myself, She will do it, she'll return to the screen! After an hour, when I had finished telling the scenario, she still said, "Wonderful!" But then she sighed and leaned back on her sofa. "Yes, it's wonderful, but not for me. Give it to Joan Crawford."

The second occasion when I saw Garbo was about five years later, I'd guess, when I was invited to a little party given by that fabulous old character actress, Constance Collier. Garbo was there and I approached her and said, "You are the only great tragedienne that the screen ever had, you've *got* to resume your career!"

Garbo jumped up and exclaimed, "This room is stifling!" She rushed across to a window, threw it all the way up as if about to leap out and stood there with her back to us for several minutes.

The old character actress leaned toward me gravely and said in a whisper, "Never speak to her of acting again. She always goes into a fit at the suggestion."

How sad a thing for an artist to abandon his art: I think it's much sadder than death . . .

There must have been something about her screen career that profoundly revolted her—in Hollywood, I mean. And so she turned into an imperishable legend and we are left with her *Camille* and her *Anna Karenina* and the vibrations of that marvelous voice that surely must have been as great as Duse's.

At the end of that December, no longer able to cope with the unremitting publicity in New York, I sailed for Europe.

I was not at all seasick but I felt strangely unwell and I was unable to write.

Being unable to write has always disturbed me as if the sky had fallen upon my head.

I arrived in Cherbourg and then in Paris.

I had asked Garbo where to stay in Paris and the dear lady had said, "Try the George V." I didn't see how Garbo could be mistaken so it was there I went. I never hated a hotel quite so much in a life full of rented rooms.

So the next day I moved to a hotel on the Left Bank called the Lutetia. This was more to my liking, although it was almost totally unheated. I was still being pursued by the press. And I was less and less well, due to the lack of good food in Europe during the early postwar years. I was, however, distinctly pleased by the night life which I was quick to discover. I went continually to the Boeuf sur le Toit and to Madame Arthur's, the latter having a very effective drag-show.

During the day I stayed mostly in the enormous bathtub at the Lutetia. They had no heat in the radiators but for some reason they had plenty of hot water. I received the press in the bathtub. I guess a part of me has always wanted to receive the press, under any circumstances. The door kept ringing with requests for interviews. I would get out of the bathtub, shivering in one of those great wrap-about towels.

*"Montez, s'il vous plaît, Chambre numéro—"*

Then I would leave the door slightly ajar and plunge back into the enormous, steaming bathtub.

I suppose I must have received a dreadful press in Paris but I never read it. I was too preoccupied with the nocturnal pleasures which the city of lights had to offer.

Even so, each morning I felt sicker. One could not get real milk in Paris at that time, only powdered milk, and the food was wretched. I drank a lot of cognac.

All at once I felt desperately ill and I went to the American Hospital in Neuilly.

The doctors informed me that I was "threatened with hepatitis and mononucleosis." I had never heard of either of those disorders and they were not explained to me by the doctors. In my journal I wrote: "The jig is up."

On the boat coming to Europe I had met a charming young lady whose father and mother were both eminent French journalists. The father, M. Lazareff, was the owner of two Paris papers, *Paris Jour* and *Paris Soir,* and the mother, Mme. Lazareff, was the editor of the fashion magazine *Elle.*

It was Mme. Lazareff who came to see me in the American Hospital, where I was expecting the arrival of the reaper.

"Get out of bed at once," she ordered. "I am taking you home, giving you a good dinner, and seeing you off on a train for the South of France."

She dispatched me to an inn called La Colombe d'Or, where her daughter was staying. It was a place frequented mostly by artists and writers and it was in the town of Vence, where D. H. Lawrence had died. Snow white doves were fluttering and cooing all about —and they made me unhappy. I stayed there only a couple of days and then went south to Italy. As soon as I crossed the Italian border my health and life seemed to be magically restored. There was the sun and there were the smiling Italians.

In Rome I took a two-room furnished apartment on Via Aurora, just off Via Veneto. It was in one of those tawny old high-ceilinged buildings that are characteristic of *Vecchia Roma* though it was not situated in that part of the city. It was only a block from the entrance to the great park called Villa Borghese. Both the park and the boulevard, Via Veneto, I was soon to discover, were favorite resorts for the sort of chance acquaintances that a lonely foreigner is apt to be seeking. This was still soon after World War II, and the dollar was very high.

A cynical old American journalist whom I met soon after my arrival said to me, "Rome is a city of thieves, mendicants and prostitutes, both male and female." The prevalence of prostitution was undeniable and not to the disadvantage of the cynical journalist who shared my sexual interests but was considerably more callous in his indulgence of that taste.

There were mendicants in Rome: there are beggars wherever there is a great deal of economic distress. You find more of them, actually, in certain parts of New York than you would have found in Rome twenty-five years ago, and certainly there are far more thieves in American cities. I never encountered a thief in Rome in those days, nor did I ever encounter violence or a threat of it. The Italians are not much inclined toward thievery or violence, it seems to me it goes rather against their nature.

As for prostitution, that is really the world's oldest profession in all Mediterranean countries with the possible exception of Spain. It is due largely to their physical beauty and to their warmth of blood, their natural eroticism. In Rome you rarely see a young man on the street who does not have a slight erection. Often they walk along the Veneto with hand in pocket, caressing their genitals quite unconsciously, and this regardless of whether or not they are hustling or cruising. They are raised without any of our puritanical reserves about sex. Young American males, even when they are good-looking, do not think of themselves as sexually desirable. Good-looking young Italians never think of themselves as anything else. And they are rarely mistaken. That is a matter that I dealt with pretty thoroughly in my longest piece of fiction, *The Roman Spring of Mrs. Stone.*

I made many friends very quickly in Rome: the American journalist's social contacts were all but limitless both in high and low strata of Roman society. I met through him most of the early tide of film people from the States. I met Luchino Visconti, who had already directed *Zoo de Vetro* in Italy and was soon to direct *Un Tramway che se chiamo Desiderio*. He remains one of the world's greatest directors for stage and screen and his intimate friend and early assistant Franco Zeffirelli has achieved an almost equal stature, especially in his enchanting film, *Romeo and Juliet*.

That winter Visconti was directing a film in Sicily called *La Terra Trema* ("The Earth Trembles"), which I think is still very likely his greatest work for the screen, although it is perhaps the least known. The American journalist and I flew down to Catania, near which Visconti was shooting—the location was a suburb called Acitrezza. There I met both Visconti and Zeffirelli, who was at that time a very handsome blond Florentine youth.

Although an aristocrat of great inherited wealth, Visconti was an avowed Communist at this time. I think it is only in the case of Brecht that a man's politics, if the man is an artist, are of particular importance in his work; his degrees of talent and of humanity are what count. I also feel that an artist's sexual predilections or deviations are not usually pertinent to the value of his work. Of interest, certainly. Only a homosexual could have written *Remembrance of Things Past*.

My apartment consisted of two rooms, a comfortably furnished living room, which was pleasant mainly because of the huge windows looking out upon the sun-drenched street and the old wall of Rome, which surrounds the Villa Borghese. I kept the room full of mimosa that winter. The other room, the bedroom, was furnished almost entirely with a huge *letto matrimoniale*. This room also had huge shuttered windows filled by day with sky and sun. It was a golden winter, the warmest I've known in Rome.

There were no privations in Rome, then, for a reasonably affluent tourist. The food at even the simplest trattorias was excellent and the wine of Rome, Frascati, had an incomparable mellowness. After a *mezzolitro* you felt as if a new kind of blood had been transfused into your arteries, a blood that swept away all anxiety and all tension for a while, and for a while is the stuff that dreams are made of.

Italians take three or four hours off for lunch (because of the wine-drinking, I suppose, and the climate), and after they've dined they go straight to bed for a siesta. And if you were young, the siesta was usually not alone, certainly not when you occupied a letto matrimoniale and had great windows that opened directly upon the street, and knew a few little phrases like *"Dove vai?"* ("Where are you going?"). My cynical American journalist told me that I needed to know only two Italian phrases to enjoy myself in Rome, *"Dove vai?"* and *"Quanto costa?"* ("What's your price?").

But I was not long in picking up most of the language. I can speak it fluently—well, rather fluently—when I'm in Italy, which I wish was all the time, even now when it has changed so drastically.

On the second night I spent in Rome, I happened to be on the Via Veneto and I strolled by the windows of Doney's, a famous patisserie on the street floor of the Hotel Excelsior. I stopped short, my eyes encountering those of a youth who appeared to be a young faun in a dilapidated old overcoat, seated alone at a table from which he could smile at strangers on the street.

We smiled at each other and I made a motion to invite him outside. He came out promptly. It was no use saying, *"Dove vai?"* and it was not yet time to ask, *"Quanto?"*—but I was sure it soon would be ...

I had not yet moved into the apartment on Via Aurora, I was still in a room across the street at the Hotel Ambasciatore. The hotel was one of the most prominent in Rome and it was still trying to maintain a respectable front, so when I entered with my adolescent acquaintance in his worn-out coat and his shoes that were tied to his feet, the staff in the lobby looked dumb-struck. I took the youth, whom I'll call Rafaello, directly to the elevator, wondering whether or not the operator would be permitted to let us enter. There were, indeed, some long moments of hesitation and Rafaello was pale and trembling, he had never entered a grand hotel before in his seventeen years.

I think I handed the elevator man a few hundred lire: then the old apparatus cranked into immediate action and we were delivered to a floor at the top of the building. I had a nice room there. I remember that it had a pink-shaded bedside lamp. I had acquired a pocket dictionary of English-Italian. I began to look up words furiously as the youth sat on one single bed and I on the other. We smiled and smiled at each other, but he kept shaking his head when I managed, through the dictionary, to invite him to pass the night with me at the grand Hotel Ambasciatore. He kept pointing to the word for Papa. It seems that his father was a *carabiniere* who punished the youth, when he stayed out nights, by tying him up in a chair in the basement for the whole next day without food or water. Then Rafaello, with the apologetically piquant gestures of a geisha, pointed out to me the word *domani,* which means "tomorrow": I felt dreadfully put down. Tomorrow seemed an interminable period to wait, for I had never seen a boy who attracted me so desperately since Kip. Or should I say appealed to me so deeply.

Well, my Italian lessons had begun. And I had a sleepless or nearly sleepless night.

A rendezvous was arranged for the next evening at

the same place, Doney's, for I had already found the apartment on Via Aurora and was to move into it the next day.

Is it possible to be a dirty old man in your middle thirties? I seem to be giving that impression.

This book is a sort of catharsis of puritanical guilt-feelings, I suppose. "All good art is an indiscretion." Well, I can't assure you that this book will be art, but it is bound to be an indiscretion, since it deals with my adult life . . .

Of course, I could devote this whole book to a discussion of the art of drama, but wouldn't that be a bore?

It would bore me to extinction, I'm afraid, and it would be a very, very short book, about three sentences to the page with extremely wide margins. The plays speak for themselves.

Life that winter in Rome: a golden dream, and I don't mean just Rafaello and the mimosa and the total freedom of life. Stop there: What I *do* mean is the total freedom of life and Rafaello and the mimosa, and the letto matrimoniale and the Frascati when morning work was over.

I had arranged things very well for myself. I had a little bedside buzzer and when I woke up with Rafaello still asleep beside me I would press it. The *padrona* was a lovely lady named Mariella. She would knock at the door and I would order breakfasts. Eggs and bacon and toast for Rafaello—for me just *caffè latte*.

Rafaello was now outfitted with a new suit, a new coat, and with new shoes and he was no longer living at home under the dominion of the fiendish father. Every other night he spent with me, the other nights at a little *pensione*.

My friends would ask me, "Is this Rafaello's night?" —or was I going to cruise with them . . . ?

I remember that one morning I received a lady journalist when Rafaello and I had just gotten out of bed. I received her in my dressing-gown in the living room: Rafaello sat quietly in the corner eating his eggs and bacon and toast.

A day or two later there was a headline in a Roman paper that read: *"La Primavera Romana di Tennessee Williams,"* and it mentioned the *"giovane"* in the corner eating breakfast—and I was at once launched upon a long period of personal notoriety in Rome which doubtless persists to this day.

The landlady, Mariella, thought that I was a lunatic because, in those days, I used to compose dialogue out loud, pacing the floor with a coffee cup in my hand.

I still talk aloud when I write dialogue for a play: it helps me to know how it is going to sound from the stage.

A line from *Camino Real:* I mean two lines from the play:

Casanova to Camille: "My dear, you must learn how to carry the banner of Bohemia into the enemy camp."

Camille to Casanova: "Bohemia has no banner, it survives by discretion."

It is now twenty minutes past three but I shall go on writing till it is milking-time for the cow, if there are cows in New Orleans.

This week alone I received several appeals for financial assistance. One came from a beautiful young hustler in Manhattan. He wanted two hundred bucks to go abroad.

Another was from a friend who wanted me to send him sixty bucks to blow up a picture of me and Dave Dellinger.

Right now I am in no position, economically or even spiritually, to gratify the requests of those who regard me only as a source of supplementary income.

I have never been able to obtain any kind of medical insurance, I have to pay all my own medical and surgical bills, and it has been three months since I've had the courage to open my accountant's monthly statement on my financial status.

I need friends very badly but even at sixty-one I don't want to buy them. Temporarily at least I feel like old Flora Goforth: "The milk train doesn't stop here anymore."

In Rome in the winter of 1948 there were very few private vehicles on the street and soon after settling into my apartment on Via Aurora I purchased an old jeep from a GI being sent back to the States. Among other disabilities, it had a defective muffler and as it raced up Via Veneto, it sounded like a jet plane taking off. Everyone along the street would stare furiously at me as I roared by. On nights when Rafaello was not in attendance, I had the practice of staying up till dawn in this jeep, up to no good. At dawn I would drive over to St. Peter's, *"molto umbriaco,"* which means drunk as hell, and I would race the jeep through the wind-blown fountains to cool my head, I would race round and round a fountain until I was thoroughly soaked and then would head home.

As traffic in Rome is now, it would have taken an hour to return from this exhilarating excursion at daybreak. Very often I would not be alone in the jeep, and my companion would not be quite so hilarious about the dousing as I'd be. But then, in those days, an *Americano* could get away with a whole lot ...

Toward early spring of '48, some well-known or notorious Americans began to appear on the Roman scene.

One evening at a dinner party given either by Henry McIlhenny of Philadelphia, the famous curator of art, or by Sam Barber, the celebrated composer, in a baroque apartment at the American Academy—I met young Gore Vidal. He had just published a best-

seller, called *The City and the Pillar*, which was one
of the first homosexual novels of consequence. I had
not read it but I knew that it had made the best-seller
lists and that it dealt with a "forbidden subject."

Gore was a handsome kid, about twenty-four, and
I was quite taken by his wit as well as his appearance.
We found that we had interests in common and we
spent a lot of time together. Please don't imagine that
I am suggesting that there was a romance. We merely
enjoyed conversation and a lot of laughter together
and we made some trips in the jeep to places on the
"Divina Costiera" such as Sorrento and Amalfi.

I believe we also went to Florence that season and
were entertained by that marvelous old aesthete Berenson.

And then one afternoon Gore took me to the Con-
vent of the Blue Nuns to meet the great philosopher
and essayist, by then an octogenarian and semi-inva-
lid, Santayana. He seemed like a saintly old gentleman. He had warm brown eyes of infinite understanding and delicate humor and he seemed to accept
his condition without the least bit of self-pity or chagrin. It made me, this meeting, a little more at ease
with mankind and certainly less apprehensive
about how the close of a creative life might be. His
gentleness of presence, his innate kindliness, reminded me very strongly of my grandfather.

"Sometimes I've seen God in old faces," said Han-
nah Jelkes. I think of Grandfather's face and Santayana's—and Grand's ...

Then that spring an old friend arrived with a companion, and the three of us, accompanied by a shame-
less Australian, picked up some Roman boys selling
cigarettes on the black market and we drove them
out in my jeep to the wilds of the Villa Borghese.
There we parked the jeep and each of us disappeared
into the wilds with one of the young cigarette kids.

It was more of a lark than a genuinely decadent
occasion. It led, however, to my third night in jail.

Last evening I returned once again to "the boards" in *Small Craft Warnings*, and I have just written Maureen Stapleton a "thank you" note and will send her roses for advancing my career in the performing arts. I called her up on stage with me, as I simply couldn't face another of the symposia I've been conducting after the performances, and the dear girl came up and read cold with me the part of Bessie—I read Flora—in that funny little skit called *A Perfect Analysis Given by a Parrot*.

It's getting a bit wearing, in my state of health, to keep attempting to resuscitate ticket sales at this Off-Broadway offering. However, I must face the fact that if it doesn't get through the summer, or most of the summer, my chances of getting a first-rate production for *Out Cry* will be further compromised. Peter Glenville and I have worked on the collation of a final script for *Out Cry* the past two days.

Rome, 1948. My first year in the golden city. It was getting into summer, and I had a professional commitment in London, no less an event than the first appearance of Helen Hayes in the theatre of London —and in *Menagerie*.

So over I went for rehearsals, which were conducted under John Gielgud. At first things seemed promising. Miss Hayes is not, in my minority opinion, one of the world's most gifted performers. I suppose in her youth she must have been very attractive and even quite accomplished. But as long ago as 1940, when I was in New York for *Battle of Angels* and she was appearing for the Theatre Guild in the Shakespearean role of Rosalind, I overheard some light-man saying, "You just can't light her, she's not possible to light." But I like the lady as a lady and I admire her off-stage style.

By 1948 she had been sensible enough to forsake all ingénue roles and was doing very well in parts that suited her age. Her husband was in England with her.

I think they loved each other. Perhaps I should underline think, to stress the fact that this is just a conjecture. There's something a bit suspicious about the decline of Charlie into drunkenness coexisting in time with his wife's indomitable advance to the status of "First Lady of the American Theatre." However, be that as it may, the great Gielgud has never been, I'd say, much of a director, but Miss Hayes should not have happened to John. During the first couple of weeks of rehearsal, she played legitimately without any of those simian grimaces that have come lately upon her. She was moving in rehearsals and giving an honest performance of Amanda Wingfield, the mother in *Menagerie*.

We went to Brighton, where we were to open. At one of the last rehearsals Miss Hayes summoned Gielgud and me and her supporting cast into her dressing room, and after an ominously long silence, she declared, "At this point in the making of a play, I know if it will go or it won't go."

More silence.

Then Miss Hayes slowly and sorrowfully shook her little head, meaning that the prognosis for the attraction was negative.

I took her word for it. I stayed for the opening in Brighton. The performance was pancake flat and her whole bag of tricks didn't help the "First Lady."

I remember meeting E. M. Forster after a performance there in Brighton. He came to Miss Hayes's dressing room and she cried out, "Oh, *Passage to India!*"

Well as I've said, off-stage Miss Hayes was and certainly still is a lady of presence and grace.

Seeing that the play was doomed to disaster, I flew back to Paris, where Gore was staying at the Hôtel de l'Université on the Left Bank. I took a nice suite there. It was a raffish hotel but it suited Gore and me perfectly as there was no objection to young callers.

At that time our favorite haunts were the Boeuf sur

le Toit and certain bohemian night clubs on the Left Bank. I met Cocteau and Bésé Bérard and Jean Marais, and quite a lot of artists, but I was most interested in meeting Jean-Paul Sartre, whose existential philosophy appealed to me strongly, as did his play *Huit Clos*.

I decided to give a big party in my room at the Hôtel de l'Université.

It was attended by most of my celebrated new friends in Paris. But I kept waiting for Jean-Paul Sartre, whom I had invited by wire. Off and on during the evening, I received bulletins concerning him. He was just around the corner in the bar of the Hôtel Rond-Point and people kept assuring me that he would show up. He never did.

I suppose he regarded me as too bourgeois or American or God knows what, but he did not appear at my party.

*Menagerie* was about to open in London and that great hostess, Lady Sibyl, had planned a big bash in the nature of an opening night party.

Mother was there with Dakin, and all the eminent London actors were there.

I kept sending wires, at first assuring them that I was going to be there. But something prevented my attendance. I never left Paris for the event, which is an embarrassing thing to look back on. At the last moment I wired Mother and Gielgud and Miss Hayes that I had taken ill in Paris, though actually I was feeling exceptionally well.

I believe that I was enjoying a little *affaire de coeur*, as usual.

When I had parted with Rafaello in Rome, it had been understood between us that I would return the following fall and meanwhile I was sending him monthly checks of a hundred dollars.

Well, I got the London notices on *Menagerie* from a very delightful young lady, a friend I'd made during the rehearsals in London, Maria Britneva, now the

Lady St. Just. I met her at John Gielgud's and we immediately hit it off together. A girl she was then, a very attractive one, three quarters white Russian, and one quarter English. She and her mother were impoverished, living upon Mme. Britneva's meager earnings for translations from Russian literature and from Maria's equally meager income as an occasional actress. We became great friends and are still great friends—she was so honest and beautiful, and still remains so. She was an actress until she married the Lord St. Just, then she became the Lady St. Just.

(I will write more about Maria later.)

Maria sent me all the London notices and they were very good for Miss Hayes and very bad for the play. I remember one was headed with this caption: "Bad Play Well-Acted."

I was not particularly surprised, having seen the rehearsals and the Brighton break-in.

About a week after the play's London opening—having soon to return to the States for the Broadway production of *Summer and Smoke*—I passed briefly through London. Gore came along. We had a good time despite the gloom at the theatre. I saw a performance and it was just as bad as I had expected. *Menagerie* can't be tricked. It has to be honestly and more than competently performed and directed.

Truman Capote was also in England. He returned with me to the States on the *Queen Mary* and it was an hilariously funny crossing. In those days Truman was about the best companion you could want. He had not turned bitchy. Well, he had not turned *maliciously* bitchy. But he was full of fantasies and mischief. We used to go along the first class corridors of the *Mary* and pick up the gentlemen's shoes, set outside their staterooms for shining—and we would mix them all up, set them doors away from their proper places.

And then there was that alcoholic Episcopalian bishop.

I do not feel particularly elated this morning since last night I resumed my symposium after the performances of *Small Craft Warnings*. I made an unfortunate attempt to hold the audience with a reading of one of my best short plays, *The Frosted Glass Coffin*, a play admired by Paul Bowles. I warned the audiences that the play was a piece of rather depressing material since it dealt with the fate of retired citizens, very senior, living at a hotel called the Ponce de Leon in Miami. I told them that, if the play did not interest them, they should feel entirely at liberty to walk out. To my distress, the greater part of them chose this option.

However, among those who remained was my old friend, the director José Quintero, and his faithful friend Nicky. We dined at P. J. Clarke's.

Back to the perhaps familiar story of Truman Capote and the hard-drinking Episcopalian bishop on the *Queen Mary*, that late summer crossing in 1948.

We had scarcely left Southampton when Truman began to notice that a portly and bibulous bishop was popping up unexpectedly almost everywhere Truman went. I began to notice it, too. We would hardly sit down at a bar on the ship when in would come the Bishop, less steadily than the calm ocean and the seaworthy vessel could possibly account for. He would cast a glazed and anxious look about the bar. Then his eyes would light up as he spotted little Truman crouching before the bar, hoping to escape the attention of this eminent churchman. No luck, never, none, whatsoever. The Bishop would invariably spot us, the gloom would disappear from his round face and he would fairly plunge at the nearest bar stool, close to those occupied by Truman and me. Or if we were at a table or at a seat in the movie auditorium, he would plump himself down (quite uninvited, needless to say) or would heave into an adjoining seat. So it went for half the crossing.

A dreadful confrontation between the Bishop and Truman was unmistakably impending and down it came like a bolt from heaven.

Truman and I were seated vis-à-vis at a table for two in the dining salon. With apparitional abruptness, the Bishop had drawn up a chair between us and started to engage us in conversation. His motive was not of an evangelistic nature. I mean not in the usual sense. Truman had declared himself quite uninterested in any church of any denomination.

On this evening, Truman began to stare at the Bishop's massive ring.

"You know," he drawled sweetly to the Bishop, "I've always wanted to have a bishop's ring."

The Bishop chuckled indulgently.

"A bishop's ring is only available to a bishop," I think was his answer.

"Oh, I don't know," countered Truman, "it occurred to me that maybe I might find one in a pawnshop. You know, one that had been hocked by a defrocked bishop."

He drawled out "defrocked bishop" in a way that left no doubt of his implication. The Bishop turned redder than usual and excused himself from the table and we were not disturbed by his persistent approaches for the rest of the voyage.

The voyage terminated, of course, in the harbor of New York. Margo Jones was at the dock to meet me. She had already found an apartment for me and I think it was the loveliest of the three or four apartments I've occupied over the years in New York City. It was the one designed and decorated by the now famous sculptor Tony Smith, who had been a close friend of mine since 1941—I was "best man" at his wedding to Jane Lawrence, the singer, in 1943, when I was "working" for MGM, where Jane was making a rather hapless film in which she was fatally miscast.

Her middle name was Lanier; we were distantly related, it seemed. In any case we had become, we are now, quite close friends.

The apartment was on East Fifty-eighth between Lexington and Third avenues. A three-story brownstone, façade freshly painted white and gray. The interior of the first-floor apartment was Tony's creation and he had created it for another old friend, Buffie Johnson, the painter. The apartment had a huge workroom in the middle, the height of two stories. Back of that great studio was a little patio full of exotic plants watered by a small fountain. It was kept at a low temperature so that the glass walls which enclosed it were always frosted over: it looked, from the studio and bedroom beyond it, like a small submarine garden. As for the bedroom, it was a piece of enchantment. Buffie's sign was Aquarius and the bedroom was full of water things. An illuminated aquarium, a great assortment of sea shells, and driftwood and old fishing-nets. The bed was huge, and marvelously comfortable—perfectly designed for the activities that it was soon to support . . .

Margo Jones was a dear friend at this time and getting me this dream place to live in was about the loveliest thing she could have done for me in her sadly brief lifetime.

Rehearsals were soon to begin on *Summer and Smoke*, which Margo had produced at her arena theatre in Dallas. I attributed the Dallas production's remarkable absence of artistry to the fact that the play was, in my opinion at that time, not a good one and the leading roles had been unhappily cast, Miss Alma Winemiller being played by a very tall, skinny girl with a Bronx accent and exceptionally large front teeth.

However, Mr. Brooks Atkinson caught the Dallas production and, for some reason still unfathomable to me, he found the play enchanting. He wrote it up in the New York *Times*. Margo was ecstatic at this premature notice. Of course Margo seemed almost always to be ecstatic over something and this condition was not always unrelated to a taste for whiskey.

For the New York production, we procured the services of Margaret Phillips and Todd Andrews for the parts of Miss Alma and the young doctor. Miss Phillips was an exquisite fresh-faced, tilt-nosed young ingénue of Welsh origin; Mr. Andrews was exceptionally handsome but not so talented, I regret to say.

Now you may think, perhaps correctly, that I am a total ingrate when I say that in my opinion Margo Jones should have confined herself to a regional theatre, preferably in the executive and fund-raising departments. But I think it was there that her genius lay, not in the direction of actors or of delicate plays.

We were scarcely past the first week of rehearsals when I had or began to have depressing premonitions about the venture. An actor or actress would approach the ecstatic Margo with a question such as "How do you want me to play this bit, Miss Jones?"

*"Play* it? Honey, don't play it, just *feel* it."

Naturally the performer would go away from Margo as perplexed as when he approached her.

It was not until a year or two later that I learned that Margo had informed the cast, in a reverential tone, that this play was the final work of a dying playwright. The young Anne Jackson was in the cast and it seems that she told this story to Truman Capote. It got back to me the following summer in Italy and it caused me a great deal of consternation. I did not like to be reminded that my apparent good health was so profoundly suspect.

Well, the play opened as plays usually did in those days, and it got another rave notice from Atkinson, but none from anyone else. Obviously it was doomed. The performers were not feeling it nor were they performing it very well, either. Of course Miss Phillips was as effective as she could be with the kind of direction that she had been given. Mr. Andrews looked handsome.

*Streetcar* was still running to packed houses and even *Summer and Smoke* was packed for the first weeks. But word got around and pretty soon attendance dropped off. I remember standing in the back of the house and being unable to watch or listen for more than ten or fifteen minutes at a time.

Only my lovely apartment kept me from despair for a while. That and, of course, the unfailing work each morning on some new project, story, poem, or play.

Why do I resist writing about my plays? The truth is that my plays have been the most important element of my life for God knows how many years. But I feel the plays speak for themselves. And that my life hasn't and that it has been remarkable enough, in its continual contest with madness, to be worth setting upon paper. And my habits of work are so much more private than my daily and nightly existence.

One evening I was passing along Lexington Avenue when I encountered, leaning against a wall near a corner, a very young man with carrot-red hair and the sort of figure that every hustler should have but rarely does, now or then. I stopped short in my tracks and said, "Hello." He grinned amiably and moved out from the wall, extending his hand to me.

"My name is Tommy Williams," he said.

This is, of course, my own real name and it struck me as an irresistibly good omen so I took him straight home to the lovely apartment and it was a night when the nightingales sang. Redheads have that wonderful skin, almost translucent and full of pearly tints.

Enough about that.

Tommy was inexperienced as a hustler and would

not, as we say, "turn over." However, one evening, when I had more or less allowed that contact to lapse, I saw him on the same corner where we'd originally met and he smiled at me sheepishly and he said, "Mr. Williams, if you'd like to, you can bugger me tonight."

Pathetic, maybe, but it was very touching.

# 9

In the early fall of 1948, I had a quite sudden and accidental and marvelous re-encounter with Frank Phillip Merlo.

It came about this way. I was once again, near midnight, walking downtown on Lexington, taking the night air, when I passed an open delicatessen. In there buying some edibles was "The Little Horse" with a wartime buddy of his.

"My God, Frankie, why haven't you looked me up?"

"I don't like to climb on band-wagons," was his characteristically direct and honest reply. "When you hit it big with *Streetcar* last year, I figured you'd think I just wanted to exploit a little meeting we'd had on a beach. That's why I never got in touch with you. But I saw the play and I loved it."

"Let's have a picnic at my place," I suggested. Frankie looked at his buddy (who was a straight) and his buddy nodded.

We went back to the Aquarius apartment and ate roast beef on rye with pickles and potato salad. Frankie and I kept looking at each other.

Frankie didn't know that his buddy knew. But his buddy did know and couldn't have cared less. Nobody who knew Frankie would allow anything like being one for the boys, not the girls, to matter in his friendship with "The Horse."

So presently the Navy buddy said, "Frankie, why don't you stay here with Tennessee and I'll go home to Jersey?"

Well, that's how it began to work out. Frankie stayed over with Tennessee, on that magical carpet of a bed back of the submarine garden. Some years later I wrote up this event in a poem called "A Separate Poem."

I did not really fall in love with Frankie all at once. In fact at first I was hesitant to make it a permanent thing. I was too used to having freedom. So one evening, with all possible delicacy, I told him that instead of staying every night it would be better if he made it every other night; the old Rafaello arrangement.

This was doubtless interpreted negatively by Frankie, and I think it hurt his feelings. In any case, this partial commitment to the romance was soon to be complete.

I went to St. Louis to see Mother. And it was while I was there under the maternal roof that it became unmistakably clear to me that my heart, too long accustomed to transitory attachments, had found in the young Sicilian a home at last.

I sent him a wire from St. Louis: "Returning New York tomorrow. Please wait for me in apartment."

I returned after midnight. When I let myself into the apartment it seemed totally empty, there was no evidence of Frankie's presence and I felt quite desolate. But that feeling persisted only for the time it took me to enter the Aquarius bedroom. There on the huge bed was little Frankie, sleeping.

So began a relationship that lasted for fourteen years.

Now I'll describe the lunatic events of last night. I was scheduled to make two appearances at the New Theatre for my resumed "symposia" after the performance. The first was to be at 9:10, after the first Saturday evening show, the second at 12:10 after the second. I was intending, out of sheer madness, I suppose, to read my new story which I call my last one, "The Inventory at Fontana Belle."

Well, the audience at the early show last night was spared that experience by a seriocomic concomitance of misadventures.

I had a dinner date with Ruth Ford and Dotson Rader set up for 7:30. I was also, at the same hour, expecting my new friend, who was to join us for dinner. Dotson left messages for me to call Ruth. I did and it was apparent that she was the opposite of eager to keep the date. She said that Dotson was now incommunicado, locked in the little attic apartment, the eyrie, in which she has lately ensconced him. I told her that my friend and I would go to Billy Barnes's for a picnic on his terrace and that she and Dotson might join us if they felt so inclined. Well, they didn't. And I felt put down about that. And there were bad vibes in the air on Billy's penthouse terrace. There were several young male beauties present and they started disappearing together, as is the wont of the beautiful and young in the States. Billy became more and more distraught in appearance. Mr. Robert Fryer of the Ahmanson Theatre in Los Angeles, where they plan to revive *Streetcar* this winter in celebration of its twenty-fifth anniversary, did not help the situation. He seemed extremely cool and quite lacking in social charm and not at all amused by my efforts to be amusing. I began to feel strange, partly due to a vodka martini and two or three glasses of red wine.

It seems that I can't hold liquor anymore; consult my liver on that subject and perhaps also my brain.

Well, when it was time to go to the theatre for the so-called "symposium" I tripped over a garden hose on the terrace and fell flat on the pavement, suffering quite a few bloody abrasions. My young friend was truly solicitous and Billy was a bit hysterical-looking as antiseptics were applied by my friend to the cuts I'd suffered.

Actually we arrived at the theatre no more than two or three minutes late, but the audience was leaving. They had not been informed of my appearance. I supposed they thought that it would be one appearance too many. I don't know why I was so upset over this, it was a trivial matter. But Candy Darling's boyfriend had a car, a white convertible, waiting at the door and he offered to drive our party home. I said, "I've had it. Please deliver me to my hotel." On the way, Mr. Fryer suggested that I return to the theatre and read my short story to the second evening's audience, *before* the play. This struck, correctly or not, as a reflection upon my sanity and I flew into a blind rage at the man. I told him to shove his West Coast theatre and the announced revival of *Streetcar*, and I told him various other things no more polite, and then I asked to be let out of the car on a corner several blocks from the hotel. They wouldn't let me out but drove me to the hotel door. Billy and Fryer remained in the car, both speechless, and the three young men went up to my "Victorian Suite" at the Elysée to see that I didn't jump out the window, I guess. I soon got hold of myself, drinks were ordered up, my friend massaged my back and talked soothingly and affectionately to me until the phone rang and one of the producers said they had failed to announce my appearance inadvertently and they would pick me up at the Elysée for the midnight show.

It appears that I will do just about anything, now, to keep the show running, that is, short of a tango with a kangaroo partner. So I went. The curtain opened. There was a fair-sized house for midnight. I took a drink of wine and informed the audience that on this occasion I intended to amuse myself, primarily, by reading a story to them.

The eccentric aspects of the story—and eccentric is a mild term for it—didn't strike me until after. The reception of the reading was, I could say, perfunctory.

Lately no one seems to laugh at my jokes on paper, perhaps they're too black, I don't know ...

I then took the three kids to P. J. Clarke's eatery and we drank and ate and I then began to reflect more and more upon the frightening compulsive note of self-destruction in which I had been indulging myself lately.

My friend took one kid: another left alone in my hat, a Dobbs Western. I'd presented it to him—and another friend took me home. He's a nice kid and he is now asleep in the twin bed while I knock out this preposterous account of the night before ...

Make of it what you will. I can make of it nothing but a sense of doom.

To return again to 1948, I have a bit more to report on that season.

Frankie and I had been out late one evening and when we returned to the apartment the transom on the front door was open and from within came the voice of Truman Capote, shrill with agitation. We let ourselves in.

In the apartment were Truman, Gore Vidal, and a female policeman: they were called "the Bo-peep squad" in those days. It seemed that Truman and Gore, still on friendly terms at this point, had got a bit drunk together and had climbed in through the transom of the apartment to wait for me and Frankie.

The lady on the Bo-peep squad had been passing along by patrol-car as they were climbing through the transom. She pursued them into the pad and she was now in the process of searching the premises for suspected narcotics and she was holding Gore and Truman for breaking and entering.

She had located some Seconals in the bedroom and she was making a big deal of it. (In those days my use of sleeping pills was very occasional and only at bedtime.)

Frankie and I managed to calm her down enough to prevent the arrest of Truman and Gore. Having only turned up the few Seconals in the way of dope, she stepped angrily out.

*Summer and Smoke* was still surviving at the Music Box in early December when Frankie, Paul Bowles and I took passage on the Italian liner *Vulcania,* which is the most charming ship I've ever voyaged upon. Outside each first class stateroom was a verandah. I breakfasted and worked out there in the mornings, while Frankie slept inside—he was always a late and sound sleeper in his years of health.

My sexual feeling for the boy was inordinate. Every evening I would cross to his bunk in the stateroom. Aware of my sexual intemperance and what its consequences could be, I began to entertain a suspicion that something was going on between Frankie and Paul Bowles. Nothing was, of course, except friendship—and perhaps they also may have shared an interest in some derivative of Cannabis, as many of the "in" people did in those days. Bowles asked me to read a short story of his which became the title story for a collection published a year or two later. This story was "The Delicate Prey" and it shocked me. This seems odd, I know. And I think it was quite incomprehensible to Paul that I, who had published such stories as "Desire and the Black Masseur" should be shocked by "The Delicate Prey." I recognized it as a beautiful piece of prose but I advised him against its publication in the States. You see, my shocking stories had been published in expensive private editions by New Directions and never exhibited on a bookstore counter.

Except for all that, the voyage was extremely pleasant. The *Vulcania* served excellent food. It had a charming little bar with Chinese décor. There was a big storm at sea which made Frankie seasick but which I found exhilarating.

We arrived off the shore of Gibraltar and there for

the first time met Paul's wife, Jane Bowles, whom I regard as the finest writer of fiction we have had in the States. You will probably think this a wild opinion but I must stick to it. She had a unique sensibility in all her work that I found even more appealing than that of Carson McCullers. And she was a charming girl, so full of humor and affection and curious, touching little attacks of panic—which I thought at first were merely bits of theatre but which I soon found were quite genuine. And I don't mean to say—God forbid—that theatre is not sometimes authentic.

When Jane Bowles succumbed to a long illness in a convent-hospital in Málaga, Spain, in 1973, she left an irreplaceable vacancy in the lives of all who were so fortunate as to have known her. When her collected works were published in a single volume about seven years ago, these works consisted of a novel of unique quality, *Two Serious Ladies*, a group of short stories truly equaled in sensibility by the work of no other writer of her time, and a curiously underestimated play, *In the Summer House.* I had the great good fortune to see this play's first American production at the University Theatre in Ann Arbor, Michigan, starring the late Miriam Hopkins, who gave a stunning performance.

Later produced on Broadway, this time starring Dame Judith Anderson and Miss Mildred Dunnock, it met with a reception that I would describe as bewildered, although Miss Dunnock's performance was one of her most poignant.

For what it may be worth, I feel impelled to offer the opinion that it is a dramatic work of such profound sensibility, mixed with Jane's unfailingly acute admixture of humor and pathos, that it stands quite superbly alone among works for the American theatre.

We spent a night at the Rock Hotel in Gibraltar and the following day we crossed on a big ferry to Tangier with our beautiful maroon Buick Roadmaster; I had stubbornly refused to drive into the mountains of Southern Spain, an excursion which Paul was anxious to make; in those days I didn't think that my heart could take even a moderate altitude. And I was eager to get settled.

We stayed a few days in Tangier and then we set off in the Roadmaster for Fez, where Paul's very young friend Ahmed was waiting for him. We had fantastic difficulty crossing the frontier of Spanish Morocco. Bowles always traveled with at least a dozen pieces of luggage. These provoked the suspicion of the Spanish authorities at the frontier. Every piece of our luggage had to be removed to the customhouse for a maniacally thorough inspection. We had passed through a terrific thunderstorm and it was still storming. While we were in the customs' shed, one of us suddenly noticed that the brakes on the Roadmaster weren't holding and that it was rolling rather rapidly backward straight toward a deep ravine.

Little Frankie dashed out and stopped the car just before it reached the drop-off. It was quite a display of courage, which he never lacked. Well, they wouldn't let us continue and they tried to confiscate my typewriter and several pieces of Paul's luggage. We had to return to Tangier: the Hotel Rembrandt.

Luckily I had some newspaper friends in Tangier, they promptly phoned all frontier stations between Tangier and Fez informing them that a group of important Americans were going to drive through the next day. Off we went again and at each frontier we were waved on without inspection.

We arrived at the Hotel Jamais in Fez about nightfall. Among the mail waiting for me there was a cablegram that plunged me into depression. It informed me that *Summer and Smoke* was about to close, due to the drop in attendance that Broadway plays have always suffered during the weeks before Christmas. I suspect, however, that, Christmas or not, it couldn't have survived much longer.

The Hotel Jamais was one of the loveliest in the world. It had been the palace of a sultan and its furnishings remained in their original style. Just next to it was the tower of a mosque, on the terrace of which the Koran was chanted softly at hourly intervals through the night.

But I could not shake off my depression over the fate of *Summer and Smoke*. I liked Fez no more than I had liked Tangier and I insisted that we drive to Casablanca, Frankie and I, and catch a ship to Marseilles, from which we would head for Rome.

Frankie turned very sulky and we came close to a quarrel during that drive to Casablanca. The ship to Marseilles was horrid. The food was bad and the passengers unpleasant and noisy.

I think it took us about three days to reach Marseilles. As soon as we entered Italy, Frankie's good humor returned as did mine.

And it was now the winter of 1949, month of January, and Frankie and I began our first of many long stays in Rome.

What is my profession but living and putting it all down in stories and plays and now in this book?

After her great success with *Streetcar*, a success which surely she deserved, Irene M. Selznick had rejected *The Rose Tattoo*, telling me rather crushingly that it was material for an opera, not for a play. Cheryl Crawford thought otherwise: she embraced it warmly and gave it a fine production, in 1950.

Young Eli Wallach was a wonderful choice to play Mangiacavallo. And that fine young actor Don Murray was perfect to play the sailor—love of Serafina's daughter. There was great trouble casting Serafina. It was I who found Maureen Stapleton for the part.

Her reading convinced us all that, despite her youth, she could do it; she was a very young girl at the time but nevertheless I thought she was so brilliant in characterization that the obstacle of her youth could be overcome. So I kept insisting that she read and read again. Finally I assisted her in "making up" for a reading: I had her dishevel her hair and wear a sloppy robe, and I think even streak her face to look like dirt stains. And that reading she gave made all agree that she was the one.

Both Eli and Maureen were very active in the Actors' Studio and had benefited a great deal from the "method" as taught by Lee Strasberg and also at that time by Elia Kazan and Robert Lewis. We opened in Chicago. Claudia Cassidy, theatre reviewer for the Chicago *Tribune*, didn't seem quite to know what to make of it, as a follow-up of *Menagerie* and *Streetcar*, but she gave us a pretty good notice and we had a pretty good run, about two months in the Windy City.

*The Rose Tattoo* was my love-play to the world. It was permeated with the happy young love for Frankie and I dedicated the book to him, saying: "To Frankie in Return for Sicily."

And the epigraph, a quote from the author of *Exile*, the poet St. Jean Perse, went something like this.

"Life is beautiful as a ram's head painted red and nailed over a doorway."

Anna Magnani was magnificent as Serafina in the movie version of *Tattoo*. I often wonder how Anna Magnani managed to live within society and yet to remain so free of its conventions. She was as unconventional a woman as I have known in or out of my professional world, and if you understand me at all, you must know that in this statement I am making my personal estimate of her honesty, which I feel was complete.

Of course I also existed outside of conventional society while contriving somewhat precariously to remain in contact with it. For me this was not only

precarious but a matter of dark unconscious disturbance. For Anna what was it? Since she has written
no memoirs of the sort I'm writing, or any sort at all,
that question is going to remain a question. I can only
say that she never exhibited any lack of self-assurance,
any timidity in her relations with that society outside
of whose conventions she quite publicly existed.

She looked absolutely straight into the eyes of
whomever she confronted and during that golden time
in which we were dear friends I never heard a false
word from her mouth.

I think that's rather a lot to say for the lady. Still,
I have a lot more to say for Anna and much of it is
inexpressible now, so much of it that these recollections are bound to be fragmentary . . .

Shyness always having been my great problem with
people (although I often come on, these days, with a
display of an assurance which is sometimes quite as
spurious as it may be startling), at first I was very
shy of Anna. But with Frankie as an intermediary
between my reserve and her beautifully natural lack
of it, the shyness was soon to go.

Merlo was a first-generation Sicilian. Magnani was
a Roman. With that sharing of the Latin, or Mediterranean, temperament, as well as an equal directness,
they had no need for a tentative period before understanding and loving.

Anna never got up for the day before it was afternoon. At about 2:30 or 3 P.M. the phone would ring.

After *"Ciao, Tenn,"* she would say, "What is the
program?"

She always offered me this courteous question,
though I suspect she had already decided what the
program was to be. I have said she never spoke false-
ly, but to permit a close friend to think he's arranging
an evening's program is not a dissimulation but a
simple act of politeness. I have the same habit. I always know pretty well what my program is going to
be, at least as far as a program can be known in ad-

vance of its performance, but when I call a friend,
with my program for the evening more or less determined, I will always say, "I have no plan for the evening, how about you."

At eight o'clock Merlo and I would arrive at her
apartment on top of the Palazzo Altieri (near the
Pantheon): a distraught-looking maid would admit us
to the living room. On the table there would always
be a bowl of ice, bowls of pretzels and peanuts, two
tall glasses and a bottle of Johnnie Walker Red Label.
We'd sit there and drink and wait, and it was sometimes close to an hour, but it passed agreeably. We
had our drinks and wandered out on her terrace to
look over Vecchia Roma, gleaming softly through late
dusk, and from the back rooms of the apartment we'd
hear Anna shouting orders that were loud but resonant
with affection.

Often her current young man would appear half an
hour before Anna. He would greet us with a sort of
suspicious civility and stretch himself out in a chair or
on a chaise with an air of sleepy detachment.

At last Anna, brilliant with animation and expan-
sive feeling, would burst into the room, and she was
ready to charge forth upon "the program." She had
her own private elevator which took us directly down
to the huge, shadowy courtyard in which she kept two
or three luxurious cars. Occasionally, not often, she'd
allow her young man to drive, but she much preferred
driving herself and was a fantastically good driver.
Roman traffic didn't seem to exist for her. The young
man would usually maintain his sulky silence while
she and Frank talked away like a pair of children on
the way to a fun-fair. We never inquired where we
were going for dinner: that was a matter which she'd
already decided and her choice was always perfect.
Restaurateurs and waiters received her like a queen:
they hovered beaming around the table while she ordered wines, pastas, salads, entrees without consulting
the menu. This doesn't sound like good behavior and

yet it was the best. Every meal was a feast which it would take Ernest Hemingway with his gourmet appreciation to describe with justice.

The evening would never let down: it was centered around the dinner, but after the coffees, Anna would demand a great sack of leftovers. And then we would start our midnight course about Rome, visiting all those places where the hungry stray cats were waiting for her to feed them: the Forum, the Colosseum, under certain bridges, in Trastevere, in parts of the Villa Borghese.

This done, she would return to the palazzo to pick up her *lupo*, a big black German shepherd which I had given her when its predecessor of the same breed succumbed to old age. It would almost pre-empt the back seat of the car; she would drive it straight to the Villa Borghese. There she'd let it out and it would race with the car along a bridle path until it was panting, and ready to hop back in.

Then we would drive to Rosati's on Via Veneto, in deference chiefly to my desire for a nightcap. Anna was not a drinker of anything but wine. Frank Merlo would have *caffè espresso*. The young man with Anna would stretch out his long, elegant legs and sip a liqueur with his eyes half open. Anna would shoot glances toward him, somewhere between two opposite emotions. And she would always comment sorrowfully on my need for whiskey. Late as it was, by this time, the Veneto would still be crowded and the sidewalk strollers would slow down to glance with wonder at this darkly shimmering woman. Of course there were frequent assaults of *paparazzi*, those kids with flash-cameras who swarm about Rome at night in search of "name faces." Anna would endure them for a few moments, then she would shout them away in a fashion that dispersed them at once but in good humor.

Our car would be waiting in that shadowy courtyard of the Palazzo Altieri. We would escort her to the glass-walled outdoor elevator.

"*Ciao, caro, ciao, bello, ciao, ciao, ciao!*"

Kisses and embraces. Then she would step into the elevator and her young man would follow and we'd see her staring at his enigmatic face with great eyes on fire, as the lift rose out of view.

She was beyond convention as no one I've known in my life, and I suspect that was our great bond and that it was the root of her proud assurance, as much as it was the root of my own lack of it and the sense of guilt that must always shadow my life.

In the early fifties Bill Inge invited me one day to lunch at the Algonquin. He appeared to be sort of sanctimoniously morose, if you get what I mean, and in the course of the dismal lunch he abruptly, out of nowhere, came up with this question: "Tennessee, don't you feel that you are blocked as a writer?"

My answer: "Yes, I do, I've always been blocked as a writer, but I love writing so much that I always break through the block."

I feel that Bill's primary problem was one of pathological egocentricity: he could not take a spell of failures after his run of smash hits: so eventually he was cared for by two male nurses.

I think of a line from *Kingdom of Earth*.

"Life is rock and man has got to be rock, too, or one of them's gonna break and the one that breaks is never gonna be life"—or something like that . . .

As I said earlier, I wrote the first draft of *Camino* in New Orleans in 1946; that was the manuscript Audrey Wood told me to put away and not show to anybody. Her reaction had depressed me so that I thought the play must be really quite awful. Then a few years later, I was in New York and dropped by the Actors' Studio. Kazan was conducting an exercise with Eli Wallach and Barbara Baxley and some other student actors—and they were performing *Ten Blocks on the*

*Camino Real.* I realized that Audrey had been altogether mistaken, that it played remarkably well, and I said, "Oh, Kazan, we must do this. We must do this with one other play maybe, for Broadway." There was no Off-Broadway in those days. He agreed. He was very excited about the idea and we exchanged letters about it all that summer (when I was in Rome, and he was in New York). Then suddenly Kazan accepted an assignment to direct some other play; I was upset and retreated to Key West. But I wouldn't relinquish the idea of *Ten Blocks on the Camino Real* so I continued to work on it and expanded it into *Camino Real.*

Meanwhile, the play that Kazan had decided to do in preference to *Ten Blocks* was a failure. *There's* poetic justice. And then he was ready to take on the revised play of *Camino Real.*

Well, it was a big thing to take on at that time, but Kazan has never been lacking in courage and he went ahead. The rehearsals were very, very exciting and the out-of-town reception of the play was very, very puzzled. A great many people walked out during the performance. People seemed outraged by its innovations.

It had felt exciting to work on. I knew that I was doing new and different things and it excited me and I thought that they would work under Kazan. They did work, except the audience generally did not want them to work; the audience wasn't with it at the time. Now they are, they love the play now. *Camino* was the first time on Broadway of which I know when actors ran down the aisles and went out into the audience. This technique was used legitimately, I thought; nobody got stepped on, except me, for writing it that way. But it was great fun out of town despite the outraged reactions of a considerable portion of the audience.

I always had fun working with Kazan.

Most critics were quite cross about the play, too, but

some of them recognized the innovations and gave them some credit.

For the Philadelphia opening, Frank and I stayed in a hotel and our suite was directly above that of the singer Johnny Ray. He was just coming on big at that time with a song called "The Little White Cloud That Cried," and we got to meet him and he was a delightful companion. Kazan and Frankie and I all visited him backstage and he inscribed photographs for us. I still have one in New Orleans. He was a very nice kid but he couldn't stay out of trouble.

One night after a performance of *Camino,* at the Shubert in Philadelphia, the producer Saint Subber was in the audience and after the show he rushed up to me and shouted, "Maestro!" and threw himself to his knees in front of me. I thought this was a most disgraceful performance, too hysterical. He made great protestations of adulation to me, which, I'm afraid, were somewhat insincere as I never saw or heard from him since. That's show business.

Kazan had cast the entire show out of the Actors' Studio, an organization that was a very important thing in the great days—I guess I should say the *prosperous* days—of Broadway, during my time in the forties and the fifties. Those were two great decades of the Actors' Studio. Nearly every great actor of promise studied there. And the Actors' Studio technique fitted so well my type of play. And, the Actors' Studio—with Kazan, Strasberg, and Bobby Lewis—was a great place for actors to go and compare notes on each other's work and it gave them a sort of home base.

*Camino Real* opened in New York in 1953. I sat in a box with Mother and Dakin and I remember thinking that, although it may have been flawed, it surpassed its flaws.

Then there was the after-opening party and the New York reviews began to come in. They were savage about this play, which freed so much of contemporary American theatre from realistic constrictions.

That night I suffered the usual apocalypse of New York opening nerves. I fled the party and the reviews to my apartment on East Fifty-eighth with Frankie. I tried to go to bed but I couldn't. Frankie was a marvel of controlled cool empathy.

At about 1 A.M., Kazan and his wife arrived at the door, and to my dismay they were accompanied by Mr. and Mrs. John Steinbeck.

Then I did go quite mad and I shouted at Kazan, "How dare you bring these people here tonight?"

Then I slammed into my bedroom and bolted the door.

I've never wished to be seen by virtual strangers at a time of crisis.

The Kazans and Steinbecks, despite this less than cordial reception, stayed on for an hour in the apartment and Frankie continued to be a marvel. He served them drinks and explained my nature to them, which I'm afraid he always knew very well but which, in a time of crisis, he would usually defend . . .

Kazan and I had lunch the next day at a fish-place and things were set in perspective.

Of course poor Cheryl Crawford, the producer, had decided to close. The last week of the run she cut out the confetti in the big carnival scene as an act of economy, despite the fact that the play, after its closing announcement, was playing to capacity.

Parties, in the fifties. I remember how Irene Mayer Selznick, daughter of that awful old Louis B., used to invite me to socially prestigious dinners at the Pierre and say, "Ask Frankie to drop in afterward."

"Tell her to go fuck herself," was his invariable and proper remark when I relayed these insulting invitations.

Again in this context, I remember when Jack Warner entertained me and Frankie in his private dining room on the Warner lot. He was bullying some subordinates who had appeared slightly late for lunch.

Frankie stared at him with an expressionless fixity which Warner finally noticed.

"What do *you* do, young man?"

Without a change of expression and in a loud, clear voice, Frank replied, "I sleep with Mr. Williams."

Jack Warner may have dropped his fork but Frank didn't blink an eye as he continued to stare steadily at the old tyrant.

Well, now, about plays, what about them? Plays are written and then, if they are lucky, they are performed, and if their luck still holds, which is not too frequently the case, their performance is so successful that both audience and critics at the first night are aware that they are being offered a dramatic work which is both honest and entertaining and also somehow capable of engaging their aesthetic appreciation.

I have never liked to talk about the professional side of my life. Am I afraid that it is a bird that will be startled away by discussion, as by a hawk's shadow? Something like that, I suppose.

People are always asking me, at those symposia to which I've been subjected in recent years, which is my favorite among the plays I have written, the number of which eludes my recollection, and I either say to them, "Always the latest" or I succumb to my instinct for the truth and say, "I suppose it must be the published version of *Cat on a Hot Tin Roof.*"

That play comes closest to being both a work of art and a work of craft. It is really very well put together, in my opinion, and all its characters are amusing and credible and touching. Also it adheres to the valuable edict of Aristotle that a tragedy must have unity of time and place and magnitude of theme.

The set in *Cat* never changes and its running time is exactly the time of its action, meaning that one act, timewise, follows directly upon the other, and I know of no other modern American play in which this is accomplished.

However my reasons for liking *Cat* best are deeper than that. I believe that in *Cat* I reached beyond myself, in the second act, to a kind of crude eloquence of expression in Big Daddy that I have managed to give no other character of my creation.

The story of *Cat*'s production in 1954 and the disaster that followed upon its enormous success must be told now.

Kazan immediately shared Audrey's enthusiasm for *Cat* but he said that it was faulty in one act. I assumed that he meant the first act, but no, it was the third act. He wanted a more admirable heroine than the Maggie offered in the original script.

Inwardly I disagreed. I thought that in Maggie I had presented a very true and moving portrait of a young woman whose frustration in love and whose practicality drove her to the literal seduction of an unwilling young man. Seduction is too soft a word. Brick was literally forced back to bed by Maggie, when she confiscated his booze . . .

Then I also had to violate my own intuition by having Big Daddy re-enter the stage in Act Three. I saw nothing for him to do in that act when he re-entered and I did not think that it was dramatically proper that he should re-enter. Consequently I had him tell "the elephant story." This was assaulted by censors. I was told it must be removed. The material which I then had to put in its place was always offensive to me.

I would not tell you this except for the consequences to me as a writer after *Cat* had received its Critics' Award and its Pulitzer.

Even though I always go crazy on opening nights, the New York opening of *Cat* was particularly dreadful. I thought it was a failure, a distortion of what I had intended. After the show was over I thought I had heard coughs all during the performance. I suppose there weren't that many, probably the usual number. And it did become my biggest, my longest-running play. But after the show was over on opening night, Kazan said, "Let's go to my apartment until the reviews are out." He was totally confident that it would be a hit. I met Audrey Wood outside, and at the time I was totally dependent on her for any creative confidence; and so I said, "Audrey, we're all going up to the Kazans' to wait for the notices." She said, "Oh no, I have other plans." I was hurt, and said something mean.

After that, I went to Italy with Frankie and for the first, no, the second time of prolonged duration, I was unable to write.

Strong coffee no longer sufficed to get the creative juices to flow.

For several weeks I endured this creative sterility, then I started to wash down a Seconal with a martini. And then I was "hooked" on that practice. That summer of 1955 in Rome this creative state of abandonment resulted in the film *Baby Doll*, the script of which has a wanton hilarity to it, in my opinion, a quality which was never fully or rightly used in the film.

It may seem as if I am blaming Kazan for the beginning of my disasters as a drugged writer. I have never blamed anyone for anything but deliberate cruelty, for there has always been in me the conviction of Blanche, that "deliberate cruelty is the one unforgivable thing."

Perhaps I do blame Audrey for her neglect, in the dreadful sixties, but even her I blame little. Kazan I blame not at all, not even for his question in a rented limousine—returning from a sad evening at Jane and Tony Smith's—"Tennessee, how long do you think you are going to live?"

I felt no shock at the brutality of the question, having been long cognizant of the fact that an element of the fire cat must exist in all artists.

"A few months more, Gadg," I answered him quietly.

For a few minutes no one spoke in the rented limousine returning us from South Orange.

I suppose we all realized that a moment of truth had occurred.

It was through *Cat* that I met Faulkner. He was in love with Jean Stein, who was working with *Cat,* and he had come up to Philadelphia when we were there working on *Cat,* and I had gotten to know him there. He never talked to me. I thought he disapproved of me. And then later that summer he was with Jean Stein again in Paris and we all went to dinner together. I felt a terrible torment in the man. He always kept his eyes down. We tried to carry on a conversation but he would never participate. Finally, he lifted his eyes once in response to a direct question from me, and the look in his eyes was so terrible, so sad, that I began to cry.

Jane Bowles, though, is in my mind the greatest writer. Of course, I'm not a critic, but I am a writer and I think writers make good critics, especially if they divorce themselves from rivalry as I do now. I consider her quite the greatest writer of our century in the English language. And Harold Pinter told me he thought so, too.

Have I yet told you about the evening when my friend "the Professor" and I went to see a work called *The Dirtiest Show in Town?*

Afterward, we strolled along a street in the East Village. We were almost alongside someone who seemed indigenous to the locale when I recognized him as my dear friend Kazan.

The good Professor was, at this moment, engaged in conversation with a black stud and I was somewhat distracted by my apprehension that he was about to get himself into serious trouble.

Precisely what preceded this remark of Kazan I don't recall, but the remark was:

"Tenn, each of us dies and each of us dies alone."

I said to him, "Gadg, I know very well that each of us dies but I don't think we all die alone."

His response was an introspective, faraway look. At this point I turned my attention to the Professor and somehow, quite atypically, managed to disengage him from his perilous flirtation on that Bowery sidewalk with the towering black.

Since that summer of 1955 I have written usually under artificial stimulants, aside from the true stimulant of my deep-rooted need to continue to write.

I could cross the room to a big bag containing my collected works—as collected and published this year by New Directions—and provide you with the list of plays I have written since that summer and I think it would make you wonder a bit at my ability to continue my work under these debauched conditions.

Of course I could cite a number of known artists, I mean writing ones, who also succumbed to artificial stimulants. I could mention Faulkner's practice of climbing into the loft of a barn on his Mississippi farm with a full bottle of bourbon when he was intending to write, which I assume was each morning. And I could cite Coleridge and I could mention Jean Cocteau, all of whose best writing was done under opium, I have heard on good authority.

I could mention many productive and honest writers who went the way of liquor, especially in middle years.

Yet I would, of course, not advise any young writer to elect that way until it is forced upon him, until he cannot continue his work without resorting to stimulants.

Not long ago, in fact just a few nights ago, a gifted and handsome young screen writer, seeing me to bed and my bedtime Nembutal, confessed to me that he was able, now, only to write when drinking.

I felt like an older brother, and I said, "You're too young for that, don't take that way yet."

He did not seem to think that there would be offered him another and his handsome face was already beginning to show the coarsening effect of excessive drink.

Is it fair not to offer to writers the same tax-exemption for depleted resources that is offered, for instance, to big oil millionaires and steel works and other corporate enterprises which own and run our country?

We are now into protest and politics.

Plays have usually happened on lovely mornings in my Key West studio, though they have happened also on all mornings wherever I may be, even in that N.Y. pad of mine called the Victorian Suite; it has served me well enough, and so have rooms at the Hotel Colón in Barcelona and although I never felt I was able to write well in my various Roman apartments, there is evidence that I sometimes did write well enough, as in the case of *Rose Tattoo* and *The Roman Spring of Mrs. Stone*.

But surely always the best was in the studio of Key West, and for a couple of weeks late this fall or early in the winter, I hope to return there, to work on a second draft of a new play.

In 1959, I met with a truly shattering setback with the failure of *Orpheus Descending*—the legitimate descendant of my first New York-managed play, *Battle of Angels*.

Alas, *Orpheus* was not only overwritten but it was

under-directed by that dear man and fine critic, Harold Clurman.

In the part of Val had been fatally miscast a young man who came on like a lieutenant of the Mafia, which was not at all right for Val. I refused to fire him in Philadelphia, I told Clurman he'd have to do it, and Clurman did it, and the poor kid came to my suite at the Warwick in tears, not angry at me but professing great love for the play and—well, I was a sympathetic and rather deeply moved audience but I stood firm. "You're just not right for it, baby. You've got a great future but you're miscast in this one."

He never got angry at me, not even when it became apparent to him that I was not going to give an inch, let alone the proper male lead for *Orpheus*.

Then Cliff Robertson came into the play and I remember his first matinée, the best performance of *Orpheus*, and I remember how that gentleman of the theatre, Robert Whitehead, during this great matinée in Philly, came up and crouched alongside my aisle seat and exclaimed with great emotion, "Oh, this is it, this is it, thank God this is it!"

Well, unfortunately Bob Whitehead was mistaken in aces and spades. This was not it at all: except that single matinée.

The play was overloaded, and the requirements upon Maureen and Clurman were excessive.

But the reviewers could have seen its passages of lyric eloquence and permitted themselves to give the play a break. This they chose not to do. It is remarkable, considering the reviews, that the play survived the two or three months it did. In repertory it ran for seven years in Russia, if that means anything, and I suppose it does.

In New York they put it down with a vengeance, and with a vengeance that shattered me and sent me to Dr. Lawrence Kubie—that, too, was a case of miscasting—for the mistake of strict Freudian analysis.

He taught me much about my true nature but he offered me no solution except to break with Merlo, a thing that was quite obviously untenable as a consideration, my life being built around him.

And why did the critics turn on me so fiercely in the late fifties and the early sixties? I suspect it was a cabal to cut me down to what they thought was my size.

And what is my size? It is, I trust, the size of an artist who has consistently given all that he has to give to his work, with a most peculiar passion.

Never mind the bit of egomania now rearing its ugly head. Truth is in that, too ... isn't egomania almost the precondition of all creative work? I have found little to dispell that notion ...

And yet through this egomania of an artist there runs the great longing to "reach out your arms and embrace the whole world." Of course that sentence betrays egomania, too.

Truth is the bird we hope to catch in "this thing," and it can be better approached through my life story than an account of my career. Jesus, career, it's never been that to me, it has just been "doing my thing" with a fury to do it the best that I am able.

It is the evening of the first reading of Kazan's production of *Sweet Bird of Youth*, a major production by all customary signs: Cheryl Crawford is presenting it, starring Paul Newman and Geraldine Page; such top-ranking actors as Madeleine Sherwood, Rip Torn, and the late Sidney Blackmer are in supporting roles and we are booked into that great barn, the Martin Beck. And there also is probably a big preproduction movie deal.

The reading begins.

About halfway through it I leap from my chair and cry out, "Stop it, stop it! It can't go on, it's too awful!"

A total hush descends upon the rehearsal hall as I stride deliriously out into Times Square. I go home and knock myself out with booze and a pill. The phone is ignored if it rings. "The Horse" has left the apartment, going serenely about the mysterious business of Horses who have ridden out many tempests in their young lives . . .

Evening comes in due course. Then there is a strong knock at the door: the sort of knock that says, Open up in the name of the law!

I open up and there stand Molly and Gadg Kazan, sweetly and genially smiling as if nothing has happened of an unusual nature.

I believe it is near Christmas and a Christmas tree is lighted in the corner and they sit cozily by it.

I am now dreadfully ashamed of my conduct before the company but not yet swerved from my conviction that the play should not go on.

Gadg and Molly talk to me as you do to a wounded animal or a sick child. Gradually my desperate resolve crumbles: I love them. I decide to trust them.

But at the next day's rehearsal, Kazan, for the first time, does not want me seated directly beside him. Beside him, in fact, is a young writer, and I paranoiacally suspect that he has been brought in to rewrite my work. I sit gloomily back against the wall: the reading of the script is tedious and lifeless and hardly, to my ears, more a presentable script than it had seemed at the previous day's first reading. But I hold my peace. At lunch break I am introduced to the young writer. It seems that he has been dispatched from the Actors' Studio as a "listener" to the production and I am now reassured that he will not touch my script, awful though it may be, but I am still jealous of his proximity to Gadg.

Gradually, as rehearsals proceed, he fades out of the picture for me and I am sitting in my rightful place next to our great white father Kazan.

This anecdote is merely inserted here to show once again the state of nerves, the panic, the long, long slide toward a crack-up that stretched appallingly before me, even that long ago.

It occurs to me at this point that I have omitted an account of one of my more prestigious "adventures in drama," a pair of short plays that were presented under the title of *Garden District*. The first was a tragicomic one-act titled *Something Unspoken;* the second was the more important work called *Suddenly Last Summer*. I believe this production was the first that I went into after the disaster of *Orpheus Descending* and my subsequent term of Freudian analysis. The summer before its production I had happened to visit Southampton, where that gifted and amusing director Herbert Machiz was vacationing. In a tentative fashion I was working on *Suddenly Last Summer*. One evening I showed it to Machiz and he was instantly enthralled. He immediately set the wheels of the production in motion by interesting John C. Wilson in the work. For the leading role of Catharine Holly he had the inspired thought of Anne Meacham.

Machiz may not be a master director but he is a ball of fire at getting things going, he has an *élan vital*, and the greatly supportive companionship of John Myers, the art dealer.

Things went full steam ahead. We obtained one of the first important Off-Broadway houses, the York, on the upper East Side, and after the all-important casting of Anne Meacham, we procured the extremely talented services of Hortense Alden (formerly married to James T. Farrell) as a supporting star in both of the two plays, which were plausibly connected by having the same background of the garden district of New Orleans.

The opening night was a stunner. Miss Meacham tore into her role like a tigress: Hortense Alden was perfect as Mrs. Venable, and as the young doctor, Robert Lansing was an attractive and commanding performer.

The curtain went down to an ovation on opening night. After the audience had filed out, exclaiming with astonishment, a small group remained down front and among them was Elia Kazan.

In those days I had the unfortunate practice of fortifying myself, morally, for an opening night with a barbiturate washed down by several stiff drinks.

I therefore had the courage to go right up to Mr. and Mrs. Kazan and their companions and holler out, "Well, how did you like it?"

Their response was ambiguous: however, they did accompany Frankie and me to our apartment to watch us sweat out the notices. As usual the TV notices came in first, and as usual they were disparaging. I flew into my usual opening night hysteria. I remember saying, "If the theatre doesn't need me, I don't need it!"—and various other wild assertions of ego at bay.

Then all at once the *Times* and the *Trib* notices came in and they were raves.

While still on the subject of *Garden District*, I should mention that Anne Meacham was followed by Olive Deering in the part of Catharine. Olive took it to the Coast, where the notices were great, especially for dear little Olive. And I should mention that my foredoomed friend, Diana Barrymore, made a great personal success of the work in Chicago, with Cathleen Nesbitt playing Mrs. Venable.

There are passages in *Suddenly Last Summer* which are perhaps as well written as anything I've done.

Some while later I was in Miami, sitting outside my cabana at the pool of the Robert Clay Hotel, when I received a long-distance call from film producer Sam Spiegel. For the first time I made a movie deal myself.

Sam asked what I wanted for the movie rights to *Suddenly*. I said, "How about fifty grand plus 20 percent of the profits?"

Sam said, "It's a deal," and it was, and the profits were as good as the movie was bad.—that figures.

How films have changed!—for the better. They have outstripped the theatre in honesty, adventure, and technique, despite the fall of Big studios with their star system. Or possibly because of it?

There is quite a difference between classical acting and method acting, and one chance I had to witness this difference was when I had the enormous privilege of seeing Edwige Feuillere in the Paris production of *Sweet Bird*. This production was put on only a couple of years ago. Now Feuillere is a classical actress, but she is such a fine actress that she could, without any apparent disruption, switch over immediately from her classical style, which is rather declamatory; she could go right from that into very contemporary exchange of dialogue. And she was totally convincing and it was one of the great performances I've seen. The play itself got mixed notices in France, but she carried it and I think she toured France with it after the Paris run. Françoise Sagan had adapted *Bird* for France, and she did a beautiful job on it. She was a close friend of mine; although we didn't see much of each other, whenever we did, the friendship continued as if there had been no interruption.

Diana Barrymore had wanted to play the princess in *Sweet Bird* in England. Well, I thought it was bad casting, I thought Diana was too much like the princess to play the princess well. She was a good friend of Marion Vaccaro and we three had stayed together at the Nacional in Cuba one time. In Cuba she didn't drink but she smoked a lot of grass. I remember her wearing a little red lady's riding jacket and black silk pants and one of those very crisply laundered white shirts with the black string tie. She was so striking in it with her dark hair and flashing eyes. She was very lovely.

Anyway, we arranged for her to read for *Sweet Bird* but, unfortunately, what I had suspected proved to be the truth. The performance held no surprise, and I had to tell her quite frankly, "Diana, this simply isn't your role." I didn't think she would take it so badly. And actually, *Sweet Bird* has never been done in England. Sometimes I wonder if I shouldn't have let her do it, but I am very selfish about my work, and I didn't want Diana to play a role that I didn't think was suited for her. I think an author has to protect himself that way. But my telling Diana the role wasn't for her had a terrible effect on the poor girl. She had her heart set on it, somehow, she identified with it perhaps. If I had known how fully she identified with it and how deeply her heart was set on playing it, I might have tried to do something. But I didn't and I went south to Key West to work on something else and about a week later Diana Barrymore died. She died rather mysteriously, she went back on booze, and smoked heavy grass. In one week's time there was a very precipitous collapse in her. It was just as though she no longer cared about living. Her manager, who found her dead one morning, said that her room was an absolute shambles, and it looked to her as if some violence had occurred. That Diana was lying naked, face down, with blood streaming out of her mouth and that there was a very heavy marble ashtray shattered against the wall and other evidence of struggle and violence. Now that mystery was not reported in the papers: the manager whispered it to me during the funeral services in New York. I'm pretty sure that, whether she had played in *Sweet Bird* or not, sooner or later Diana would have done the same thing, because she was a girl with talent but not enough talent and it haunted her and was destroying her. There was a sort of curse on the Barrymores, I think. Diana was a great person and a great lady, though, and I was deeply disturbed by what happened.

Shall I attempt to entertain you, now, with my theatre or my life, assuming that there is much difference between them? I feel that I have hit the high spots among the plays, though possibly with all the grace and subtlety of a meat-ax in the hands of a butcher's butcher!

But I have hardly touched at all upon my prose works aside from these memoirs, and I have written a goodly quantity of prose works, some of which I prefer to my plays.

Faye Dunaway is dedicated to the project of starring in a film based on my short story "The Yellow Bird." She has it on a record which she has played for me twice, a record that I made for Caedmon and that is a steady seller.

It seems to me that quite a few of my stories, as well as my one-acts, would provide interesting and profitable material for the contemporary cinema, if committed to such lovely hands as Miss Dunaway's. Or Jon Voight's. And to such cinematic masters of direction as Jack Clayton, who made of *The Great Gatsby* a film that even surpassed, I think, the novel by Scott Fitzgerald.

But time is not on the side of anyone over thirty and I am over sixty and it is dubious that I will survive to witness these transmutations.

It is sweetly comfortable to be back in the apartment on Dumaine Street and to find that the furniture shipped so gradually from Morgan-Manhattan Storage to New Orleans has at last arrived and been beautifully arranged. I had—with my characteristic suspicion—expected to find it all somehow sitting on the ceiling.

So many forgotten items have reappeared!—relics of the apartments which I once had in New York, and all in surprisingly good condition. On the large walnut desk sits the brass student-lamp with its swinging globes of green-shaded glass, perfect for these old eyes at three o'clock in the morning.

My stay in New Orleans will be very brief, only two weeks, before I set out on the wild pilgrimage to the

Venice Film Festival in a planeload of such of the "beautiful people" as Andy Warhol, Joe Dallesandro, Sylvia Miles and Rex Reed, not to mention dear Billy Barnes, who has arranged the thing for me. It will be wonderful to be back on the Lido of Venice, at the stately Hotel Excelsior: the main object of the trip is to achieve a reconciliation with the raging Tartar, Maria, the Lady St. Just. After a week on the Lido, seeing the films and mingling with the beautiful people, I plan to fly down to Rome and then Taormina to swim, swim, and swim in that still fresh, cool, water with the tourists mostly gone—but, of course, that depends upon having a traveling-companion. I couldn't hack it alone. I mostly want someone to drive me about the coastline of Sicily, searching for that mythic little farm on which to retire and raise goats and geese for what remains of my leftover life.

I really do think that at the end of September I will come back to the States for a play production. Glenville and I had a good script session yesterday; then Glenville, after terrifying me with his statement that Genevieve Bujold had given him a terrible reading, said that he had up his sleeve a great young actor with stage experience and charisma of box-office draw, to play in *The Two-Character Play* (*Out Cry*).

Ah, God. My life is hung on that production like a hat on a hook. It seems to be the last objective of my life in theatre, the rest of me going to Italy and into these memoirs.

# 10

The longest and most appalling tour I've had with a play was that interminable trek of *Iguana*, in 1961, beginning badly in Rochester and going on to Detroit and Cleveland and then for an excessively long stay in Chicago.

It was highlighted, from my point of view, by the company of that huge black Belgian shepherd dog, Satin. At some point of the tour I had told Frankie that I needed the companionship of that dog and he had it shipped up from Key West.

Now it was my impression that Satin was devoted to me but this was the opposite of the fact. He used to sit directly in front of me at the Book-Cadillac Hotel in Detroit, staring into my eyes with those lovely yellow eyes of his, and occasionally sticking out his tongue to give my hand a lick. I remember that I was somewhat disconcerted by these continual attentions.

Well, the shit hit the fan with a vengeance.

One morning, having completed my work, I went into the bedroom, where Satin lay like a guardian by the twin bed of Frankie. As I stepped over him, to enter Frankie's bed, he uttered a low, displeasured, in fact ominous and guttural growl; but I crawled in with Frankie.

That night Satin attacked me with those great fangs of his.

An idiot hotel doctor was present, he had come up to our suite to treat me for a persistent head-cold, and while he and Frankie were in the bathroom, discussing my condition, Satin sprang upon my bed and bit me clean to the bone on each ankle. He was starting for my throat when Frankie rushed out and pulled him off me.

I said, "Frankie, turn this animal loose in the woods where he belongs."

Frankie said, "No, he's better off dead." And that morning he took Satin to the vet and had him put to sleep there.

Since Frankie adored that dog, acquired in Rome at the advice of Magnani, the death of Satin cast a dreadful shadow over Frankie that didn't lift during the long, long tour ...

About a week after the dogbites I discovered that my ankles had swollen up almost to the size of an elephant's. I had been too involved in the vicissitudes of the play to notice the pain, but when I couldn't get into my shoes, I put in a call to the fool who was the doctor. He didn't appear until evening.

However, he had the wit to recognize a staphylococcic infection, full blown, in both my ankles. He proceeded to fill a horse-syringe with a variety of antibiotics and to shoot me in the arm with it. I went almost immediately into a curious state. There was a blizzard in the dark outside. It was icy cold. However, I couldn't breathe well, and I staggered to a window and opened it wide for air.

"My God, do you want pneumonia?" inquired that pillar of the medical profession.

"I'd prefer it to instant suffocation," was my furious retort.

The doctor then summoned an ambulance and I remained gasping at the open window till it arrived. Then a couple of medics charged in with a wheelchair, I was rushed down the freight elevator to a back entrance, laid out on a stretcher and shoved into a spectral white vehicle with a scarlet lamp on its roof. Off it rushed, siren screaming, Frankie seated gravely beside me clasping my icy hand, it was for all the world like a scene from one of those doctor serials so popular on TV.

At the hospital I was wheeled directly to the emergency ward, a nightmarish arena for the life-death struggle, each contestant in a white canvas-curtained cubicle, separated from the sight of his fellow contestants but not from the sounds of their struggle.

Drugs to combat the overdose of antibiotics were pumped into my blood stream: it took three hours for me to come out of shock and my panting breath to subside to more normal respiration.

(Close shaves with death are a fascinating experience. It is especially strange how fear is eclipsed by the violence of one's struggle to hang on: it must be very much like what gladiators felt in mortal combat at the Roman Colosseum.)

When it was deemed possible to remove me to a hospital room above, I was rolled up to one. But there I discovered that I had no "pinkies" with me. A nurse reluctantly provided me with a half-size Seconal. I swore at her, "I can't sleep on this and I've got to have sleep." She shrugged and flounced out of the room, saying that no one just out of emergency would be given a grain and a half of Seconal. Well. There was a phone in the room and I dialed the hotel and got poor little Frankie on the phone.

He had gone to bed after his three-hour vigil beside me in emergency, but I said, "For Christ sake, get up and run over here with my Seconal bottle."

I guess he was too sleepy to distinguish one bottle from another, since what he arrived with, not long after, was a bottle of diuretic pills which I was on at the time. He slammed the bottle down before I had time to recognize its contents and he dashed back out.

Well, I want you to know that when I saw it was the wrong bottle I got out of bed, and dressed myself except for the shoes that didn't fit over the ankles, and I started down the corridor of the hospital. On the way down the corridor, I encountered the nurse.

"Mr. Williams," she said, "what are you thinking of?"

"Nothing," I said, "but getting the fuck out of here."

"But, Mr. Williams, a hospital isn't a hotel that you can check out of before we dismiss you."

"Fuck that, I'm dismissing myself and I only want you to get me a cab at the door."

Further attempts were made to restrain me. I had to summon the taxi myself. It came and I got in and went straight back to the Book-Cadillac, which is probably now the Sheraton something or other.

Frankie had long since stopped being surprised by my erratic behavior. He opened his sleepy eyes and moved over in bed to make room for me and, to complete this story stranger than fiction, I proceeded to make love to that sweetly permissive Sicilian.

The ankles remained so swollen that I had to wear bedroom slippers to rehearsals in Cleveland and even in Chicago for the long stay there.

It was there in Chicago that Bette Davis said she'd not take further direction from Frank Corsaro and ordered him barred from the theatre. He stayed out of the theatre but remained in Chicago; but Bette said she could sense his lingering presence in Chicago and that he must be returned at once to New York and that goddam Actors' Studio, which had spawned him.

Then it was that Chuck Bowden and I took over direction, though Corsaro's name remained on the bill. And there in Chicago, the unpredictable Bette, having won her battle against the "method," gave a great Christmas party for us, presenting us each with a gift. She had with her a lovely tall blond girl, her daughter by one of her husbands, and it was as fine a Christmas as I'd known since childhood.

A gentleman of the theatre is the rarest of aves. Shall I now give you my list of them? I mean those I've known in my time?

José Quintero, Elia Kazan, Robert Whitehead, Joe Losey. And, yes, David Merrick, who always allowed me to bring in a play doomed for destruction on Broadway, and who is now on probation to be assessed according to his treatment of my new play "Red Devil Battery Sign." And, of course, dear lost Tallulah.

I put her in the gentlemen column not to disparage the lady, but because she was a lady who had that intransigent and vocally powerful presence of a "gent."

Naturally this list could be extended...

Here comes a flashback.

It was as early as 1960, I believe, that Frankie began to lose his vitality and turn moody. Of course I attributed this to drugs, not conceiving the possibility that he might be ill.

But Frankie knew that he wasn't well, and he went up to New York from Key West for a medical checkup. At about this time—due to his disinclination toward sex with me—I had taken up with a young queen of New Orleans who was known as the "Dixie Doxy" and had really earned his nickname. He was a handsome blond kid of about twenty-two with creamy skin and a very seductive backside which he was eager to offer.

When Frankie returned from his medical checkup, the Dixie Doxy and I were in a posh hotel on Key Biscayne, living the life of Riley. The first full draft of *Iguana* was being put on at the Coconut Grove, nearby. Frankie somehow got word that we were there and he arrived unexpectedly on the spot, while the Dixie Doxy was promenading about the pool in crimson nylon swim-trunks, three-sheeting the scene.

Frankie gazed at him with contempt. The Dixie

Doxy felt himself quite secure in my favor and was not at all disconcerted by Frankie's disdain.

But needless to say, Frankie got me back to home territory, Key West, the next day and I did not see the blond again. But my sexually incontinent behavior continued.

When the two-week run of the early version of *Iguana* had been completed, I invited the young director, Frank Corsaro, who had done a still earlier version of it in Spoleto the summer before, to come down to Key West, along with a very pleasant and personable kid who played one of Maxine's male concubines in the play. The kid pretended to be able to drive a car but it became almost immediately apparent that he couldn't. He couldn't drive at all, the car kept sashaying from one side of the highway to the other, and I had to take over the wheel, although I had no driver's license.

Frankie was much taken with the kid himself, and our first night in Key West, Frankie wouldn't come upstairs to bed. He sat smoking on the downstairs sofa and I may have been quite wrong in my suspicion that he was waiting for a chance to lure the kid out of the master bedroom downstairs—projecting my own desire.

I flew into a jealous rage, and after going to bed and fuming upstairs for a while, I rushed downstairs and Frankie was still sitting like a male Lorelei on that sofa.

"Come to bed," I shouted. "I know what you're up to! You don't have to fear that I'll subject you to any advances tonight, cause I wouldn't touch you, now, with a ten-foot pole."

Frankie shrugged and came upstairs with me and was soon snoring while I lay awake until dawn.

Things between The Horse and me continued to deteriorate, with short periods of reconciliation. Actually he never denied himself to me but he created an atmosphere with which I, with my fierce pride, could not very often compromise.

One afternoon three queens from Miami came in town and checked into a motel on South Beach.

I knew them only slightly, but, being in wanton spirit, I spent the afternoon and the early evening with them and it appears to me, now, that I had intimacies with all three—in a state of drunken abandon, all of it hardly more important than leaping a pig-sty.

Frankie had prepared dinner or was still preparing it when I came home to Duncan Street. His silence was ominous. I set myself down at our patio table like a king, waiting to be served. The kitchen door banged open and past me sailed a meat loaf, missing my head by inches. Then came a bowl of succotash, once again missing its target, then the salad and even the Silex of coffee.

I was so drunk that these missiles did not alarm me. And when the kitchen door banged shut and Frankie had charged off in the car, I picked the meat loaf up off the tiles of the patio and ate it with as much gusto as if it had been served me on a golden platter.

Frankie during this period had begun, mysteriously, to lose energy and weight. Now once again he went to New York for a medical checkup, and during his absence a very talented young painter whom I had met a year or so before in Tangier happened to call me from Miami to say he was there and I said, "I'm alone, come on down to Key West."

He came down that night and we spent several innocently idyllic spring days together. I was also into painting myself at that time, not at all well, only as a diversion from writing. The very gifted young painter from Tangier worked at one side of the patio and I at the other. He painted me—the excellent semiabstract portrait still hangs in the living room of my Key West house—and I painted an imaginary boy holding a guitar and wearing pink tights.

One evening while this was going on, Frankie's best friend dropped over for dinner. And after dinner the handsome young painter and I went inside while the others remained on the patio. I had not been to bed with the painter but that evening we turned off the lights in the living room and stretched out beside each other on the long sofa and hugged and exchanged long kisses.

Frankie's pal entered abruptly and observed the goings-on and he promptly called Frankie in New York, at the hospital where he was having the check-up.

Frankie flew home at once, without warning.

That evening he declined to eat and he hardly spoke. He sat in a corner of the living room, looking drugged, his great eyes fastened balefully upon the painter and me. We made conversation as best we could under Frankie's fierce scrutiny.

Then the scene exploded.

Like a jungle cat, Frankie sprang across the room and seized the painter by the throat and it appeared to me that the painter was being strangled to death— that is one evening when I am pretty sure that Frankie was deep under drugs.

I snatched up the phone and called the police and said there was a dreadful emergency in the house.

Frankie let go of the painter. The cops arrived in a few minutes.

"Mr. Merlo is not at all well," I told them. "I think he'd be much better off at a friend's home for the night."

The cops took in the situation with understanding that is rare in their profession.

All the cops of Key West were fond of Frankie—as was the island's whole population, I would say. I often thought that Frankie could have run for Mayor of Key West and have won the election by a landslide.

The officers took Frankie to a friend's. He returned the next morning.

It was that day that the real disruption between Frankie and me took place. Without a word to him, I packed up all my papers in the studio and piled them in the car. Then the painter and I got in. Frankie was sitting silently on the porch with Leoncia, our faithful housekeeper, who was equally silent. But as the motor started, Frankie ran down from the porch.

"Are you going to leave me without shaking hands? After fourteen years together?"

I shook hands with him. Then the painter and I drove away. I drove so badly, swerving from side to side of the Overseas Highway, that the painter crouched in the car in voiceless panic. But we arrived in Coconut Grove without a crash. We checked into some depressing motel. The next day, having fucked ourselves into an exhausted sleep the night before, we had lunch at Marion Vaccaro's and I told her I'd quit Frankie.

The painter was too much for me, he simply wouldn't let up on the sex bit and after a couple of days I told him he'd better continue upon his course to San Francisco and I paid him for the portrait left in Key West, to aid in the cost of his journey. Then I went alone to the New York apartment at 134 East Sixty-fifth Street and occupied it alone for a month or two.

It was about this time that I began a serious flirtation with a gifted and handsome young poet. He was living with a much older poet and it was going to pieces between them, since practically every night the older poet would assuage his time-ravaged vanity with liquor. He would be exhilarated and amiable for his first hour on booze: then turn sullen: then he would lash out at all about him like an old caged lion, totally unreconciled to the cage.

The gifted lad, whose name I must withhold, took to spending several nights a week with me. As you may have gathered at this point, I fall in love rather easily, and the ease is easier when the object is warm, willing and "a joy forever."

I have trouble with placing events in exact chronological order. I can only tell you that this romance with the poet came after *Night of the Iguana* and of course after my Key West quarrel with Frankie.

I do know that in the late spring of '61 or '62, the young poet and I flew to Tangier, to occupy a lovely little rented house just above the beach.

It was a curiously difficult summer, both for me and my new companion. Despite the turbulence which had attended my break with Frankie and despite the charm of the little white house and of the beautiful poet, I was beset by inner torments, the most explicable of which was an inability to talk to people. There was a good deal of social activity that summer in Tangier. The beauty of my companion made us desirable as guests. But at cocktail parties and suppers I sat in silence that was seldom broken. Even with the young poet I could barely communicate except in bed.

He was very sweet and understanding about it. I remember, in particular, a long night of rain.

He said to me, "Rain is the purest water."

We opened the bedroom shutters and leaned out the window, catching the rain-water in cups and then profaning it with whiskey.

Moments of holy communion . . .

One afternoon I was alone with Jane Bowles, and I said to Janie, "Janie, I can't talk anymore."

She gave me one of her quick little smiles and said, "Tennessee, you were never much of a conversationalist."

For some reason, perhaps because it made me laugh, and laughter is always a comfort, as Janie was always a comfort, this answer to my anguished confession was a relief for a while.

(I have described that summer in Tangier in a poem, titled "The Speechless Summer," in the first issue of the magazine *Antaeus*.)

During this period I was gloomily at work on *The Milk Train Doesn't Stop Here Anymore*, and so it would be suitable to insert, at this point, the history of that play, which was more dramatic off-stage than on and which reflected so painfully the deepening shadows of my life as man and artist.

People have said and said and said that my work is too personal: and I have just as persistently countered this charge with my assertion that all true work of an artist must be personal, whether directly or obliquely, it must and it does reflect the emotional climates of its creator.

In the late spring of '62 Frankie came up to Manhattan; I was as frightened of seeing him as I was of seeing Santo after the violences of 1947. Through intermediaries I heard that Frankie, staying at the Hotel Dover, was insisting that we have a meeting. I sent back word that I would talk to him only in the presence of Audrey Wood.

During all this period of separation Frankie was kept on salary and he was not at all in financial straits, having owned 10 per cent of *Cat* and of *Rose Tattoo* and *Camino Real*. It's strange that I don't remember what his weekly salary was: I would guess about $150. And not until now did he have any "living expenses."

The meeting occurred with Miss Wood present in the apartment on Sixty-fifth. Frankie was on his best behavior: dignified, calm, and expressing hurt and bewilderment over our estrangement. Miss Wood was her coolly diplomatic self.

When she left, I insisted that Frankie leave with her. All that had been "arranged" was that Frankie was to be kept under salary—but that our separation was to be "final."

About ten minutes after Audrey and Frankie left together, Frankie called me on the phone and said it had been quite impossible for him to talk things over with Audrey's presence and that he was coming back to talk with me privately in the apartment.

"Oh no," I told him. "If you feel there has to be further talk between us, I'll meet you in a bar around the corner."

At the meeting in the bar I remained curiously resolute in my attitude. I remember saying to him, "Frank, I want to get my goodness back."

He looked at me silently and with understanding.

What did I mean, exactly? He seemed to know but I am not sure now.

He went away, then; I returned alone to the apartment. And not long after that the young poet, whom I'll call Angel, and I flew to Tangier ...

When we returned to Manhattan early that fall, I received a phone call from Marion in Coconut Grove. She told me she had some very bad news for me: she had just received a phone call from Frankie, who was on his way to Manhattan to undergo an operation for suspected lung-cancer.

He had already taken a plane and would be checking into Memorial Hospital, surgery was scheduled to be performed in a few days.

I learned later that Frankie had been sitting with his close friend Dan Stirrup and others at an outdoor café in Key West when all at once he leaned over at the table and a stream of blood poured from his mouth. He'd gone to his Key West doctor, X-rays had been taken and the dark lung area discovered.

I was stricken with remorse.

What I didn't know was that I was as much in love with Frankie all that difficult time of the early sixties as I had ever been before. The love had gone sick, yes, but it was as deep as ever. I visited him at Memorial the day before his operation; he was quite matter-of-fact about this thing of which I would have been crazed with apprehension.

Memorial is the cancer hospital of New York and to be there is in itself a certificate of the disease, I would guess.

Have I mentioned that Frankie was a chain-smoker? At least four packs a day.

The operation was performed and I next saw The Little Horse in the recovery room, barely conscious and only able to whisper a few words.

I sat by his bed in "recovery" pressing his hand, until an orderly advised me that my visiting time was up. After that I visited him each day until he was released from the hospital.

Then one day—just before his release or possibly just after the surgery—I called his doctors and was told that Frankie's lung-cancer could not be operated upon. It was situated right alongside his heart and its condition was too advanced for surgery to be effective. So they had sewed him back up, just like that.

"How long?" I asked.

The answer was six months.

I hung up and burst into tears. There was someone with me, the young poet Angel, I suppose, and he tried to comfort me.

As soon as he was released from the hospital, Frankie went straight back to Key West—alone. There he took a small house for himself on the property of one of Frankie's writer friends whom I had suspected (probably wrongly) of having a secret affair with him.

It was a small but pleasant little frame cottage.

I lost no time in following him down there.

Frankie was quite unaware that effective surgery had not been performed and during the first month or two he gave every evidence of thinking himself quite recovered. I remember him doing one of his wild "Lindy hops" in a local Key West night spot, but also remember that at its conclusion he seemed about to collapse.

I bought a TV for him in his house on Baker's Lane. Gigi, our dog, was with him; they were inseparable. And then he took a fancy to a little monkey I'd bought in New York, a very bad-tempered and nervous creature whom I had appropriately named "Creature." I don't know why this creature appealed so strongly to Frankie. It didn't to me.

One day I took Creature in its cage over to Frankie and I said, "Keep it with you a while and you'll be disenchanted with the thing."

Still I think I liked it, since I've never met an animal I didn't like . . .

Late that evening Frankie phoned me and his voice was almost hysterical. He'd let Creature out of its cage and it had disappeared.

The evening was spent in frantic search for Creature. After two or three hours I gave up the search but The Horse kept at it. I think it was near midnight, or maybe the next morning, that Frankie phoned.

Again his voice was hysterical.

"*It's back, it's back!*" he cried out.

"What?"

"It just crawled out from under the bed, the one place we didn't look for him, and he had been there all the while."

Then he started to cry . . .

After a few weeks, I asked Frankie to move back into the house on Duncan Street. I was afraid he might refuse, since Angel was still with me, but he did not demur.

He took our old upstairs bedroom and Angel and I occupied the one downstairs.

I could see that he was beginning to fail pretty fast and I could also see that he was desperately denying this fact to himself and all others. He was still pretending, fiercely.

Frankie's writer friend said to me, "I don't know if he really thinks they took the cancer out or if he's giving us the biggest snow-job of all time!"

The six months which the surgeons had allowed Frankie had now expired and he went past that time steadily weakening, but giving not an inch of his fierce pride. He seemed annoyed that I remained so long in

Key West that spring, as late as the middle of May. This was not because he resented Angel—the poet was wonderful to him; but he treated Angel almost as if he didn't exist, which was close to the truth, by this time: I mean in my heart.

Frankie didn't want a witness to his decline, not such a close one as I. So in the middle of May, Angel and I flew North and we took a house on Nantucket. As soon as we'd settled in it, I called Frankie and begged him to join us for the summer.

Surprisingly, he accepted.

I went over to the mainland to meet him: it was a bitch of a night. An unseasonably cold blast of wind was sweeping across the water: we missed the regular ferry to Nantucket. I hired a small boat to take us over, Frankie and Gigi and I. The cold wind turned icy. Frankie held Gigi tight against him, sitting bolt upright and silent during what seemed an endless crossing.

Almost immediately it was apparent that the Nantucket move wouldn't do. Frankie disliked the cute little cottage as much as I did: but he wouldn't go out except for meals at which he barely nibbled. I don't think we stuck it out for more than a week. Then he returned to Manhattan and from that point on there were continual trips, for Frankie, between the East Sixty-fifth Street apartment and Memorial Hospital. The cancer was spreading relentlessly, quickly, from organ to organ. He ate almost nothing and his weight dropped under a hundred.

One time when I took him back to Memorial for cobalt, that ghastly treatment which burned his chest black, his doctors said, "All we can do is see where it hits him next."

I sent Angel back to Key West and Frankie and I were alone in the apartment. He had the bedroom and I slept on the long sofa in the narrow study.

And each night—this is what is particularly painful to remember—I would hear him turn the bolt on the

bedroom door. Did he, poor child, suppose that I
would still be apt to follow him in there and use his
skeletal body again for sexual pleasure? That hardly
seems conceivable. But why did he bolt the door,
then?

I think it was a thing he did automatically: perhaps
it was death that he thought he was locking out.

Off and on during the night my sleep, always light,
would be broken by the fits of coughing, loud through
the wall, and I didn't dare to call to him.


Today was one of possible great significance in my
professional life—Genevieve Bujold had arrived in
New York the day before and has now indicated to
Bill Barnes and Peter Glenville that she will undertake the female lead in *Out Cry*—tonight she flew
back to Montreal and Bill will call her there for a final
confirmation.

When I met her today at Bill's apartment I saw an
incredibly perfect Clare. I exclaimed, as we met,
"You're beautiful! And slightly mad!"

Of course her unspoken reply may well have been:
"You are ugly and totally insane."

Be that as it may . . .

Afterwards, I picked up my beautiful new suit,
gave my best performance so far—not a single fluff
—and afterward took Candy Darling to Sardi's. Her
entrance was, of course, sensational. We were given
one of the prize tables and in a while were joined by
the very touching young writer Nelson Lyon and a
beautiful girl who is a publisher. I said to Lyon, "You
are at the beginning of a career that I am now finishing." I meant that I was now finishing my own career,
not his—let's make that clear. We delivered the ladies
to their respective homes—Candy next to the Christian Science Church—and the girl publisher to a mansion in the East Sixties or Seventies—then I took
Lyon to the Victorian Suite for a nightcap and he
stayed with me until I had dropped my Nembutal.

He is handsome but my behavior was admirably restrained.

These final recollections of the living Frankie are sad to recall. Yet they contained much to remember with wonder at his strength of spirit and of his pride never broken.

Stirrup came up from Key West and Al Sloane, a close friend of Frankie's, was also with us almost continually during the day. The disease was ravaging Frank, now, with ferocious intensity. Stirrup kept suggesting to Frankie that he make out a will—Frankie ignored these somewhat insensitive suggestions and continued stubbornly with his little life. Each morning about noon he and Gigi would come out of the master bedroom and sit side by side on the love seat facing the TV, their faces equally stoical and almost having an identical expression in their eyes.

I think that they would sit there almost all day, Gigi occasionally going onto our little balcony for calls of nature.

Then suddenly he went for a last time to Memorial Hospital. As he dressed to go, I entered the bedroom to assist him but he would accept no assistance. He threw off his robe. His body, that of a little Hercules in the past, had turned to something more like the skeleton of a sparrow.

For the first time when he entered the lobby of Memorial, he was too weak to walk to his ward and accepted a wheel-chair. They put him—and this I think is quite awful—in a ward where all the patients had undergone surgery for brain cancer. It was a nightmare to look at them. I begged him not to stay in that ward but to take a private room. He said sharply, "It doesn't matter at all to me now, I think I like being with them."

Since he had been in and out of Memorial so often, I did not recognize this time as the final one.

It happened to coincide with the opening of the

second version of *Milk Train* at the Barter Theatre in Abingdon, Virginia—with Donald Madden, brilliant as Christopher, and Clare Luce, handsome but inadequate as Goforth. Direction was by Adrian Hall, and set by Bobby Soule.

Audrey Wood flew down for opening night. Audience response was enigmatic, and perhaps I should have said apathetic.

The next day I received a phone call from Al Sloane that Frankie was unmistakably taking a turn for the worse. He described his condition to me. I said, "He'll die this Thursday. I'll fly back at once." —And I flew back before the reviews of the Barter Theatre production came out. The morning after my return I visited Frankie at Memorial. He was now receiving oxygen from a bedside tank. I stayed on that day and it was a dreadful vigil for me to keep. He would not stay in his bed for more than a minute or two. He kept staggering out of it and sitting for a couple of minutes in the chair. Then staggering back to the bed.

"Frankie, try to lie still."

"I feel too restless today. The visitors tired me out."

"Frankie, do you want me to leave you now?"

"No. I'm used to you."

He had, during my vigil that day, been transferred from the ward to a private room—which he doubtless recognized as a room to which he was removed to die.

There are some things that I can't forgive "Memorial" for. It took them about half an hour to bring up the oxygen tank after moving Frank from the ward to the room; he was gasping like a hooked fish all of that endless half hour.

When the tank arrived and when he had said, "I'm used to you now," he turned on his side away from me. The statement of habituation was hard to interpret as an admission of love, but love was never a thing that Frankie had been able to declare to me except over a long-distance phone.

He lay there silently on his side. I thought he'd fallen asleep. I stayed on a while and then I quietly left.

On my way home I thought, This has gone too far. I went to my doctor's office, Dr. William G. Von Stein, and told him rather hysterically what a nightmare Frankie's last days at Memorial had turned into. Von Stein gave me a sedative shot and he said, "I am going to call Frank's doctor."

I went out that night and my hysteria took a different turn. I got quite drunk with a group of friends in a gay bar and came home about eleven that night. I'd hardly returned when the telephone rang. Frankie's most devoted friend was calling. He was calling to let me know that Frankie was gone. He did it with great humanity.

"Tennessee, we've lost him. It happened in a few minutes. The nurse gave him a shot, he sat up with a gasp and fell back on his pillows and he was gone before the floor doctor could reach him."

My first reaction was a hard thing to analyze now. I think it must have been relief that his and my torture was finished.

His, yes. Mine, no.

I was on the threshold of an awful part of my life. It developed slowly.

As long as Frank was well, I was happy. He had a gift for creating a life and, when he ceased to be alive, I couldn't create a life for myself. So I went into a seven-year depression.

All of Frankie's New Jersey family arrived at the Frank Campbell funeral home. Frankie was laid out in a coffin. His older sister, Anna—a fine woman—said to me, "Go up and touch his hand."

I obeyed her with a feeling of terror. He looked very peaceful and grave and noble. But to feel his hand so dead and so cold, laid upon his chest, was a shocking contact.

Two funerals had been arranged, one at a Catholic church, arranged by his family, and the second at

Campbell's. I had invited all of Frankie's many friends
in the theatre to attend the one at Campbell's and for
my cousin the Reverend Sidney Lanier to conduct the
service there, as he had for Diana Barrymore three
years before.

But the service at the Catholic church came first,
quite rightly, and it was a beautiful service, a high Re-
quiem Mass.

Then Frankie's body was taken back to Frank
Campbell's funeral home for the second service. The
big chapel was full. And just before the service I had
Frankie put in a different coffin as I didn't like the
pink quilted lining nor the light color of the wood. He
was transferred to a much handsomer casket with
plain white satin lining.

Afterward, I couldn't go out to the cemetery but returned to my apartment with Kazan and his wife
Molly. I kept up a good front but I noticed them exchanging looks. They knew that I had lost what had
sustained my life.

The first version of *The Milk Train Doesn't Stop
Here Anymore*, an interesting but rather extended
title, grew out of a short story of mine, one of my best
stories, I believe, called "Man Bring This Up Road." I
wrote this story one golden summer at the Hotel Miramare in Positano on the Divina Costiera of Italy. I
was there with Maria and we were both supposed to
be at work on Luchino Visconti's film *Senso*.

I have always had trouble sticking to an assigned
piece of work, and this was especially true in the case
of *Senso* because I did not regard Farley Granger as
an interesting actor. Also, the fact that I was working
without remuneration on the film-script did not en-
hance my interest in it. Actually what little work I did
on it was done because of my admiration for Visconti
and my gratitude to him for giving my dear friend
Maria a much-needed job in the production.

When I returned to the States, I picked up the short

story one morning and it began to shape itself in my head as a long-short play, and I wrote it as such and as such it was produced the following summer in Spoleto's Festival of Two Worlds. This initial production was distinguished principally by the performance of Hermione Baddeley in the role of Flora Goforth. We had a gala opening night to a packed house. Anna Magnani drove up from Rome for the event and she shared a box with me. She stared at Baddeley with growing amazement.

"*Come magnifica!*" she kept exclaiming under her breath, and I knew that she was referring to the star and not to the play.

Anna was a great and very strict judge of acting talents and she recognized in Hermione Baddeley an actress of a magnitude that approached her own and she was not envious, as a lesser woman might have been, but quite genuinely delighted. After the show, her greetings and felicitations to Miss Baddeley were all Anna and all heart.

The play itself made no particular impression and received only one subsequent performance in Spoleto that summer. Of course I have always been a little skeptical about the seriousness of the annual Spoleto festivals; they always strike me as being, mainly, an ego-trip for the Maestro, Gian-Carlo Menotti, and his friend Tommy Schippers. The highlight of the festival is always Menotti's huge birthday party for himself. There is a great display of fireworks all over the charming little town: and at the climax Menotti and Schippers appear in white tie regalia and are charioted about the packed streets in a big new convertible, probably a Caddy or a Rolls ...

However, never mind. It was his kick, and I don't think I should knock another man's kick, nor his ego-trips, nor the fantasy world he lives in. There are worse things than a fantasy world to live in. I wonder, indeed, if a fantasy world is not the only world inhabitable by artists.

That next season Roger Stevens decided to produce *Milk Train* on Broadway. At first, he wanted Tallulah Bankhead to play Goforth. But I had seen Hermione Baddeley in it and I stood my ground against the mighty Stevens and insisted that Hermione Baddeley remain in the starring role. You see, I still had some clout in those days . . .

Paul Roebling, who had created the part of Chris Flanders in Spoleto, was also retained for the Broadway production and it rolled into action.

Opening night in New Haven was somewhat disastrous. Hermione was as great as ever but the audience was far from sympathetic to the play.

There was a sort of Green Room set up for an after-opening confab among the persons involved in the production but it began to fill up with persons who had no connection with the production and I flew into one of my Wagnerian tantrums.

"What the fuck are you crepe-hangers barging in here for? Take your drinks and get out, we have a play in trouble and we've got to discuss it strictly among ourselves."

The Boston opening of *Milk Train* was much the best that it received, despite a number of hilarious mishaps that occurred in the first scene. Almost immediately after her entrance Hermione's red wig fell off, but she appeared to ignore this incident. She swept about the desk at which she was dictating her memoirs and when she arrived at the wig, she snatched it up— and put it on backward, and the audience howled. It seemed like the natural thing for "Sissy" Goforth to do. To the best of my recollection—as a Watergate conspirator might say—the notices were mixed but mixed in an interesting way, and certainly that dean of Boston critics, Elliot Norton, recognized it as an exploratory but important stage-work and was deeply impressed by Miss Baddeley as was everyone who had the privilege of seeing her.

We did good business in Boston at the Wilbur and it was nice being back in a suite at that lovely hotel the Ritz-Carlton with its fireplace and its view over the snow-white Common in winter.

But then we hit Philadelphia and things began to go sour.

The notices were less interestingly mixed and business not so good.

However, what I chiefly remember about the Philadelphia gig was a party given by Mrs. Roebling for the cast. The Roeblings, Baddeley, and of course the director, Herbert Machiz, were seated at a large central table which was festively decorated and I—ah, me—was shunted off to a little table apart, the sort of table that is called a "deuce."

I did a slow burn as I took in this insulting situation. Then I rose to the occasion with a vengeance. I stalked over to the festive center table, from which I had been excluded, and I went directly up to Mrs. Roebling, seated at its head, and kissed her hand. I said this, to the best of my recollection:

"You've given a lovely party for the cast and thank you very much but I am sure you must understand why I am leaving at once!"

I then started for the elevators, but that nice boy and talented actor, Paul Roebling, rose from the center table and pursued me and tried to detain me.

At this time I was going a little zany and I made the most arrogant remark I can remember having ever made in a life that seems to lead me frequently into arrogance.

As best I recall my lines, I said to dear Paul, "When I attend a party for a play that I've written and am shunted off to the side of the big table, it is not an insult that I'm inclined to suffer gladly. This is all a Machiavellian trick played on me by Herbert Machiz and I'm very surprised that your mother and you would permit it to happen."

Then the elevator arrived at the banquet floor. Paul

made an effort to restrain me from entering the elevator but my outrage made me stronger than I was and I pushed him back and entered the elevator and savagely pushed the down button.

The play arrived in New York during a newspaper strike and so we received no written reviews in the papers, but copy of the notices were distributed and they were all ecstatic about Hermione and a bit cool toward the play.

The next day I entered the office of Roger Stevens and I said to him, "This woman has received the greatest notices, in a play of mine, since Laurette Taylor in *Menagerie*. I think you can have a run with the play if you exploit her notices. What are your intentions?"

His intentions were negative.

I like Roger very much but I felt he'd let me down and I said, after a few moments of verbal evasion on his part, "I get the message, good-by!"—and stalked out.

If you write a play with a very strong female role, such as Flora Goforth of *The Milk Train Doesn't Stop Here Anymore*, it is likely to surface repeatedly, since female stars of a certain age have a rough time finding vehicles suitable to their talents, personalities, and their public images. To call *Milk Train* a vehicle is somewhat unfair to it. In that play—really only successful, scriptwise, as the movie *BOOM*—I was fanatically obsessed with trying to say certain things. It was a work of art manqué. It is very sad that Tallulah didn't play it about five years earlier, but it didn't exist then. When it was ultimately given her, it was simply too late. Tallulah no longer had the physical stamina to put it over, she was too deep into liquor and pills, and she had great difficulty in projecting clearly past the front of the house.

The production came about in an odd way. The English director Tony Richardson got hold of the script and phoned me one day, heaping upon the re-

TENNESSEE WILLIAMS: MEMOIRS     251

vised version the most frighteningly extravagant praise.

(I don't know why directors and producers think they have to bullshit a playwright in this way when all they have to say is, "I like it and want to do it.")

Richardson was very "hot" at this time and the production was sure to be dominated by him, since Tallulah had kept her rebel spirit but lost her strength to fight, and the same was more or less true of myself. Richardson did not want Tallulah but the producer and I did. A curious compromise was made, one with which neither Tallulah nor I felt at all happy. They said to me, "Tenn, I will accept Tallulah as Goforth provided that you'll accept Tab Hunter as Chris Flanders." I was reluctant to accept this proposal since I could not see in Tab a mystic and ambiguous quality which the part demanded. Tony said to me, "I have a moral obligation to Tab Hunter and casting him as Chris will pay it off." I can only surmise what the "moral obligation" may have been, and I shall leave you in the same uncertainty.

(Tallulah was once asked if Tab were gay, and she replied wittily, "How would I know, darling, I never fucked him.") Considering his prior performances, I'd say that he peaked out in *Milk Train*, he showed more talent than I would have expected, but an ambivalent mysticism was not so apparent in his performance as a lingering talent for exposing his skin and physique. Around me, he was always affable, but he and Tallulah did not hit it off at all. That's surprising, since Tallulah was usually very fond of her male associates.

Rouben Ter-Arutunian provided a poor set for the play, lacking in Mediterranean atmosphere and featuring his penchant for the stark and bizarre. I was deep in depression because of Frankie's death. And Tallulah's on-stage liquor and pills were the real thing. The production limped through several cities, rarely getting a good notice and supported only by Tallulah's special and fanatic fans. When we arrived in Baltimore we were abruptly deserted by Richardson. He had to fly back to London to attempt to patch up his confused marriage to Vanessa Redgrave.

There was much about Richardson that I liked and much that I deplored. He had a female assistant at rehearsals who rushed backstage at intervals too frequent to fetch him a drink which was not water. Despite his preliminary gushing over the play, he showed a strange indifference to its disintegration on the road. And once when I became outspokenly disturbed over something, he said to me, "I don't think you're insane but you are a chronic (or natural) hysteric."

(Which was true at the time he said it, if not quite always.)

Good-natured and gifted he was, if responsible seldom.

David Merrick, the producer, came to our last roadstop in Baltimore and had the decency to ask me whether or not I wanted to bring the play onto Broadway. I answered, "I think it would kill Tallulah if we closed it." So in we came. The first preview was practically pre-empted by Tallulah's gay following, and they gave her an ovation. Merrick remarked to me, "If we had this audience every night, we'd have a smash." However, on opening night, the audience did not buy the play and the critics demolished it.

Nevertheless, it was purchased for the screen. The negotiations, which were very involved, took place in England. The lively little fingers of Lester Persky were hotly engaged in the project. The part of Chris was offered to Sean Connery, who could have played it well but turned it down with grace. Then Joseph Losey was engaged as director, an excellent choice. Losey is a master. Then a dreadful mistake was made. Persky offered the film to the Burtons. And he told me that if I invested thirty G's, he could deliver them and that they would make me a million. That was not how it worked out, exactly. The film (called *BOOM*) was shot on Sardinia. The direction, the script and the sets were stunning, but Dick was too old for Chris and Liz was too young for Goforth.

Another detriment to the film's reception was that it was an unmistakable attack on imperialism, represented by the American Goforth, whose personal emblem was a golden griffin, who was guilty of murder for which she went scot-free because she had *"droit de domaine"* over the island and all its inhabitants.

Despite its miscasting, I feel that *BOOM* was an artistic success and that eventually it will be received with acclaim.

History moves toward the fall of Babylon, again and again, as irresistibly as a mountain torrent rushes to the sea.

I began this account of *Milk Train*'s fourth production, the one with Tallulah (the first was at Spoleto and the third was at Virginia's Barter Theatre), with the somewhat extravagant statement that a play which contained such a strong female part as that of Flora Goforth is likely to "surface repeatedly." On reflection, I'm afraid this claim has yet to be justified. A production of *Milk Train* was undertaken at London's Royal Court Theatre (one of my favorite English-speaking theatres in the world) under what appeared to be propitious circumstances. Ruth Gordon in the role of Goforth, Donald Madden as Christopher Flanders. But the production went up in smoke while in the first week of rehearsals. Not being present, I can't tell you precisely all that went wrong but I have heard it reported from a cast-member that the brilliant Miss Gordon was not happy with the brilliant Mr. Madden, and vice versa. I have heard that, when Mr. Madden delivered a line, Miss Gordon would interrupt the rehearsals to inquire of him, "Is that how you're going to say it?" And that this was naturally quite disconcerting to Donald's Irish nature.

The whole thing was apparently more than disconcerting to the director, dear George Devine, for the production was indefinitely suspended when he suffered a coronary.

I hope I am not implying that there is something spooky or ill-starred about the play itself. But it has not escaped my attention that aside from a San Francisco revival, under the inspired direction of John Hancock—the only director who has ever suggested to me transpositions of material that were artistically effective—*Milk Train* appears to be on a side track, shunted there, I'm afraid, by the excessively beauteous Goforth of Liz Taylor in *BOOM.* However, I stick by this much of my original assertion: it remains a marvelous vehicle for an equally marvelous female star, and I don't mean the planet Venus. Miss Hermione Baddeley is very much around to support that contention of the playwright.

Who could play Goforth now? Perhaps Miss Baddeley would take another shot at it. Perhaps Angela Lansbury and perhaps Sylvia Miles.

Meanwhile Bacchus is both willing and patient.

(Let us reflect a few moments about plays that are deeply concerned with human mortality. I am afraid that the audience is afraid. I believe that John Hancock in San Francisco even scared the playwright when, at his production of *Milk Train,* he had skeletal figures of white plaster seated here and there in his theatre [what a brilliantly bizarre invention!], and when he invited the playwright to get up on the stage and read Goforth aloud to the cast, which he did to their enthusiastic applause.)

The nicest thing about this short stay in San Juan has been my reunion with José Quintero. He and his friend Nicky the Greek have rented and furnished a charming residence here. It was intended to be a guesthouse but the only permanent transient thus far on the premises is a charming young dog who was taken in from the street after it suffered a slight but

nervously traumatic collision with a passing car. I have
known José a long time, ever since he resurrected
*Summer and Smoke*, with the witchery of his staging
and the witchery of Geraldine Page. Later we were
both tenants of a high-rise next door to the Dakota on
West Seventy-second and we had hilarious poker
nights at least once a week.

Last night we played poker again, here in San
Juan, and he presented me with the first copy (in
bound proofs) of his forthcoming memoirs. The book
is titled *If You Don't Dance They Beat You*. It is an
enchanting book and the pertinence of the title has
emboldened me to consider changing the current (un-
published) title of my own memoirs. After all, one
should not refer to one's life as a sad hotel when it has
often been a merry tavern, and it is quite dishonest
to pretend one is eager to vacate it.

It is difficult to write about a period of profound,
virtually clinical depression, because when you are in
that state, everything is observed through a dark glass
which not only shadows but distorts all that is seen.
It's also hazardous to write about it, since the germ of
it still lingers in your system and it could be activated
again by thinking back on it.

This is a chance that I'll have to take this morning,
despite the fact that I am already depressed by the
situation of my oldest and closest friend, Professor
Oliver Evans, who has returned to his native city, New
Orleans, as a patient at Ochsner Clinic, after symptoms of recurring illness. (A few years ago he had a
brain cancer removed: afterward, cobalt therapy. In a
few months he appeared to have made a truly remarkable recovery: he resumed a full-time teaching
schedule in the English Department of a university in
California: there was an impressive renascence of his
writing career: everything boded well until the last
few months when he started to suffer from attacks of

vertigo without warning, resulting in falls which fractured his sacroiliac, and various other serious injuries. Now he is immobilized and in terror that a close relative's husband, whom he regards as hostile, will have him committed to a public asylum.)

Almost immediately after Frank's death, I flew down to Key West, where I had dispatched the poet Angel months before. But Angel was unable to help me now and it is hard to think of a single person who could. Probably I should have been hospitalized for a few months, willingly or not. It is strange how alone you are at times of great personal crisis. Strange is too convenient a term, and too euphemistic. The hard and cold fact of the matter is that nearly everyone who knows you draws back from you as if you bore some terrible contagion. At least, that's how it seems to you.

Going to pieces in "the sixties," my stoned age, suggests to me a slow-motion photo of a building being demolished by dynamite: it occurred in protracted stages, but the protraction gave it no comfort.

In Key West I resumed my relations with Angel. But even angels are subject to the weaknesses and defections of humanity which invented their existence.

Angel had defected emotionally (and understandably) to a young man, formerly a commercial air-pilot and then, at that time, a pill-freak with suicidal impulses but with a great deal of charm and a very attractive appearance.

If there was a suicidal impulse connected with my own combo of pills and liquor, an impulse distinct from increasing alienation, it was almost entirely on the unconscious level. That's a silly remark, I know. I am certainly not at all eloquent upon the difficult subject of my collapse in the sixties. I can't give you a detailed account of it without boring the pants off us both. I'll only attempt to record some of the most memorable symptoms and occasions, such as—

One day the Key West garden club ladies came en masse for a tour of my house and little compound on Duncan Street.

Bradley and Shirley Ayres, the widow of Lemuel Ayres, took me out to South Beach and Leoncia and Angel received the garden club ladies.

I couldn't bear the beach that day. I took a Seconal and went home while the house and grounds were still crowded with the curious ladies.

I entered and started to shout to them, "Out, out, out, out, out!"

They flew in all directions like hens in a thunderstorm: I took another pill and went to bed . . .

(The occasion is still a legend in Key West.)

Late that spring I dismissed Angel. I remember his saying to me, with tears in his eyes, "I thought I'd found a home."

You see, Angel was really a dear boy: and I a ravaged man.

I suppose it marked the beginning of my social downfall on that southernmost island. It would be "sour grapes" to say that I had never cared much about conventional Key West society. I had the Quixotic notion that I could continue to enjoy all kinds of society, the bohemian and the elite, the straight and the gay. I know many persons in "the gay world" who accomplish this trick with apparent ease: however, I think it still requires a good deal of hypocrisy, even now that society in the Western world is presumed to have discarded its prejudices. My feeling is that the prejudices have simply gone underground.

In any case I was too bizarre in my behavior, during this decade, for even the conservative members of the gay world.

(Please don't misunderstand me—unless I misunderstand myself.)

The direction of my life was away from both social and sexual contacts, not by conscious choice but through the deeper and deeper retreat into the broken world of my self.

I arrived at the nadir of this long period of depression when I began living totally alone. I forget the year and the season of the year but instinct drew me back to New Orleans and I made a last solitary effort to pull myself together. By this time, I could still make such an effort but it was always doomed to collapse. I believe a depression is classified as "clinical" when the victim stops moving, stops eating and bathing. I never descended to quite that point, but despite my efforts to go on, I think I was aware of death's attraction. The most painful aspect of the depression was always an inability to talk to people. As long as you can communicate with someone who is inclined to sympathy, you retain a chance to be rescued.

By the time I arrived in New Orleans I was almost reduced to mutism. And yet something was frantically, almost hopelessly, attempting to find a solution.

Through some friend, I discovered an ideal place to make this last-ditch attempt. He or she, I'm not sure who it was, arranged for me to take out a six-month lease on a lovely little pink house with white shutters on Dauphine Street in "the Quarter." It had been beautifully renovated and furnished by the late Clay Shaw and it was part of a group of little houses that faced Dauphine and St. Louis streets, forming an "L" about a lovely patio which contained a swimming pool, and each had its own little garden. The weather was bright and mild, an amiable black girl came in daily for house-cleaning: but in spite of all these favorable conditions, I turned the house into something as psychologically tenable as Kafka's "Burrow."

Each morning I attempted to write, but it was as difficult as trying to talk.

After two or three weeks some last remaining contact in New Orleans managed to persuade me to give

a party, and this was the most calamitous and ludi-
crous event, I should think, that's ever been called a
party.

It was a "catered affair" and almost everyone I'd
ever known in the city was invited to it. I was only
able to greet them and few of them by name. I sat in a
corner and regarded them all with a look of frozen
withdrawal.

You see how difficult it is to write about a depression of this depth?

Someone had recommended a psychiatrist to me. I
went to him daily but almost as soon as I entered his
office, I would cry out, "I'm too sick to talk, I feel
panicky, please give me the green bottle."

"The green bottle" contained a liquid that was briefly soporific. It would reduce the level of panic but it
wouldn't permit me to talk.

I am uncertain about the time-sequence of certain
occurrences during that dreadful period of depression.

I know that from time to time I returned to the
charming little apartment on East Sixty-fifth Street.
I went out just once every twenty-four hours, to a
little grocery store around the corner on Lexington, to
purchase a box of spaghetti. This was my sole and
solitary meal each day, and I don't recall embellishing
it with any kind of sauce.

I never answered the phone or the downstairs bell,
which buzzed beside the speaker in the kitchen.

Two ladies managed to penetrate my otherwise
total seclusion. One was a remote cousin by marriage,
Nan Lanier. She kept ringing all the downstairs bells
till some other tenant buzzed her in. She came to my
door and knocked and called till finally I admitted
her. She looked at me and asked, "Tom, have you
been sleeping?"

"Here? No, not a bit that I know of."

She gave me the name of a psychiatrist and dispatched me there. He took my blood pressure. It was
so low that he said he didn't know how I had man-

aged to climb the single flight of stairs to his office. He gave me an injection to raise it. When it had risen, he wrote out for me a prescription for Doriden and Mellaril tablets and said to take two of the Doriden and one of the five-hundred-milligram Mellarils each night. And he promised they'd put me to sleep. That they did.

The other lady who visited me was a friend of happier times whom I had encountered on a ship returning from Europe. She was very tall and stately, with an exceptionally lovely voice. For some reason her name eludes me. I thought of her as "Eleanor of Aquitaine" and I persuaded her to record some of the *Camino Real* passages of the character Marguerite Gautier. Her home was in Baltimore and she had a very high social position there.

One evening she penetrated my reclusive retreat at East Sixty-fifth in the same way as Nan did.

I recognized her voice at the door and I let her in.

"I can't talk," I told her.

"Not necessary," she said.

Then she sat beside me on the little apricot-colored love seat in the living room and with her long, thin hands she massaged my forehead. We didn't talk, but her hands on my forehead gave me a bit of comfort.

Sometime later this great lady called me from Baltimore and told me, "I am dying, Tom."

I said, "Oh, God, no."

"Yes, I am."

In her voice, not a trace of self-pity.

"It's now quite certain," she said, "and I want you to pray that it will be soon, as soon as possible now."

She died a short while later.

In my life I have known some heroic people.

I believe it is possibly because of the tragic circumstances of her death—no, that isn't the right way to put it, it was a most admirable and noble way to die, by informing an old friend by phone with more concern for his reaction than for her own mortal illness.

Still, it was terribly shocking to me, then and now, and possibly that explains why I can remember this lady only as Eleanor of Aquitaine.

During one of those periods in New York I somehow got in touch with my grandmother Dakin's great-nephew, Jim Adams. I persuaded him to accompany me to Key West. After observing me there for a few days, he said, "Tom, this won't do. My sister Stell and I know a wonderful analyst in New York and I think he can help you." So back we went to New York.

It was better there. Jim found us a two-story pent-house in the same block as City Center and turned me over to the analyst, one of the Karen Horney school, named Ralph Harris. He saw me daily and inexpen-sively, he seemed to be humanly, not just profes-sionally, concerned. He even allowed me to have a highball beside my couch, and I gradually began to be able to talk to him.

Jim occupied the upper floor of the penthouse and I the lower. My new sleeping medications had a eu-phoric, or hypnotic, effect, and for at least half an hour before I fell asleep, I would be visited by a wave of peace, the fierce knots in my head would relax, and it was like the presence of an angel beside my wide bed.

My stoned age had partial remissions, mostly coinci-dent with theatre productions in the sixties, all of them disastrous—due to my inability to cope with the preparations for them and with a turn, in my work, to-ward a new style and a new creative world with which the reviewers and the audiences found it very hard to empathize so abruptly.

My life was erratic. I went from place to place, of-ten in the company of dear Marion Vaccaro—I no longer traveled with a male lover. I remember going with her to Tangier, going with her to the Greek is-land of Rhodes, and I remember our partnership in booze.

In Rhodes a funny thing occurred. The American

fleet was in and the harbor was brilliantly illuminated by the warships. Marion and I sat at a waterfront restaurant table, alfresco, and I complained to her of the hotel in which we were staying and which Marion had named "the concentration camp."

"Honey, why don't you go over to the Hotel Des Roses and check us in there if you can?"

Marion never refused a request from me during the many years I knew her. Drunk and reeling, off she went down the road to the Hotel Des Roses.

I sat at the waterfront table, sodden with drink, and looked about, lizard-like, for an attractive and available member of the American Navy personnel on shore leave.

I sat there, luckless, for a long, long time, wondering what the hell had happened to Marion.

At last she returned and she was a sight to behold. The front of her dress was drenched with what was, to my olfactory sense, unmistakably urine.

"Honey, how'd you get so wet?" I asked her with surprising discretion.

"Well, baby, about halfway to the Hotel Des Roses I had to pee so I just pulled up my skirt and I peed in the road and I just now discovered I peed all over my skirt."

"Then what'd you do?"

"Why, I went on into the Hotel Des Roses and tried to book us in there, but the fool at the desk said the place was booked solid for the next three months."

"Oh."

We both began to laugh.

Two things of great consequence in my life occurred in the middle sixties. The lesser of the two was my alliance with a sort of caretaker-companion of great charm, humor, and almost suspect glamour of appearance whom I shall provide with the fictitious name of Ryan. I am still fond of him but I must avoid seeing him as an encounter with him, even brief and accidental, brings back to me the disastrous decade of my life, the sixties. I am afraid of associating him unfairly with the misfortunes that I suffered and barely survived in that period of profound depression and paranoia. Perhaps he came closest to representing Chance Wayne in *Sweet Bird of Youth* in my life, although—as best I can remember and I am trying hard to remember the best that I can—the sexual content of the attachment was minimal and was elected by him.

The more consequential occurrence in the mid-sixties was my becoming a patient of a physician sometimes called Dr. Feel Good. I had reached such a state of depression that somebody who cared about me had to do something to help me, and it turned out to be a gentleman with whom I was associated professionally—I think he would rather I didn't mention his name. He had been a patient of Dr. Feel Good's for a long time, taking the Feel Good therapies as a substitute for a period of alcoholism in his past and he sincerely believed that this doctor could rescue me from my condition. And so one evening when I had just returned, in a state of near-collapse, to New York, this gentleman, deeply concerned, took me over to the office of Dr. Feel Good and there I received the first of my "feel good" injections. I must admit that I was terrified of taking it, but the doctor had about him a magical atmosphere of understanding and compassion. He did not submit me to the usual physical examinations: I don't think he even took my pulse or blood pressure or had me fill out a questionnaire about my medical history. He just looked at me. His inspection was deceptively casual. He was not only looking at me but probably right through me. Then he started concocting the shot, drawing a bit of fluid from one bottle and another and another as my suspense and my alarm increased. He chatted away while this was going on in the most reassuringly jocular manner. At last he told me to let my trousers down: he jabbed a hypodermic full of mysterious fluids into my hips and within about a minute a miracle took place. I felt as if a concrete sarcophagus about me had sprung open and I was released as a bird on the wing.

The gentleman who had taken me there had gone home, but a young actor of my acquaintance was present: in fact, he was a part-time assistant as well as patient of the doctor. He drove me home to the empty apartment on East Sixty-fifth, but by a long detour, as I had left my luggage at Kennedy Airport. I kept saying, "My God, I feel so wonderful." Then I asked him, "How long will it last?" He smiled rather sadly and said, "Tennessee, don't think about that."

At first I only went to Dr. Feel Good's for injections, but soon he was also providing me with vials, each one a little different from the ones preceding, and I was injecting myself intramuscularly when I got up in the mornings.

Perhaps if I had given up liquor, and my nightly sedation of two Doriden tablets and a five-hundred-milligram Mellaril tablet, not to mention the morning barbiturate which I took immediately after the intramuscular injection, I would have had no adverse consequences from my involvement with the doctor.

When I traveled, which I continued to do a great deal, Dr. Feel Good would mail me vials of the stuff wherever I might go. If they arrived a day or two later than expected, I would be panicky about it: but they would, eventually, reach me. They kept me working. They kept me going. Until—but that comes later.

Now I'll revert to the tall young man whom I have named Ryan.

For nearly five years in the sixties I lived with him. I met him in that penthouse apartment, two stories, which I occupied briefly with cousin Jim Adams. Ryan and Mike Steen appeared one day and took me out somewhere in Ryan's English sports-car, a Triumph.

Ryan asked me if I didn't recall our first meeting: I

did not. He said he had come over to my place with a group of friends one night in the fifties and I had immediately commented upon the beauty of his ass.— Well, that sounds like me, for sure . . .

A short while later Ryan began to drop in more and more regularly at night. I recall how delicious were his old-fashioneds, made with orange juice. I recall our listening to Billie Holiday's last album, "Lady in Satin," and my enchantment with it.

Many people would say that Ryan was the handsomest of my companions, but I assure you that my long stay with him had more to do with his managerial expertise—that he *did* have—than to my emotional attachment. True, he had a rollicking nature and we laughed a lot together. But it was somewhat ruthless the way that he got young cousin Jim out of the apartment and took his place.

I am still fond of Ryan. He had much to do with my gradual (?) breakdown, perhaps. But he must have endured a good deal himself. It's not easy to live with a writer who has elected to be a zombie except for his mornings at work. I was only interested in working. I didn't know if I wanted to live or not, and Ryan had to cope with that and naturally it was a burden.

Ryan did devote much of his time to me, escorting me to my last analyst and to the "Y" for swims. Yet I'm afraid he considered me mostly as a convenience, and I tell you truly as ever that during our nearly five years together he offered himself to me only three or four times, and, as best I can remember, I had no carnal knowledge of anyone but him during his time with me.

All close relationships are turned later to poems. This thing could include portraits of Ryan and me in such places as Rome and Key West and New York: of Ryan embracing Elizabeth Taylor during the shooting of the film *BOOM* on the island of Sardinia. He was bisexual and very attractive to ladies with the exception of the Lady Maria St. Just and Miss Ellen McCool, both of whom objected to his very beautiful and very blue eyes.

("God bless your eyes," his mother had said to him when he left for legitimate work in the mornings.)

I remember a night in the sixties when Ryan and I were living (separate bedrooms) at that ghastly highrise next to the Dakota, on Central Park West. We were living on the thirty-third floor, and one night, very, very late, I received a frantic call from a lady friend who had been a vanished lady—deep into pills —for several years. She said she didn't have money to get back to her parents' home. I told her to come over and I'd give her cab fare.

She had been there only a few minutes when she begged me to give her some Seconals. "I know you've got some."

I did, but I feared that she'd never get to her parents if she took any more of my precious "pinkies." I gave her a couple of Miltowns instead.

Then Ryan returned from his habitual night prowlings. She silently observed him for a moment or two and then said, "I want to talk to you privately, Tennessee." We went off on that ghastly little concrete balcony which had scarcely room enough for two chairs. There she said to me, "Tennessee, how do you dare to live on the thirty-third floor of a building with a man with eyes like that and with a balcony he could throw you off of?"

Well, being a madman, then, I called Morgan-Manhattan Storage the next morning and had the apartment emptied of all furniture, just like that.

I moved alone to a hotel—the Alrae?—but in a day or two Ryan discovered my whereabouts and moved in with me. I accepted his return. We took a suite of two bedrooms. The advance rent on the highrise apartment was sacrificed. Ryan probably started, then, to hate me. But he disguised it, if he did. We resumed our daily roamings about Manhattan, shopping and having lunches at a charming little French restaurant called L'Escargot and swimming at the "Y."

One little story of an occurrence in Positano, Italy. We were summering there and Nan Lanier, then separated from her husband, had met us in Naples at the Excelsior and we were a trio at Positano. I was having difficulty walking, due to my speed-shots and pills. We were going somewhere in a cab. Ryan and Nan and I were in the rear seat, Ryan's arm seductively about the shoulders of Nan, a very sexy lady. He turned to me and with that superb arrogance of his said, "Tennessee, why don't you get in the front seat with the driver?"

He had somehow miscalculated my reaction to such an insult.

"Ryan, get the hell out of the cab!"

And out he got . . .

I was never deep enough into the oblivion of the sixties that I could be put down. I would fall down often, yes, but was put down only by reviewers . . .

In 1967, with a $400,000 bit of "front money" from a Hollywood studio, with David Merrick producing for Broadway, and with José Quintero directing—I put on *Kingdom of Earth*, a play I'd written for Maureen Stapleton but which was played by Estelle Parsons.

Things went not well at all.

Merrick wanted to fire Quintero, but I insisted that he remain and Merrick acquiesced to my insistence.

We opened disastrously in New York despite the superb performances of Parsons and Brian Bedford.

Certain biased reviewers were particularly nasty about the play. They said that they couldn't wait for the threatening flood to occur, the house to be demolished and everyone in it drowned.

Strangely, it was Walter Kerr, in his Sunday piece,

who observed that it was a play that contained excellent and funny characterization and that he hoped I'd rewrite it someday.

What it actually needed was cutting, and dear José was not the one for that. Humor he has, but it's a delicate humor that exists in a heart full of sorrow.

I may have mentioned seeing a perfect revival of *Kingdom of Earth* in a small, remote house on the Coast. It was cut to its proper length, beautifully cast, and the lady who directed it brought out its bawdy and yet touching style and its strong thematic content.

More about plays in the sixties, "The Stoned Age."

*Slapstick Tragedy,* a double bill of two short plays, was produced in 1966 and once again the press hit me with all the ammo in their considerable and rather ruthless possession.

Margaret Leighton was superb as *The Gnadiges Fraulein* and Zoe Caldwell was also superb. But this one-act play was dismissed by Walter Kerr with this devastating one-liner at the end of his notice. "Black Comedy is not for Mr. Williams."

It was I who invented American black comedy and he was surely smart enough to know it.

He also spoke with patronizing compassion about the other of the two plays, *The Mutilated,* a work that had potential but never got off the ground. It was an overextended piece, inflated, and in my opinion badly directed by Alan Schneider, the little grinning director in the red baseball cap. It ran for four performances under the aegis of Charles Bowden and Lester Persky.

The evening after it opened I took Maggie Leighton and Michael Wilding to Sardi's. An act of sheer defiance. Ryan was with us, and we entered ahead and I heard Maggie remark to Wilding, "Poor thing, it's pitiful, he doesn't know what hit him."

I knew what had hit me, but I held my tongue ...

I will never forget the superb performance of Leighton in *Fraulein,* and neither would anyone who saw it.

My next play in the sixties was *In the Bar of a Tokyo Hotel.* I was still always falling down during this time and I would always say, before falling, "I'm about to fall down," and almost nobody, nobody ever caught me.

One morning during this "Stoned Age" was that awful morning when I stumbled out into the living room to find it filled with Mike Wallace and a TV crew, that time when Mike finally said, "Okay, let's pack up, we're not going to get anything from him today."

The husband and wife who produced *Tokyo Bar* came down to Key West and although I saw them daily for about a week I had afterward no recollection of their visit, nor of their plan to produce this work given them by Audrey.

Donald Madden and Anne Meacham starred in it and they were superb.

Mother and Dakin came to the opening. Mother said to me, "Tom, it's time for you to find another occupation now."

Oh, Christ, I'm lonely this morning. Do you know what I mean, I mean how much I mean it?

No one, really, since Frankie—except old friends.

That sounds like self-pity, which is a human emotion which is sometimes unavoidable, regardless of its abnegation of pride.

But I've had a wonderful and terrible life and I wouldn't cry for myself: would you?

It seems that I am about to lose my mother. When I called her two days ago in response to her strange letter begging me to come home and take her wherever I am, I told her that I was about to leave for New Orleans and would be happy to receive her there, that Dakin could put her on a plane and I would meet it.

"Oh, Tom, I've just returned from New Orleans. I was in Deaconess Hospital there and I caught a dreadful sore throat from sleeping on unwashed sheets. Hurry home to St. Louis."

"Mother, I'll call Dakin. Where would he be now?"

"At his law office, I think."

"What's his number there, Mother?"

"Oh, Son, I'd have to go upstairs to find it and I can't go up."

Of course I was awfully disturbed. I got Dakin's office number through directory assistance in Collinsville. His secretary answered, quite coolly, and said that Dakin could not be reached at the moment, but I could call him that evening at Mother's, at about six.

He called at six and was at Mother's. I told him that she'd informed me she'd just returned from Deaconess Hospital, in New Orleans, and I asked him if her hardly coherent story was true.

He told me that she had not been to New Orleans but had just been released from Deaconess Hospital in St. Louis.

"How is she?"

"Very weak. It's hard for her to walk."

Then she came on the phone and said again, "Tom, hurry home."

Today I am going to call her doctors and get a report on her actual condition.

I was so disturbed last night it was scarcely possible to give a performance at the New Theatre.

If the Deaconess doctors' report is bad, as I expect, I will have to go to St. Louis, a place I dread, when I am, myself, just hanging on by my teeth.

I have given what I expect will be my final performance in *Small Craft Warnings;* it was also our farewell to Helena Carroll and so I bought a couple of bottles of Piper-Heidseck champagne and at the curtain I announced to the audience, after we'd taken our group bow, that tonight "was Miss Carroll's hundred and fifty-second and final performance in the play and we wish to express our appreciation of her brave and brilliant work." Then, as arranged—we all turned to her and applauded her with the audience. When the curtain fell we toasted her and her sister, who was attending the performance that night, with the champagne and so her engagement ended upon a gracious note—which I feel was fitting since she has, indeed, worked very hard under difficult circumstances.

The scuttlebutt is that the producers wanted her out of the play and told her it was going to close in order to get her resignation: in other words, her departure was engineered by the management, and I feel the little woman is bright enough to suspect this fact and to be hurt, now, that she is being replaced by Peg Murray.

I know that these are the cruel exigencies of life in the theatre: there is little or no sentiment to be encountered in its machinations. It is a mirror of nature. The individual is ruthlessly discarded for the old, old consideration of profit.

After the performance I rushed home. Jane and Tony Smith were waiting in the lobby and we went up to the Victorian Suite, along with Billy Barnes, to make our planned phone call to the indignant Lady St. Just. Domestics who answered the phone both at her London townhouse and at the country estate in Salisbury told us icily that "Her Ladyship" could not be reached. I remarked to Tony that I am beginning to fear, now, that "the lady is afflicted with *folie de grandeur*"—and he smiled.

Billy and I were luckless in getting Genevieve Bujold on the phone in Montreal. I am increasingly fearful that she is scared of the play *Out Cry* and of moving to New York for its run—which leaves us where with Merrick and the planned production in late September?

We dined at Casey's in the Village and I got quite high on Margaux. I stumbled over a curbstone, on our way home, tearing the pants of my best suit and skinning my knee. Of course I'm alarmed by this resumed tendency to fall over things. Now both knees are scabbed.

Rest is indicated and less dependence on liquor, in the evening, to disguise my growing exhaustion—especially since the disguise turns out to be a further exposure ...

Having arrived home, I called Mother. She was very slow to answer the phone: when she did, she said she was having to "wait up until midnight" to admit Dakin and "some young black woman" living with him upstairs. This struck me as most improbable even for my improbable little brother. I asked her to have Dakin call me soon as he came in last night—since she could not recall the name of her physician.

Dakin called about midnight, New York time. He laughed at Mother's charge of his cohabitation with "some young black woman upstairs," provided me with the name of Mother's doctor, whom I shall try to contact today for a diagnosis of her condition. Dakin says she can only walk a few steps at a time without catching hold of something—he also admitted, most astonishingly, that he himself had not talked to the doctor.

One fantastic night in the summer of '67, Bill Inge attempted to have me put away. I was living in a house up in Hermit's Glen, near Los Angeles. On that strange night, Ryan and a guy I'll call Pat had a fight while I lay drugged in my back bedroom. I woke up and staggered into the kitchen-living room of the house to find the floor stained with blood and a strange and formidable man in the house who subjected me to a piercing inquisition. My secretary pro tem, "The Virginian," spoke not a word, just stood in the kitchen area washing dishes.

I rose to the occasion and demanded that the strange man—Inge's current psychiatrist, as it turned out, dispatched by Inge—leave my house at once or face a charge of illegal entry. Finally the psychiatrist saw that he could not question or stare me down.

"Let him make a phone call to William Inge," he said, "if he promises not to call the police!"

I phoned Inge about the situation at Hermit's Glen and asked him to come right over and clear it up. Inge replied loftily, "I'm sorry I can't come over, I'm entertaining tonight."

I instantly dialed "O" for operator and shouted into the phone, "Get the police at once up to Hermit's Glen! My house has been invaded and there's blood on the floor!"

The psychiatrist fled down the steps and hot-footed it out to his car. Ryan and Pat got down on all fours to swab up the bloodstains on the carpet.

Having won this bout, I then called Audrey Wood —who hated Pat and was fond of Ryan—and gave her a breathless account of what had taken place.

"Right now," she informed me, "Ryan is being bailed out of jail to which Pat sent him as a house-breaker. I told him to go straight to the Hollywood-Roosevelt Hotel and wait for you there."

I left the house up in Hermit's Glen under police escort—to the Hollywood-Roosevelt, where I was shortly joined by Ryan. The next day we flew back together to Manhattan . . .

But I was headed for the bin, and in '69, following the vicious put-down of *In the Bar of a Tokyo Hotel* —and my flight with Anne Meacham to Tokyo when she'd told me that *Life* was coming out with a statement of my professional demise—I really began to crack.

Oh, I'd been cracking for years but then the cracking

was like that subterranean fault, under the West Coast.

I like the crowd I'm with, here in Venice, all of them: Sylvia Miles, Joe Dallesandro, Paul Morrissey, little Andy Warhol so much like a lost little boy, lost in time.

Morrissey strikes me as someone very special. I would like him to make a film of one of my short stories: why not "Two on a Party," which may be the best of the lot? I will ask him to read it. But I respect him too much to hustle him about it.

I am hoping that some moral change for the better may occur soon, as well as relief from loneliness, and I hope that the two wishes are not in complete contradiction or counterpoise to each other . . .

I think I like Rex Reed. From the moment we met, we could talk to each other but I suppose I talked too much when he interviewed me for *Esquire*. No, I take that back. It's true that I didn't pinch the ass of a black waiter in Brennan's, but still he caught my nature.

Last night was a lovely evening. After sleeping all afternoon in my suite here at the familiar old Excelsior, the Adriatic washing gently and constantly below my balconied windows, I had a little swim. You have to wade out too far at the Lido and the water cannot be described as translucent as the Mediterranean is, or was, at Taormina—it was time to have drinks with Pat and Michael York. Billy Barnes had arranged it while I slept, and, oh, a call from London —Maria arrives tomorrow and she sounded warm and elated on the phone.

Of course I met with some of the familiar irritants of traveling alone. I feel that I am traveling alone, even when I am with a party of people, when there is no one sharing my rooms. I can't get things together. It took me forty minutes to assemble my tuxedo and accessories. The pants had fallen into the bottom of the Val-pack and, of course, I started cursing, being convinced that only the jacket had been packed. But when I got all assembled and was dressed in my finery—the shirt with the lace cuffs flaring discreetly and the ruffled shirt front and the black tie eventually secured precariously—can a thing be precariously secured?—I was still early for the six-o'clock cocktail date.

Impatient, I called Billy and said I thought it would be more fun if we met in the hotel cocktail lounge, instead of the salon of my suite and of course I was quite wrong, as usual, it was not better at all but distinctly worse. I sat with Billy at a table for four and a wretched queen started playing the grand piano directly behind us.

"Some damn child is banging on that piano," I said loudly to Billy.

"I'm afraid it's their professional pianist," said Billy, "and we'd better move someplace where we can talk."

From the point that the Yorks met us it was a lovely evening. Pat had just had her hair dressed, so she remained in the cabin of the launch with Billy—I sat on the open-back bench with Michael and the lagoon was as lovely as I remembered it.

"Ah, Venice, city of pearls," I said, quoting from *Camino*.

We dined simply and quickly on the Gritti terrace (spaghetti alla vongole) while a three-quarter moon floated gradually from behind the white dome of a church across the canal and I got nicely high on Frascati, first, and then on a better wine indigenous to Venice.

You see, we had to hurry back to the Lido as Michael's film, *Cabaret*, was to be the inaugural *spettacolo* of the festival.

Now back in the Excelsior bar, I sat on the arm of Pat's chair with beautiful ladies such as Marisa Berenson across the table while Michael was being interviewed just behind us. Cameras were flashing continually.

I asked a producer at the table if he had any money. He said no. And I said, "Then I'm not talking to you."

In the late summer of 1969, Anne Meacham and Gigi and I returned from our dismal flight to Tokyo and I returned to the little compound in Key West. I was not with it there, I was not at all with it, the collapse had started.

The construction of the big new kitchen had also started, the kitchen which was to cost twice the 1949 purchase price of the entire property. And the erection was to last for nearly four months, which is a much longer-lasting erection than even Casanova might have desired.

The stove had been removed to the patio so I could prepare my morning Silex of coffee. And one nocturnal morning, a few days after the return to Key West, I prepared one Silex of coffee too many. I was, at this time, always falling down, you may recall, and as I removed the boiling coffee from the stove in the patio, I came a cropper on the patio tiles, spilling the boiling coffee over my bare shoulder.

I was so spaced out that I felt no pain and went about my morning's work as usual.

At this point the fog sets in. I remember going to a doctor who bandaged the lobster-red shoulder and then I remember that Dakin was in Key West. Then I remember we were in Key West airport and poor Edie Kidd came by my table and I said to her, "I like your painting, Edie, but have no other interest in you at all."

And then I was in the house on Wydown Boulevard in Clayton, Mom's old Spanish stucco dwelling, and it was morning and I had firmly decided not to enter a hospital.

"Mother, have you ever heard of sibling envy?"

"Oh yes, I think so," said Miss Edwina coldly.

A bit later I said I would go to the hospital provided an ambulance was summoned to take me. Dakin talked me out of that. He got me into his car and drove me to Barnacle Hospital. At first, that first day, I was put in the Queen's Division—and I didn't make up that name, that's just what it's called. It is the rather posh division for the "mildly disturbed." I was placed under the "care" of three neurologists and an internist.

All that I remember of my first day in Queen's Division was lying in bed watching TV. Every program seemed to be directed at me with some thickly disguised hostility, even Shirley Booth's soap opera struck me as a personally menacing thing.

About 6 P.M., in comes Dakin, grinning, with a bunch of yellow flowers and some remarkably talentless crayon drawings that were drawn for my delectation by his two adopted daughters.

Mother marched in, a little Prussian officer in drag.

There was now, quite clearly, something impending of a fearful nature. I sensed this and I scrambled with remarkable agility out of bed and said, "I'm going home right now," and I ran into the closet to get into my clothes.

"Oh no, Son."

"You all will drive me right home or I'll walk."

I got myself dressed with amazing alacrity, all the while shouting abuse at Dakin.

"God damn you and your two adopted children. How dare you give them our family name."

Dakin: "I don't have to sit here and listen to this abuse."

Now fully dressed and totally out of my mind, I charged into the corridor and down to the elevators. I started to enter one, was blocked in this escape effort by a huge young man in hospital uniform. He was blond, I remember, with a beefy, sneering face. I somehow slipped past him into the elevator but he wouldn't let the doors close.

Raging and storming invectives, I rushed back past him to the room where Mother was asking a nurse for smelling salts. Jesus!

Then I lit into her with a vengeance.

"Why do women bring children into the world and then destroy them?"

(I still consider this a rather good question.)

Said Miss Edwina—sincerely?—"I just don't know if we're doing the right thing."

I turned again to the corridor but now the door was obstructed by a wheel-chair with straps and by a goon squad of interns.

Now suddenly I recognized defeat and gave up.

Clutching the flight bag that contained my booze, my pills, my vial of speed, clutching it despairingly and tightly, I was strapped into the chair and rocketed out of Queen's Division to Friggins Violent Ward —there the flight bag was snatched from me, and at this point I blacked out . . .


I am in the violent ward of Friggins Division of Barnacle Hospital. I said I had blacked out and so I did —when they snatched my flight bag from me.

Now I am going to tell you as much as I can about my closest brush with death.

After I blacked out, I don't know whether I came to or not.

And I don't know how long the convulsions lasted. I know that there were three of them in one morning and there was the "silent coronary," which is the only thing during the apocalypse that's clear to me, as I felt, through my convulsions, the stabbing pains of it.

I went through a time of total fantasy.

I recall being strapped to a table and wheeled about. But never medicated.

I refuse to ascribe to paranoia my conviction that

the resident physician intended to commit legalized murder upon my person and very nearly succeeded.

I had a most extraordinary experience which may or may not have occurred the evening after the convulsions.

I am walking very, very slowly down a corridor toward a lighted room and I am chanting a poem.

The recurrent line of each verse is "Redemption, redemption." And I am performing, as I move slowly down the corridor, a mincing exaggeration of the walk of a drag-queen. What was I chanting about? About the birth of my brother Dakin when I was eight and my first sight of him, suckling the bare breast of my mother in the St. Louis hospital.

Redemption from what? A never-before-spoken sibling rivalry with him, I would suppose. And also a redemption from the "crime" of my love-life with boys and young men . . .

The truth is that I don't really want to go back over the time in Friggins Division of Barnacle Hospital in the city of St. Pollution. It's all been fairly well taken care of, in a documentary way, in "What's Next on the Agenda, Mr. Williams?"

I shall only recount a few bits omitted from the "poem."

After my convulsions and my indeterminate period of delirium, I woke up in a narrow cubicle in a bed with barred sides like a big baby's crib. And when I say I woke up, I mean my eyes were open and I was experiencing some degree of cogitation but I wasn't really awake for an hour or two, I couldn't have been since I remembered nothing and didn't know where I was.

The realization came upon me like death.

Strange figures passed my open door on a narrow corridor, I couldn't believe they were real. I literally thought I was dreaming.

I don't believe I was visited, perhaps not even brought food, before evening, at least I have no recollection of it.

But in the evening I was outside my cubicle and Dakin was in the "dayroom." He had a sort of triumphant smirk on his face and he bore a copy of *Esquire*, the issue which contained that horror piece of fiction, an article called "A Dream of Tennessee Williams" and his first words to me, beside his grin of greeting and hearty handshake, was the devastating question: "Do you know that you have had a silent coronary? And several convulsions?"

Then he presented me with that issue of *Esquire* and made a grinning departure and I began my desperate effort to hang onto myself in the Violent Ward at Friggins.

In what way was I violent there?

I dutifully came to their atrocious meals and the rest of the time I crouched like a defenseless animal in a corner while the awful pageantry of the days and the nights went on, a continual performance of horror shows, inside and outside my skull.

I intended to survive.


Little mementos of it.

A huge nurse with a great Germanic blond head and a fixed grimace of jubilant authority kept stalking about, arms swinging like a wrestler's before he catches hold of an opponent, oh yes, lovely Miss Rothschild she was, and let me tell you this: I gave that lady no mouth!

Speaking of mouths, there was this fantastically exhibitionist middle-aged queen who paraded about, Miss Rothschild's opposite number, and he was continually arranging his gray hair with his fluttering fingers as he sashayed about and then one day this glowering Irish truck-driver type sprang up and fetched him the most terrible clout in the mouth I've ever witnessed. All of the faggot's front teeth were knocked out as if he'd been struck in the mouth by a sledge hammer. For days, his face was a baboon's ass to look at, the mouth swollen out as far as his nose and its interior a crimson cavern. But this did not diminish his concern with his gray hair, the fingers went on fluttering over the carefully arranged waves.

Then—God help me!—his assailant began to draw a chair up beside mine, in the corner where I crouched, and to stare at me, from time to time, with the same look he had given the Narcissan old queen.

There was the day a young girl with a great head of brilliant red hair was dragged screaming into the ward and thrown into a padded cell and left there screaming all night and when I next saw her, in place of the brilliant and thick head of hair was a mound of bloodstained bandages.

I had begun to ask questions of a young intern who was friendlier than the others and he informed me that the girl had torn all of her hair out while screaming in the padded cell that night, torn it all out by the roots.

I had a few suits in my locker. Dakin had brought them over.

Surreptitiously I searched the pockets and discovered a little cache of "pinkies," about five capsules: I would take one at bedtime to supplement the totally ineffective sleeping medication prescribed by my doctors, who had not yet found time to call on me in the ward.

When these capsules were exhausted I began to spend three and four sleepless nights and days in a row.

Finally there would be a night of such exhaustion that I would sleep an hour.

One night as I was falling asleep—yes, really drifting away—the door flew open upon a young intern who was scarcely describable as friendly.

"My God, what do you want?"

"You didn't turn in your electric shaver at the desk!"

"What of it?"

He snatched the Norelco off the tiny bureau and said, "Patients in this ward are not allowed to keep anything in their rooms that they can hurt themselves with."

I went out into the hall after him and I went up to the night nurse's glassed-in box from which she monitored the inmates.

I pounded on the door. Several nurses and interns gathered and I went into hysteria over the incident just related.

"I was falling asleep, I was really falling asleep after not sleeping four nights and he burst into my room for my electric shaver."

I kept repeating it and I began to sob and the night nurse turned to a woman and she spoke to me gently.

"Go back to your cubicle, your medication may start working again."

It didn't though.

My cubicle was right next to the garbage disposal plant, a huge one, and an hour before first light it would start its grinding thunder and that was the only way I knew when day was approaching, for my watch had also been confiscated since it contained glass and nothing containing glass was permitted to remain in the possession of a patient in that ward.

At first light, a brisk, expressionless nurse with a voice like an automatic drill would charge into the cubicle for an inquisition and the taking of temperature and pulse-rate.

"Bowel-movement yesterday?"

Sometimes I'd give no answers and sometimes I'd groan and cover my face and so my stay in the violent ward was prolonged to a full month—for unco-operative attitudes, I suppose.

In my nature I think that a basic pride of some kind will remain the last thing to go when all else is gone but breath . . .

The resident physician was very friendly with Da-

kin and when Dakin came to see me—about once or
twice a week—he would chat with him in my presence. He would tell Dakin how I'd had three convulsions in one morning and he told these things with an
inflection of pride—as if the convulsions were an
accomplishment upon which he congratulated himself.

I had long since read the "Dream of Tennessee Williams" in *Esquire* when one evening a doctor brought
me a copy of the issue and said with his evil grin,
"I see you've got a very good write-up in here. Want
to read it?"

"No, I think not. I've read it."

"Resident physicians are envious of us," said Dr.
Levy, "and so they take it out on our patients . . ."

Even in the violent ward, the patients had an hour
of occupational therapy in the morning and another
in the afternoon.

Each day those whose names had been called as
acceptable for O.T. lined up at the elevators. We all
had an option of refusal, we could refuse to go down
in the elevator for the simplistic occupations that were
available to us down there.

Most times I'd decline to go down but then I discovered that I was being monitored badly if I declined. So I started going. I accepted water-colors as
the least tedious of the occupations, and for some reason I began to do a water-color of my left hand.

I remember it was just about finished and huge old
Dr. Levy came puffing up to me.

"Your little finger isn't that big, Tom."

Did he mean that I still suffered from *folie de grandeur?*

Dr. Levy was the least inhuman of the triumvirate
of neurologists and the one who eventually—after I'd
survived a month in Violent—transferred me to what
is called an "open ward."

What kept me enduring the confinement at Friggins Division were boxes of books sent to me by Andy Brown of the Gotham Book Mart, and the nightly bridge games that occupied the four hours from dinner till lights out, after I'd been transferred to an open ward. There were several excellent female bridge players in the first open ward I went to. I played every night for about four hours. One of the players was a seventy-five-year-old lady who was being put under a relentless series of shock treatments of which she had mortal terror. She would not know until late evening whether or not she was to be subjected again to a shock treatment in the morning. The notice of it would be posted on the door of her cubicle and she would be shattered, trembling and in tears.

After a shock treatment she had difficulty playing bridge. I remember with a warm feeling how we all ignored her memory failures in the card game and how we all comforted her and tried to assuage her panic when she saw that posted notice of a shock treatment scheduled for the next morning.

She had grown sons who dropped in to see her about once a week; why didn't they stop this torture of their old mother? I am just cynical enough to suspect they wanted her "out of the way"—and one of them was a professor at St. Louis University, a Catholic institution.

I am happy to report that some months later in Key West I received a postcard from her that stated that she had been released from Friggins Division and was "back home."

Survival! What an epic capacity of the human heart, young and old!

However dreadful they were at the time of their occurrence, there are incidents and characters whom you recall, at a safe distance, with a shocked amusement. There was, for instance, this great, monolithic black woman who would sit in the center of the dayroom. Whenever I went past her, she would grin at me and say, "You're so sweet, you're a lump of sugar, just a sweet lump of sugar."

Ingenuously, I thought she meant it. And then one day, while delivering this saccharine greeting, she abruptly rose and took a swing at me that would have flattened me on the floor had she not swung off target.

I have incorporated her in my television special *Stopped Rocking*.

Then there were the two very attractive young ladies who had gone on a bad trip on drugs in Istanbul and who could sleep only if they were given, for sleeping medications, the chemical components known to the underworld as a "Mickey Finn." Each night when the sleeping medications were passed out, they would stand up to receive their potions. The moment they had downed them, they would start a mad dash for their cubicles, about twenty-five yards away. And invariably they would collapse to the floor before they reached their doors and would have to be dragged unconscious to bed.

Oh, how I envied those girls! I begged Dr. Levy to let me have the same potion, but he said, "No way."

I was now being permitted to go outside but for at least a month it was only for a walk around the block and I would be followed by a little vehicle from Friggins to make sure that I didn't attempt an escape.

Toward the very end, I was at last allowed to take a cab into downtown Clayton for an hour.

I went straight to a drugstore and bought a non-prescription box of sleeping pills called Nytol.

I found that it blurred my vision so I gave it up.

Then one day, in downtown Clayton, I went into a doctor's office, identified myself as Clemence Otte— the name of a brother of my German grandmother— and said that I was in town for a convention and was unable to sleep and would he please prescribe some Seconal for me.

The doctor insisted upon giving me a physical examination. He noted my cardiac trouble and gave me an EKG. After that he wrote me a prescription for exactly three pinkies . . .

That very same afternoon, when I returned to Friggins, I was summoned to Dr. Levy's office. He announced that I was to be released the next day, after my confinement of three months.

My first night home, the Christmas holidays, 1969.

Mother and I sat before the downstairs TV to watch a showing of my *Roman Spring of Mrs. Stone*. Mother would not shut up, she chatted all through it despite my continual pleas that she let me hear the dialogue.

Foiled in that, I just sat and watched the grace and tragic style of Vivien Leigh. I think that film is a poem. It was the last important work of both Miss Leigh and of the director, José Quintero, a man who is as dear to my heart as Miss Leigh is.

In the last months of Frankie's life, Vivien gave a party to which she invited Frankie.

It was his last time out.

Vivien centered the whole dinner party around him with an intuitive sympathy that will always endear her memory to me. She did it without seeming to do it . . .

Having known madness, she knew how it was to be drawing close to death.

Drawing close to death she was, too, although it was not yet known . . .

My first night out of Friggins, after the TV show, I asked Mother if I could have a cup of cocoa. She searched endlessly, it seemed, about the kitchen and then she said, "Susie has 'toted' it home."

Susie was her black maid for half a lifetime. And later Mother found the cocoa in the kitchen cupboard.

Poor Susie and poor Miss Edwina!

When Susie went home at night, Mother would loosen the four bolts on the front door, peek out fearfully, then slam the door shut, and cry out to Susie, "Susie, you can't go yet. There are some blacks on the corner waiting for the bus."

And one night, Susie laughed and said, "Mizz Williams, none of 'em blacker than me."

And now Miss Edwina accuses Dakin of keeping "a young black lady" upstairs so she, Miss Edwina, has to remain on the first floor of the house . . .

Frankie's enlarged passport photo stares at me from the back of the writing desk: it disturbs me. I turn it face down among the pages of my poem "Old Men Go Mad at Night."

It is extremely unattractive and humiliating and sleep-destroying to still be at my age a sensualist as well as a romanticist.

Earlier in the day, in fact at noon, I learned that Michael York had read *Out Cry*, the latest version of it, and had made a verbal commitment to costar in it. There is a difficulty about taxes—but my agent Billy Barnes thinks that he and Merrick can work that out.

Once I was dining at Joe Allen's with the wise and lovely actress Ruth Ford, who seems to have been born with more worldly wisdom than I have accumulated even at this point in life. I began to speak of my loneliness, the need for a hired companion.

"Hire a companion," she advised me, "but don't have him double in bed. You can always find a pickup on the street."

"Oh, Christ, you don't understand. There's nothing emptier, nothing more embarrassing than a street-corner pickup. Usually you get crabs and you're lucky if you don't get the clap and each time a little bit of your heart is chipped off and thrown into a gutter."

She had no answer to that: her beautiful face was enigmatic and grave.

"Then what is the answer," I asked?

(No change of expression on that noble Southern face.)

So many people seem to have been unable to comprehend why I found it necessary, in the summer of 1971, to sever my professional relationship with Audrey Wood.

The break has been attributed, I suppose, to paranoia, gross ingratitude, and to a general collapse of moral fiber in me. I think I should give you, as honestly as my own perceptions allow, my own side of the story.

It is true that Audrey had represented me from 1939 to 1971, but the representation had somehow worn itself out, during the last ten years of its exceptionally long duration.

Perhaps because of her husband's failing health, as well as my own alienated life-style and addiction to pills, liquor, and "feel-good" shots, Audrey became, or appeared to me to become, detached from my increasingly desperate circumstances in the sixties.

After Frank's death, no one was able to help me out of the almost clinical depression into which I sank.

It appeared to me that only Maria made a true effort to provide me with the personal concern that I needed so critically at that time.

The break with Audrey occurred through one of my hysterical "mad scenes" before the opening of a new play. It took place, I am ashamed to say, in the presence of several witnesses, convened in Donald Madden's dressing room after a preview of an early production of *Out Cry* at the Ivanhoe Theatre in Chicago, in 1971.

I had worked a very long time on *Out Cry* and it was especially close to the marrow of my being, wherever that is. The first preview of the play had been attended largely by young people who had given the play, brilliantly performed by Donald Madden and Eileen Herlie, a very heartening response. But it did not seem to me that Audrey responded to the play and its reception that night with any appreciable warmth. If Audrey had not still been so very close and important to me it might not have mattered so much.

The second preview had been pre-empted by a society of theatre-goers called something like the Sarah Siddons Sisters. They were mostly matrons with an austere and outdated attitude toward theatrical adventures such as *Out Cry*. They gave it a very cool reception that night. And—about this I may have been deluded by my inbuilt anxieties—it seemed to me that Audrey was more agreeably affected by the Sarah Siddons reception than by the relative enthusiasm of the younger audience the night before.

In Donald Madden's dressing room I became a sort of madman. I glared at Audrey and said to her, "You must have been pleased by the audience reaction tonight. You've wanted me dead for ten years. But I'm not going to die."

I did not shout at her, I spoke to her with a quiet ferocity, but it was a dreadful thing for me to say, even though Audrey must have known from long experience the shattered state of my nerves before the official opening of a play in which I am very deeply emotionally involved.

With her customary dignity, she made no response to my outburst in Madden's dressing room. But she did not remain in Chicago for the opening. She flew back to New York.

Some very wild stories have accrued about that occurrence. It was even said that I had "beaten her up" physically. I protest! I have never struck a woman in my life. (It has also been said that I locked Maria in my bedroom at the Hotel Ambassador East in Chicago and threatened to jump out the window if she tried to escape!)

None of these stories—need I say?—have a grain of truth in them. But certainly much grotesque humor. However, what I did and the way that I did it do very little indeed to reinforce whatever claim I may have to being a dependably rational person on all occasions.

I sincerely doubt that I've ever wanted to hurt anyone in my life, but it is all but impossible to go through a lifetime without inflicting hurt on someone, and it is most likely to be a person you care for deeply.

I cared deeply for Audrey and I believe I still do, though to an extent quite naturally reduced by the decade of neglect.

With passing time I trust that those ten years will be dimmed out of my recollections of a truly remarkable woman who has deserved the esteem of the professional world in which she worked and who has been a brilliant representative for some notable writers.

To me she was much like a family member on whom I was particularly dependent. Her reaction to a new piece of my work was always that which first and most concerned me: that is, hers and Kazan's.

Perhaps if my feelings for her had been limited to professional ones, I would not have been so disturbed and finally so outraged when her concern for me—once so great and sincere, or so it seemed—appeared to ebb, so that I found myself alone as a child lost or an old dog abandoned. . . .

# 11

What is it like being a writer? I would say it is like being free.

I know that some writers aren't free, they are professionally employed, which is quite a different thing.

Professionally, they are probably better writers in the conventional sense of "better." They have an ear to the ground of best-seller demands: they please their publishers and presumably their public as well.

But they are not free and so they are not what I regard a true writer as being.

To be free is to have achieved your life.

It means any number of freedoms.

It means the freedom to stop when you please, to go where and when you please, it means to be voyager here and there, one who flees many hotels, sad or happy, without obstruction and without much regret.

It means the freedom of being. And someone has wisely observed, if you can't be yourself, what's the point of being anything at all?

I am not a frequent reader nor quoter of Scriptures and yet I love a piece of advice which occurs among them:

"Let thy light so shine among men that they see thy good works and glorify thy Father which is in heaven."

There is a New Journalism, there is a New Criticism, there is a new look and style of cinema and theatre, of practically everything that we live with, but what I think we most need is a New Morality.

And I think we've arrived at a point where that is a necessity of continued and bearable existence . . .

I woke up just now explaining to the dark bedroom, sweetly shared not by a stranger of the night, this very Blanche sort of cry, "Oh, but my heart would break."

I am sure it was just a sort of Southern extravagance of statement and not a true *cri de coeur:* and be assured that I do not mean that "a Blanche sort of cry" isn't or couldn't be a true cri de coeur. In fact nearly all of her cries to the world in her season of desperation have survived because they were true cries of her embattled heart; that is what gave them the truth which has made them live on, echoing in the hearts of so many known and unknown ladies. But this sounds not like me, not even me in the Victorian Suite. It lacks the humor of Blanche, and it is that humor, along with the truth, that has made a Blanche a relatively imperishable creature of the stage, reincarnated on stage in major productions in recent years, one on the West Coast with Jon Voight as Stanley and one on the East Coast, at Lincoln Center, directed by Ellis Rabb and starring as Blanche his former wife, Rosemary Harris.

This day got off on three wrong feet and does not seem likely to acquire the distinction of a normal tripod, assuming there is such a thing and I take nothing for granted.

I slept late yesterday morning and had to lunch alone in the restaurant downstairs. I killed a half bottle of Chianti Ruffino and went back up to bed. Loneliness assailed me like a wolf pack with rabies, so—lacking my little red address book left in Venice —I had to consult the telephone directory for a madam I knew of, to send over a paid companion. I think he must have read and remembered my story, "Desire and the Black Masseur" as he gave my tired old body the roughest pounding and squeezing I've experienced ever.

"Hey, now, I'm not a masochist."

Well, he had me turn front and back, back and front several times, it went on for an hour and I must confess I began to feel relaxed.

I do have plans for the near future in addition to the inevitable one of death. I will move to Southern Italy or Sicily and I will fulfill my promise to acquire a nice bit of land on which to raise goats and geese and to finish one more play.

I can't stand the present kind of Italian "*borghese*" hustlers as exhibited in the north of that phallic peninsula, but I'll never forget the sweetness of the "*contadini*," especially on that occasion when, having quarreled with Frankie, I split for Barcelona in my town-coupe Jaguar with a thermos of martinis and wrapped that elegant car around a tree when a truck swung out of a side road and my car wouldn't hold the road when I turned to avoid it and my portable Olivetti flew out of the back seat and hit me right smack on the back of my head, knocking me out for I don't know how long. And I came to and discovered myself surrounded by contadini, nearly all holding toward me in trembling hands their little glasses of vino or *liquore* and their sweetness and concern.

I want to be among them when I die on a *letto matrimoniale* and with that euphoric image of a lovely young gardener who can double as chauffeur.

Why not? A persistent dream has meaning, and is sometimes fulfilled.

Out of Friggins in 1970, and home to Key West, where I was confronted by what seemed to me maddening evidence that Ryan had not expected me to survive. He had not only built an exorbitantly costly kitchen with a big stained-glass window as if it were a cathedral but he had had erected a completely new patio that seemed to belong in Beverly Hills. My survival and my return to Key West were such an obvious disappointment and—yes, you might say an affront—to His Lordship.

He had been gaily cruising the town in the steady company of a lady who shared his profligate habits. She came, at his invitation, to dinner one night. I slammed into the bedroom and informed him, when he followed, that I would not come out until she had left the house.

Pitiful! (For him.) He had to drive her home . . .

A week or so later Ryan himself was evicted. It was my dear friend Mary Louise Manning who engineered that imperative action.

I had refused to host a large party that he had arranged at a very expensive restaurant; he had gotten up in a rage and stalked out when I said I had not invited any of the guests and that I was not entertaining them.

About midnight I was seated in the living room with Mary Louise Manning, the composer Alec Wilder, and John Young, when Ryan came in drunk and evil and began to taunt me.

I took him on, verbally. Mary Louise grabbed my wrist and then said to Ryan, "Tom's pulse is racing, he's in no condition for this, pack your things and get out of the house right away."

She told John Young to stay with me that night and he remained there, as secretary pro tem, through the spring of 1970 as I gradually and painfully recuperated from the nearly fatal confinement at Friggins.

Confinement has always been the greatest dread of my life: that can be seen in my play *Out Cry*.

I considered *Out Cry* a major work and its misadventure on Broadway has not altered that personal estimate of it, especially since I was able, between production and publication, to edit out the material

that impeded its flow, and to improve that opening
monologue which had been mangled by dissension between author and director and by the latter's refusal
to attempt rewrites submitted in Washington. My
feelings toward the director became very bitter because of his autocratic behavior. I was still convinced
that Genevieve Bujold opposite Michael York could
have given the play a drawing power that would have
held it on Broadway until it found its audience. Cara
Duff-MacCormick is a gifted young actress but her
name and her stage presence were insufficient for
*Out Cry*'s very special requirements. At the interval
on opening night at the Lyceum, I heard someone
descending from the balcony with me observe that
the play had been better in its Chicago tryout the year
before, and I turned to the stranger and said, "Thanks,
I agree."

Still, it held the audience on opening night: there
were no coughs, no fidgeting in seats: there was an
atmosphere of attentive gravity. Nevertheless I felt
the production was doomed and had arranged for a
limousine to pick me up at the theatre half an hour before the final curtain and whisk me (with my friend)
out to La Guardia, for a red-eye flight to Miami. I
understand that the actors received an ovation at the
curtain and certainly both deserved them. Dear Michael had worn himself to the bone. Little Cara had
stood her ground like a Trojan, and possibly she, best
of all involved, aside from the author, understood and
loved the play's meaning. She had a tendency, off-
stage, to be carried away by emotion, and at a lunch
in Washington she had turned to me and said, "I
think it's the best play ever written."

And she blushed when I laughed at this youthful
extravagance of feeling.

Oh, but my God, how I do need these youthful ex-
travagances of response which are now the breath of
life to me!

The daily papers of Manhattan did not destroy the play: they were not "money notices" but exhibited no impulse to destroy.

Clive Barnes was cautiously respectful. With the exception of Leonard Harris, I disregard TV reviews. I suppose they were generally negative.

To say that I disregard TV reviews is hardly the total truth. How could I dare to disregard any review which determines the life or death of a production? What I meant was that I place no particular value upon their critical faculty. However it was not I, but David Merrick, who barred a TV critic from the Manhattan premiere.

It took me a full year, at least, to recover from the Lyceum production. I suspect that I am not yet recovered from it and that this languid attitude which I feel toward completing *The Red Devil Battery Sign* and the other play, *This Is*, stems from that year-old wound: the bleeding is slow and protracted.

Suddenly one gets the act together again and goes on: there is no alternative to it but death in my case ...

I have suddenly undertaken to correct what I've gradually come to recognize as the principal structural flaw in *Small Craft Warnings*, the long monologue of the bartender Monk coming directly after the long monologue of Quentin, the homosexual film-scripter, which is much the most effective piece of writing in the play, and since the play's values are so largely verbal, Quentin's speech is obviously the climax, at least of Act One. I have, for the past few days, submitted three drafts of rewrites, opening the play with Monk's monologue and having him open the bar. This gives a feeling of form to the play: its beginning with Monk opening his place, alone and frightened of his angina, and in the end closing the place, having accepted as a companion, *faute de mieux*, the pitiful derelict, Violet, whom he has at least persuaded to take a shower upstairs.

I realize how very old-fashioned I am as a drama-
tist to be so concerned with classic form but this does
not embarrass me, since I feel that the absence of
form is nearly always, if not always, as dissatisfying to
an audience as it is to me. I persist in considering *Cat*
my best work of the long plays because of its classic
unities of time and place and the kingly magnitude of
Big Daddy. Yet I seem to contradict myself. I
write so often of people with no magnitude, at least
on the surface. I write of "little people." But are there
"little people"? I sometimes think there are only little
conceptions of people. Whatever is living and feeling
with intensity is not little and, examined in depth, it
would seem to me that most "little people" are living
with that intensity that I can use as a writer.

Was Blanche a "little person"? Certainly not. She
was a demonic creature, the size of her feeling was
too great for her to contain without the escape of madness. And what about Miss Alma? Was she a "little
person"? Certainly not. Her passion gave stature to
the drama as it does to Lee Hoiby's opera.

Make of the paradox of my life what you will, I
have made an honest effort to make sense of it.

Well, it's true I'm a fighter and have come a long
way from St. Louis, but there has been a long period
of defeat in my life, ever since Frankie left. But
then I felt my life was as finished as his and I gave up
the battle. It's different now. I have a desire to continue, and there are important new projects.

My God, I sound like Nixon!

Here I would like to insert, more briefly than its
dramatic content may seem to call for, my voyage to
Bangkok in 1970. I went on the voyage under the
bizarre misapprehension that I was to undergo there
an operation for suspected breast cancer, the surgery
to be performed by none other than the surgeon of the
King of Thailand.

During my long and inadvertent cruise of the Mediterranean earlier that year I had noticed a little swelling under my left nipple. It gave me no pain and caused me little concern. But when I was visiting New Orleans shortly afterwards, I visited a well-known doctor for consultation about my heart condition. He noticed the swelling in my chest.

He said to me, "Carcinoma of the breast is extremely rare in men but rare things do occur."

I assured him that I would certainly agree with him on that.

He advised me to cancel my plans for a trip to Bangkok and to have the swelling removed at once. But I had my heart set on continued voyaging, and my determination to proceed to the Orient was reinforced by the assurance of a friend that he knew the king's surgeon personally, and I would be accepted as his patient.

The American doctor was unhappy about the delay involved in another transoceanic cruise before the surgery could be performed, but my course could not be shaken, and so early that fall I set out upon a lovely cruise of the Pacific, shadowed only slightly by the progressive swelling and the prospect of surgery in the fabled city of Bangkok.

The S.S. *President Cleveland* put in at several ports on the way there, including Honolulu, and I believe it was in Honolulu that I had a couple of mai tais on the night ashore and revealed to some talkative persons that I might, at the end of the voyage, be subjected to an operation for cancer of the breast.

It astounded me what a commotion this casually mentioned prospect caused among the journalists of Yokohama, our next port of call. I was surrounded, immediately on debarkation, by photographers and newsmen and interpreters.

As the flashbulbs bedazzled me, the interpreters

kept shouting: "Is it true you've got cancer, Mr. Williams?"

This visit, lasting only a couple of days, was to be my last encounter with Yukio Mishima. I was staying at a hotel in Yokohama while the ship was in port, and Yukio drove out to the port one evening to have dinner with me.

At this point I suspect he had already decided upon his act of hara-kiri, which took place only a month or two later while I was still in Bangkok. I noticed when he entered the hotel bar that there was a tension and gravity about him which leads me to believe that he had already decided upon the act, which I think was performed not because of political concern about the collapse of the old traditions in Japan but because he felt that, with the completion of his trilogy, he had completed his major work as an artist.

It was touching to me that his principal concern was over my drinking, although I had, at dinner, only a cocktail and a little wine. He phoned me the next day, to tell me to watch my drinking habits . . .

After Yokohama we put in at Hong Kong. From there I flew to Bangkok. I stayed at the Hotel Orient, occupying a suite which had been sanctified by the former occupancy of Noël Coward and Somerset Maugham.

The news of my (alleged) breast cancer had followed me there. No sooner was I settled in my suite than the social hostess of the hotel phoned me to say that newsmen were awaiting me for a conference in the dining room below.

This was true. A long table was occupied by excited journalists, interpreters and cameramen.

The first question put to me was a shocker.

"Is it true, Mr. Williams, that you have come to Bangkok to die?"

Having come to Bangkok with quite different purposes in mind, I burst into laughter.

"The only place I'd go to die, if I had any choice," I told them, "is Rome, not because it's the home of the Vatican but because it's always been my favorite city in the world."

I promised you a brief story and I'll try to stick to that promise.

It turned out, unsurprisingly, that the surgeon who was to perform the operation for suspected breast cancer was not only *not* the king's surgeon but had never, he laughingly admitted, met a single member of the royal family. He was just a surgeon of the Siamese army with medical training in the States.

I liked him, though.

The operation was performed under casual, if not primitive, circumstances: I was still more worried about my heart than this alleged breast cancer, and all the while the operation was performed I held my little bottle of nitroglycerin tablets in my hand. It was performed under local anesthesia which wore off *in medias res;* the operation lasted about an hour, and the pathological report was gynecomastia, which is a fairly commonplace enlargement of the male mammary gland in cases where the liver has been abused by heavy drinking at some earlier time in life.

I had no hospital room reserved in the little clinic. Immediately after the operation's conclusion I had a long swig of sherry. Then I left with a little company of Thai youths to the best restaurant in town, where we feasted on steak *au poivre* with vintage wines.

The rest of my stay in Bangkok was a dream which I hope to have again someday. I wish that I had space here to extol its exotic delights!

I returned to the States via San Francisco, and for the first time in my life I found my name hitting the headlines. The headline went something like this: "Tennessee Williams jokes about Cancer and Death." And I was described as "ugly, elegant and arrogant."

All that was five years ago and now I am looking for

another good excuse to return to Bangkok: perhaps I
already have one, of a nonsurgical nature.

This is the first time since the summer of 1946 that
I have attempted to write with another person in the
room with me. In 1946 it was Carson McCullers who
sat at one end of the long Nantucket work table and I
at the other, she dramatizing *The Member of the
Wedding* and I struggling with the tortures of the
damned, meaning Miss Alma Winemiller of *Summer
and Smoke*. But the other person now is a young
prodigy—not yet protégé—and I am quickly forget-
ting his presence, it is a warm and dreamy presence
like that of Carson, and he is as absorbed in working
on the rental typewriter the management sent us up
as I am on knocking out these trivialities.

I have just hung up the phone on a call from Eric
Mann, the revolutionary who once, last winter, spent
the night sleeping on the living-room floor here. He
had gotten in the habit of sleeping on hard surfaces
in the prisons of Amerika, as he'd call it. I don't know
how deep I am into this Kafka spelling of a beautiful
word like America; in fact, I suspect it is not my
thing at all.

My thing is revolution, personal and artistic, I
trust, but not militant and not underground, and I feel
it will accomplish itself, possibly even during my lifetime, without general violence.

Violence! All of my old psychiatrists, but especially
Dr. Lawrence Kubie, the Frenchman, told me that I
had it in me, and right he was about that. Except
that my violence is all verbal.

And yet I do not run away from possible physical
combat, and this brings me to a startling incident
which occurred during intermission last night at the
New Theatre. I was seated in the men's dressing room
when all at once all the technical people and the
beautiful (bit-part) policeman rushed into the audi-

torium where violence had erupted. I leapt up and broke through their ranks to confront the chief instigator of the disturbance. I didn't know what I was saying or doing, it had been a strange day, but I heard myself shouting, "We've all put our hearts in this play. If you don't like it, I am the man who wrote it, talk to me!" Then I found myself confronting a young man about twice my height, his face inflamed with frustrated fury. At once everybody was around me, trying to hustle me out of the fracas. The important thing is that I wasn't scared, although he might have plastered me into the woodwork, so to speak. It seems that I am dangerously impervious to what may happen to me when I'm insulted and confront the insulter.

You see, I do love my "Small Craft."

I felt disoriented, because of the shock of learning that *Small Craft* will run two weeks short of the six months I had in mind for it, at the New Theatre. So I went to my doctor and he gave me a fairly powerful shot of Ritallin, a drug related to speed, and one which was given me by a hotel doctor in Chicago last summer when I called him and told him that I didn't feel strong enough to get out of bed but I did get out of bed after he gave me the shot.

I've always gotten out of bed after shots of speed so yesterday evening, coming down from the Ritallin injection, I performed like a mad creature at the top of the play. I garbled my lines and then I said to Gene Fanning, who plays Monk, "Have I said that already? Okay, I'll say it again." And when that goddamn weather broadcast comes over the (fake) radio: Monk says to me, "Small craft warning, Doc." And I turn to the audience, full front, and I say, "Yes, that's the title of the play and I'm the star," the audience howled with merriment. But I can assure you that poor Gene Fanning—who loves the part he plays and plays it legitimately always—glared poisoned daggers at me.

Unfortunately I am the "star": they put my name above that of Peg Murray and I hasten to assure you that I have protested. Hell, I'm not even an actor, I am just appearing on stage to beef up the summer box-office. Yet I have something. I know how to be outrageous. And when I wish to play legitimately now, I think that I do it and well. For instance last night, when I (in the role of Doc) came back to the bar after killing off a pregnant woman, whose premature child was stillborn—well, Doc doesn't exactly kill her off, literally, but, as Doc confesses to Monk, while she was hemorrhaging to death he could have called for an ambulance for her. But Doc says that he considered the probable consequences to himself, and while he was considering these consequences, the woman died.

But I'm not really like Doc, you know. I wouldn't have paused a moment to call the ambulance for her, despite the probable consequences to me as a doctor who'd lost his license through alcoholism and was still clandestinely practicing.

Oh, there are similarities between me and Doc, age-wise and even perhaps in depth of self-abasement. But thank God I would have called the ambulance for the little woman regardless of consequences, not just given the man living with her in the trailer a fifty-dollar bill I'd received that day for performing an abortion.

You see how this play, closing at the New Theatre the end of this week, lives hauntingly in me still? I will not permit it to close. In New York, yes, but I'll somehow compel ECCO to give it the tour it has earned.


After several nights without sleeping medication, I managed yesterday to score for two dozen Nembutals from a doctor and I made up for the nearly sleepless nights past by sleeping on a single yellow jacket, as Marion called them, from midnight until 9 A.M. I got up with the expectation that the long sleep would restore my energy for work, but the reverse was soon apparent.

My condition as I attempted to resume work on my story "Sabbatha and Solitude" was next of kin to comatose, so I gave it up after the slight accomplishment of getting the pages into some kind of order.

About that story: it is a satire of sorts but I'm afraid it doesn't come off.

As a matter of fact, it is almost incoherent at points. Something is happening to me that's not very propitious and at a most inconvenient time, since I am very close, now, to the production of my last major work for the theatre. It may be that the imminence of this event has unnerved me. But haven't I always been unnerved? —So that excuse doesn't hold much water or even—what's less than water?—precipitation or dew?

Still, the story will someday come together. Given time enough, a piece of work does. And what's the hurry?

I look back on the months during which I have kept this chronicle of time present and past. I realize that it puts me in a less than flattering light but that doesn't violate the premise—can a premise be violated?

I need somebody to laugh with.

Since my release from Friggins Division in the holiday season at the end of '69 I have almost constantly needed someone to laugh with, and I realize, now, that this has been somewhat to the detriment of my work. Too much of it has been in the form of hysterical laughter, as humorless, at heart, as it was loud in volume.

It wasn't easy to live as a writer with a brain damaged by three convulsions in one morning and a heart so damaged by coronaries that going to sleep each night is always attended by the uneasy and sometimes fearful suspicion that you may not wake up in the morning.

Mornings, I love them so much! —Their triumph over night.

It sometimes appears to me that I have lived a life of morning after morning, since it is and has nearly always been the mornings in which I've worked.

A friend tells me that she has phoned a friend who works for the New York *Times,* to ask for a copy of the obituary which that *éminence grise* of American newspapers has undoubtedly already placed in its files, since she has survived to a certain age, and obituaries must be produced with expedition when a "celebrity" dies.

There is something macabre about this journalistic practice.

I say this not because I doubt that the death of American artists should be reported quickly after their demise but because I feel that the chief endowment of any true artist is the honesty of his intention, and that this cannot be explored in a bit of copy listing his dates and honors, and mention of his principal works, but that he is entitled to a reflective study of both his life and his "ouevre."

The word "ouevre" is pretentious. Why not just his work?

Work!!—the loveliest of all four-letter words, surpassing even the importance of love, most times.

What most alarms me is my progressive difficulty in sleeping: it has never been this difficult before.

It is as if I were unconsciously haunted by something that prevents me from sleeping more than the minimal time that the sedation is active.

The impending productions?

All possible misadventures can be survived with a little old-cat licking of wounds, especially since I will be free to immigrate permanently to that "little farm in Sicily" to "raise goats and geese."

I suspect what I am haunted by is something that

I am concealing from myself, unconsciously but wisely.

Perhaps the desperate condition of my mother, which does continually prey upon my "mind" but to which I have hardly given adequate attention. I might attempt to justify myself by my dread of returning to St. Louis, so great that I feel not physically able to undertake it.

The illness of my sister? That seems closer to being a plausible cause. And yet even that does not seem to suffice . . .

Someone interviewing me asked me why writers are so preoccupied with disease and death.

"Any artist dies two deaths," I told him, "not only his own as a physical being but that of his creative power, it dies with him."

A play is submitted to so many people and to so many conditions, alterable or not, and to such bafflingly varied interpretations by those to whom it's submitted that it's a wonder the author isn't stricken with incurable vertigo and plummeted irretrievably into a pit of snakes and madness.

And yet, today, as I complete my revisions for the published version of *Out Cry*, I don't feel any disequilibrium at all. The weather is fair; I'm surrounded by close friends; and tonight I will see a preview of *A Streetcar Named Desire*, the leading parts performed by actors who understand and love it, and the revival staged by the gifted young director James Bridges.

If there are stop signs ahead, they are not yet visible enough for me to stop going on . . .


A man must live through his life's duration with his own little set of fears and angers, suspicions and vanities, and his appetites, spiritual and carnal.

Life is built of them and he is built of life.

The umbilical cord is a long, long rope of blood that has swung him as an aerialist on an all but endless

Trapeze, oh, such a long, long way, from the first living organism that gave birth to another.

Define it as the passion to create which is all that we know of God.

Is that an agnostic thing to say? I think not.

Perhaps you will accede to my claim of exceptional honesty, both as writer and man. And if you knew me outside of this book, you would find me a man who values kindness and patience with others.

Most of my life has been spent with intimate companions of a complex and difficult nature. It is only recently that I have learned how to accept the bargain, by which I mean to treasure the lovely aspects of their natures, which all have possessed, and to stoically live through their abrasive humors. After all, none of them have found me exactly easy to exist, and travel about, with.

For two and a half years I have been companioned by a stormy young man, given to verbal abuse in the lingo that he acquired during his military service in Southeast Asia. He says that he loves me. I ask myself, "How could he?"

If he should leave me today, I would have the deep satisfaction of knowing that while he lived with me he had completed two of the most distinguished modern novels that I have read.

If he should leave me today—but I don't think he will...

We are both Southerners, we are both writers, and both of us are committed to honesty in our work and our lives.

About honesty in work: There are two kinds: honesty with taste, and honesty without it.

I started out on this book in 1972: it is now 1975. Consequently, the present passages skip back and forth in time.

This is not a precedent in a book concerning the life of a man. The very clever, and often brilliant, Garson Kanin wrote a biography of Somerset Maugham with even more disregard for chronological order than I've attempted: and I liked it that way. Now time past and time present have come to a point of convergence in this thing.

This evening Miss Rose came down from Stoney Lodge for dinner. Dear Tatiana, her companion, was not available so the young writer and I escorted her to the St. Regis for dinner.

Did I mention that the last time she came into town, conversation among us turned to foreign travel and I asked her if she wouldn't like to visit England? My friend Maria, the Lady St. Just, has offered her a standing invitation to be her guest at Wilbury, which I think would enchant Miss Rose. I mentioned this invitation, and added that I thought it could be arranged for her to meet the Queen of England. And without a moment's hesitation or the least lack of conviction, she replied, "I *am* the Queen of England."

I suppose if you live in a dream world, it is nice to be a queen in it.

Often she does have a regal air about her which seems completely natural. When entering a restaurant, she lifts her hand or nods to strangers.

This evening her attention was particularly taken to children we passed in our short walk to the park. She waved at them delightedly and they all waved back.

"Who was that child, Rose?"

"My son," she said.

(Heir to the throne of England?)

The last two times she's come here she's brought along her toothbrush and dental cream, apparently hoping to spend the night. It would obviously be nice for her to have a trip: and why not England?

Maria still has her fantastic love of fun, and it would be fun to establish Rose at the lovely Palladian mansion, Wilbury, as a lady sovereign, with ladies curtsying to her and gentlemen bowing. And after her

heroic endurance of the ordeal of madness, head un-
bowed, spirit never broken, why should she not be
accorded such homage, as Queen of England or not?

And have I mentioned that she now thinks that
Mother (Dowager Queen?) is among the patients at
Stoney Lodge? Tatiana says that she gives this surrogate parent a little pat on the shoulder and says,
"Hello, Mother." Receiving and expecting no response,
she goes on by. Tonight I asked her, "How is Mother
doing at the Lodge?"

"Oh, she's fine."

"What's she doing?"

"Sitting."

Carson McCullers was very fond of Rose and we often took her to visit Carson in Nyack. Always over-
flowing with *tendresse*, Carson once said, "Oh, Rose,
come here and kiss me."

"No, thank you," said Rose, "I have halitosis."

Another evening Carson had invited us to dinner
which was intractably delayed, and Miss Rose, accustomed to eating early, became more and more restless.
She always addressed Carson as "C" for some reason,
and at last she insisted on going into the kitchen to
see how dinner was progressing. Well, it was retro-
gressing, in fact the roast had burned.

"C," said Rose, "I'm afraid the roast has burned."

Carson was too dreamily involved in her Bourbon to
be concerned about this report, but Miss Rose was not.

"C, will you please get up and put on your clothes
and my brother can afford to take us out to a restaurant."

It took Carson quite a while to get up, of course,
and then she asked Rose to help her dress.

Miss Rose was not so disposed.

"I'm afraid you'll have to manage alone."

Carson and her husband Reeves have come into
Paris from their "Ancien Presbytère" in the country.
They are staying in the same hotel as Frank and I,

the Pont Royal. It is the evening of the Paris premiere of a Magnani film, and, having received a summons to attend it, I'm getting into my tux when the phone rings. Carson is on the wire, greatly agitated.

"Oh, Tenn, darling, we've had to move from the fifth floor to the second because Reeves is threatening to jump out the window. Please come at once and try to dissuade him."

This was a summons even more urgent than Anna's, so I rushed to their room.

"What's this about suicide, Reeves? You can't be serious about it!"

"Yes, completely."

"But why?"

"I've discovered that I am homosexual."

Not foreseeing, of course, that he was really going to kill himself a year or two later, I burst out laughing.

"Reeves, the last thing I'd do is jump out a window because I'm homosexual, not unless I was forced to be otherwise."

Both the McCullerses were amused by this, and Reeves's suicidal threat was put aside for a time.

I arrived late for the Magnani premiere. Her eyes were daggers as I slunk into her box.

At the Ancien Presbytère, to which the McCullerses returned, there was a cherry tree which Reeves kept suggesting to Carson that they should hang themselves from.

He even had two ropes for the purpose. But Carson was not intrigued by this proposition.

One of her relentless illnesses forced her to return to Paris for medical treatment.

Reeves drove her in, but on the way he produced the two ropes and again exhorted her to hang herself with him.

She pretended to acquiesce, but she persuaded him to stop at a roadside tavern and get them a bottle of wine to fortify themselves for the act.

Soon as he entered the tavern, Carson clambered out of the car and hitchhiked a ride to the American Hospital in a suburb of Paris.

She never saw poor Reeves alive again. He killed himself, some months later, with a bottle of barbiturates and booze.

How lightly I write of these dreadful remembrances!

How else could I present them to you, so few of whom have known Carson and Reeves?

Yesterday evening I was interviewed, for the first time in my life, by a drama critic of New York, no less than Walter Kerr.

I was scared. He declined to have lunch in La Veranda downstairs and wouldn't share the bottle of Soave that I brought up to the suite—I think I drank it all since no remnant of it remains in the living room.

But being with this reassuringly human man who fumbled quite a bit with his tape recorder and left one of the cassettes behind him—I didn't babble nervously about irrelevant matters.

Of course one never knows how an interview will come out any more than one knows how a review will. —Nor, indeed, how a play will.

My New Orleans cardiologist advised me, four years ago, to return to Key West and live like a crocodile, a piece of advice that I have ignored, not knowing how crocodiles live except sluggishly in a swamp, and that sort of life attracting me about as strongly as death.

"Walk softly and you'll go far"—As far as what?—I shall certainly try, despite this continual itch for action and travel.

Speaking of travel: This is the first summer since 1947 that I haven't been abroad, at least to Italy. Suddenly, lunching at the Woman's Exchange with my young friend, I dismissed the idea of Montreal, which isn't really abroad, and all thought of retreating again to New Orleans or Key West. The Cocaloony Key has little appeal for me in the hurricane season. And I began to discuss enthusiastically the idea of flying to Italy for September. It's probable I could take a pleasant little house for a month in Positano with most of the summer population gone, the water cool and clean, and I could do a few paintings and let some new writing project come to the surface, preferably not like a drowned cadaver but some living creature whose elements are water, air, and fire like Cleopatra's.

I could return stateside via London, spending a while with Maria; and the young writer, who dislikes her nearly as much as she does him, could fly back from Rome. In London I could try to interest the Royal Court or Hampstead Club Theatre in *The Latter Days of a Celebrated Soubrette* with Anne Meacham, with whom we dined this evening as her guests. She is still hopeful of getting a commitment from Peter Cook and Dudley Moore to appear with her: I am less hopeful of it and less interested. I think all the project needs now is an off-West End house and a good director who digs its fantastic humor and —Anne would say "Terror" but I think that element is exorcised by the wild black comedy that envelops it.

Quoting *Camino*'s Byron: "Make voyages, attempt them, there's nothing else."

I think it is now time for me to consider the question of whether or not I am a lunatic or a relatively sane person. I suspect that most of you who have read through this thing have already come to your own conclusion on the point, and it is probably not in my favor. With those of you, the suspected plurality, I say *non contendere*. You have your own separate world and your own separate standards of sanity to go with it. Most of you belong to something that offers a stabilizing influence: a family unit, a defined social position, employment in an organization, a more secure habit of existence. I live like a gypsy, I am a fugitive. No place seems tenable to me for long anymore, not even my own skin.

Sane and insane are legal terms, really. I don't believe that Lieutenant Calley, now become a legend, a symbol of mindless brutalities as the young officer who turned that muddy ditch red with the blood of defenseless civilians, from grandparents to infants, has been declared legally insane.

The question could be pursued with countless other examples of what passes for sanity in the world but it is a tedious question. And I turn back to its pertinence in regard to myself and I confess that I find myself exceedingly peculiar.

I have made a covenant with myself to continue to write, since I have no choice, it is so deeply rooted as a way of existence and a form of flight—but I shall probably not involve myself in any further productions except as writer and as spectator. I shall not flay myself nor permit myself to be flayed by the anxieties, the tensions, of participating in the transmutation of a written script to a Broadway stage.

Do I mean that? I must always wait and see, nowadays.

Death is the unavoidable eventuality which in most cases we avoid as long as we can, but which, finally, when all the possible options have expired, we must attempt to accept with as much grace as there remains in our command. None of that is surprising except perhaps to some hard core Christian Scientists. The nicest thing about death that I've read lately was in Stewart Alsop's book *Stay of Execution.* He wrote: "A dying man needs death like a very tired man needs sleep."

Of course needing a thing is not quite the same as wanting it.

In *Cat on a Hot Tin Roof*, Big Daddy remarks at one point in Act Two that a pig squeals but a man can keep a tight mouth about it. He says that the pig has an advantage. He has no idea of mortality. Animals go without knowing that they're going but when they go, they howl or squeal about it. A man, though, he can know and keep a tight mouth about it.

Ironically, in Act Three, Big Daddy howls vociferously with pain, and poor Big Mama, who did love him, rushes into the bedroom of Maggie and Brick for morphine to relieve his terminal anguish.

A couple of summers ago, when I had an operation at Doctors Hospital in Manhattan, I kept a tight mouth about my terror when they wheeled me into surgery and the anesthetist gave me the spinal injection from which I suspected I would not emerge. But when I did emerge in my hospital bed and they tore away the surgical gauze, I howled like an animal, or like Big Daddy in Act Three. Thank God they immediately gave me a strong Demerol tablet that put me out again. But soon the merciful sleep wore off, and the next day I described the night which had preceded it as "the night of the long knives."

I hope to die in my sleep, when the time comes, and I hope it will be in the beautiful big brass bed in my New Orleans apartment, the bed which is associated with so much love and Merlo in our New York apartments on East Fifty-eighth and East Sixty-fifth streets.

I have read that as brilliant a man and artist as Yukio Mishima had faith in reincarnation. If he did, he never discussed it with me.

I am unable to believe that there is anything but permanent oblivion after death. It is a dreadful apostasy with which to live a human life. I've been told that all straight lines in the universe are eventually curved and a curving line may eventually curve back to its beginning, which might be something in the nature of rebirth. But what a long time to wait, and if the thought of its remote possibility is a comfort, what a cold comfort it is, for you would be born again upon a planet turned to a slag-heap, if it existed at all. And among what other conditions I dread to imagine.

I am not sure, even, that it has been incontestably proven that space and the universe are curved in our sense of what is curved.

So, finally, we are left with either the simple faiths of our childhood, unacceptable to a mature person, or to—what?

What, indeed! The trivial distractions of daily and nightly existence with which we obscure the hushed but giant footsteps of our approaching end? The practice of meditation in solitude and, through it, the slow, the marvelously stoical transcendence of bodily self and its concerns?

I am certainly aware of the attractions in this Far Eastern way of reconciling one's self to the end of being one's self, but I am too Occidental a creature to follow it through without an opium pipe.

For me, what is there but to feel beneath me the steadily rising current of mortality and to summon from my blood whatever courage is native to it, and once there was a great deal.

Not long ago we dined with a very talented young black who was writing a history of jazz and popular music in Harlem. During the course of the meal he made such a wise and amusingly "black" remark, that I wrote it down on a paper napkin.

"God don't come when you want Him but He's right on time."

While waiting, what? Of course I will continue to work, but not to trick myself into supposing that what I now accomplish still has the vitality of my work at full tide, when it sprang like the torrents of spring.

*How perilously do these fountains leap*
*Whose reckless voyager along am I.*

(Lines from an early poem when I was bursting
with images but had not yet broken the confines of
iambic pentameter.)

What else while waiting?

Being a sensual creature—and why do I keep saying creature instead of man?—I will go on doing what
I am doing while waiting. I will comfort myself with
good wine and food but not to drunkenness and sati-
ety and grossness of the flesh. I will try to hang onto
those friends who have remained friends despite my
difficult, angry years which I think are now past. And
I will have, I still hope to have, both spiritual and carnal knowledge of a desirable young companion: not as
frequently, now, but at prudently spaced intervals.

I shall not indulge in vanity but I shall cling to
pride, two very different things, one being weak and
indulgent, the second being strong and a necessity of
survival with honor.

Do you think that I have told you my life story?

I have told you the events of my life, and described
as best I could, without legal repercussions, the dramatis personae of it.

But life is made up of moment-to-moment occurrences in the nerves and the perceptions, and try as
you may, you can't commit them to the actualities of
your own history.

The work of a fine painter, committed only to vision, abstract and allusive as he pleases, is better able
to create for you his moments of intensely perceptive
being. Jackson Pollock could paint ecstasy as it could
not be written. Van Gogh could capture for you moments of beauty, indescribable as descent into madness.

And those who painted and sculpted the sensuous
and the sensual of naked life in its moments of glory
made them palpable to you as we can never feel with

our fingertips and the erogenous parts of our flesh.

A poet such as the young Rimbaud is the only writer of whom I can think, at this moment, who could escape from words into the sensations of being, through his youth, turbulent with revolution, permitted articulation by nights of absinthe. And of course there is Hart Crane. Both of these poets touched fire that burned them alive. And perhaps it is only through self-immolation of such a nature that we living beings can offer to you the entire truth of ourselves within the reasonable boundaries of a book.

If that's the case, well, the inadequacies of this attempt to tell my life story, and believe me, I've tried to tell it, may be, surely must be, to my advantage, and I trust no serious disappointment to you.

This year Rose's Christmas was celebrated on New Year's Day (1975) since I had spent Christmas traveling "up country" and Rose received in advance only the token gift of a pair of pearl earrings. They match the pearl necklace that I had purchased at Saks with her dinner-gown, a lovely silvery dress called "pistachio green." I had visited Saks again the day before New Year's to get her important presents for the delayed Christmas: a beautiful silvery fur jacket and two silk blouses patterned with spring flowers. (Rose has by no means lost her frustrated passion for clothes, which caused her to devote so many pleasant hours in her girlhood to window-shopping in St. Louis's county stores. The problem now is finding closet space for her wardrobe at Stoney Lodge—most of her clothes have to be stored outside her room.)

Her *most* important gift of all, however, was conferred by the medical staff at Stoney Lodge. They consented to her spending three days in New York City with me and her companion whom I mentioned earlier, Tatiana, a white Russian refugee from "St. Petersburg." Tatiana is a charming lady in her seventies who is working "on call" as a practical nurse in New

York. It is necessary for Rose to be attended by a nurse because she is subject to occasional attacks of petit mal, a result of the scar tissue that remains as a memento of the lobotomy performed at Missouri State Sanitarium. I regard that as a tragically mistaken procedure, as I believe that without it Rose could have made a recovery and returned to what is called "normal life," which, despite its many assaults upon the vulnerable nature, is still preferable to an institution existence.

And so on New Year's afternoon, Tatiana and I went to Ossining in a hired limousine to pick up the *soi-disant* Queen of England. It was to be Rose's first real holiday in more years than I can easily remember, at least twenty-five, and both Tatiana and I were somewhat worried about how it would go.

Rose received us cordially and invited us into her new room, which was rather small but pleasant. She had no traveling bag but Tatiana had brought one along and Rose packed all that she could into it with amazing alacrity. She knew precisely where everything was and as she packed she announced that she was intending to stay with me for good. We thought it better not to advise her that the stay was limited to three days. While the nurses were providing Tatiana with Rose's medications, Rose and I waited in the reception room. On the floor was a girl stretched out on the carpet and going through grotesque contortions and facial grimaces. Miss Rose was not impressed. She stepped right over this prostrate figure, saying politely, "Excuse me," and sat on a sofa to light up a cigarette.

At Stoney Lodge, Rose is limited to three or four cigarettes a day but when she comes into town she is a chain-smoker. I showed her the Surgeon General's warning, on a pack of cigarettes, that they were dangerous to health. Rose pretended to be unable to read it, although, later, she could read a French menu in a restaurant with ease.

Aside from her snatching, at every opportunity, for cigarettes, the visit went off with great success. The second night Billy Barnes entertained us for dinner in his penthouse apartment, the delicious meal prepared by his sixty-eight-year-old black gentleman's gentleman whose name is Ernest Williams. Sometime before, when Rose first met Ernest, he told her that his name was Williams, too, and Rose smiled and said to him, "Just say that you are Welsh."

Rose is fond of the blacks, as I am, perhaps because of our devotion to our beautiful black nurse Ozzie when we were children in Mississippi. She always used to conclude her letters to me with, "Love to my children, white or black." I noticed that in New York, on the streets and in stores, Rose was continually waving to children of both races.

I feel a great affection for Tatiana. She is valiant and so warm-hearted. Afflicted badly with arthritis, she now has alarming dizzy spells when she moves suddenly. She makes light of it, but I am troubled, especially since she must continue to earn her living.

On the afternoon of the third day we went to the Fellini film *Amarcord*. Rose watched it delightedly. There were some scenes of far-out comic erotica which I thought would shock her. Not at all! When the visit was over, and Rose had reluctantly accepted the news that she couldn't stay permanently with us, Tatiana asked her what she'd enjoyed most. "That wonderful movie," Rose said. The film does not need more "quotes" but Fellini is welcome to that one from the self-proclaimed ruler of the British Isles.

The success of this little vacation has revived my old hope that Rose, with a nurse-companion, may be permitted to occupy the Coconut Grove, Florida, property which Marion Vaccaro and I selected for her so many years ago and which has increased in value from its purchase price of $40,000 to $150,000 and will probably still increase. She and Tatiana could, perhaps, both retire there with a nice housekeeper, or they could occupy an apartment in my New Orleans rental property.

Of course the realization of this dream is contingent upon a reversal of the downward trend in my own health.

In any case, you couldn't ask for a sweeter or more benign monarch than Rose, or, in my opinion, one that's more of a lady. After all, high station in life is earned by the gallantry with which appalling experiences are survived with grace.

# INDEX

"Accent of a Coming Foot, The" (Williams), 48
Actors' Studio, 204, 208, 210, 220, 230
Adams, Jim, 261, 264, 265
Adams, Stell, 261
Ahmanson Theatre, 197
Albus, Joanna, 140, 163, 166, 168
Alcohol
  Inge, 110–12
  McArthur, 186
  Taylor, 114
  Vaccaro, 82–83
  Williams, 25, 214, 220, 233, 245, 256, 261–62, 264, 272, 275, 288, 293, 299, 316
Alcoholics Anonymous, 112, 171
Alden, Hortense, 221
Alexander, Dr., 150
Algonquin Hotel, 134, 208
*All My Sons* (Miller), 163
Alpha Chi Omega, 44
Alpha Delta Pi, 34
Alpha Tau Omega, 31–34, 37–41, 54
Alsop, Stewart, 313
*Amarcord* (motion picture), 319
Ambasciatore Hotel, 180

*American Blues* (Williams), 6
*American Gothic* (Wood), 81
American Hospital, 176, 311
American Shakespeare Theatre, The, 50
Anderson, Dame Judith, 201
Andrews, Todd, 192, 193
*Anna Karenina* (motion picture), 174
*Antaeus*, 236
Appalachian Club, 148–49
Atkinson, Brooks, 107, 144, 191, 192
Austen, Jane, 56
Ayers, Bradley, 257
Ayers, Lemuel, 59, 61, 96, 99, 257
Ayers, Shirley, 257

*Baby Doll* (Williams—motion picture), 214
Baddeley, Hermione, 247–50, 254
Bankhead, Tallulah, 124, 231, 248–53
  Williams on, 76–77
Barber, Samuel, 183
Barnes, Billy, 43, 100, 160–161, 197–98, 226, 242, 271, 274, 275, 287, 319
Barnes, Clive, 296
Barnes Hospital, 41

Barrymore, Diana, 222–24, 246

Barter Theatre, 244, 253

*Bateau Ivre* (Rimbaud), 155

Batista, Fulgencio, 85

*Battle of Angels* (Williams), 65, 74, 76, 79, 80, 87, 131, 185, 217
  Boston closing, 78–79
  rewriting of, 81

Baxley, Barbara, 110–11, 114, 208

Bedford, Brian, 267

Bedford, Patrick, 43

Bedinger, Mrs., 18

Bedinger, Albert, 17–18, 19

Bérard, Bésé, 187

Berenson, Bernard, 184

Berenson, Marisa, 275–76

Bergman, Ingrid, 95

Bernhardt, Sarah, 108

Bernstein, Leonard, 117–18

Bible, the, 291

Bigelow, Paul, 4, 65, 113

Black, Mrs. Cora, 80–81, 82, 83

Black, Reverend George, 79

Blackmer, Sidney, 113, 219

Blanch, Arnold, 81

*Blanche's Chair in the Moon* (Williams), 109

Bogart, Humphrey, 95

Book-Cadillac Hotel, 227, 230

*BOOM* (motion picture), 250, 252, 253, 265

Booth, Shirley, 113, 227

Bowden, Chuck, 50, 161, 230, 268

Bowles, Jane, 73–74, 201, 215, 236
  Williams on, 201, 215

Bowles, Paul, 73–74, 189, 200–2

Brando, Marlon, 64, 104, 212, 164–65, 172

Brecht, Bertolt, 51, 178

Brett, Dorothy, 129

Bricktop, 50

Bridges, James, 306

Britneva, Maria. *See* St. Just, Lady

Brooks, Stella, 166–67

Brown, Andy, 284

Brownlow, William G., 147–48

Brownlow, Mrs William G., 147–48

Bujold, Genevieve, 226, 242, 271, 295

Burke, Billie, 82

Burton, Richard, 252–53

Bynner, Witter, 129

*Cabaret* (motion picture), 275

Caedmon Records, 225

*Cairo, Shanghai, Bombay!* (Williams), 50, 52

Caldwell, Zoe, 268

Calley, Lieutenant, 313

*Camille* (motion picture), 174

*Camino Real* (Williams), 182, 208–10, 237, 260, 312
  critical response to, 209, 210–11
  New York opening, 210
  Philadelphia tryout, 210

Canadian Broadcasting Company, 119–20

*Candles to the Sun* (Williams), 55

Capote, Truman, 188–90, 192, 199, 200

Carroll, Helena, 64, 144, 270–271

*Casablanca* (motion picture), 95–96

Cassidy, Claudia, 108, 204

Castro, Fidel, 84, 85–86

*Cat on a Hot Tin Roof* (Williams), 86, 106, 212–13, 215, 237, 314
  critical response to, 214
  New York Drama Critics' Award for, 213
  New York opening, 213–14
  Pulitzer Prize for, 213

as Williams' favorite play, 212–13, 297
Chapin, Betty, 155
Chekov, Anton, 51
Chicago *Tribune,* 108, 204
*City and the Pillar, The* (Vidal), 184
Clayton, Jack, 225
Clift, Montgomery, 121
Clurman, Harold, 6, 218
Coconut Grove Theatre, 231
Cocteau, Jean, 187, 216
Coleridge, Samuel Taylor, 216
Collier, Constance, 174
Colombe d'Or, La, 176
Columbia University, 155
*Come Back, Little Sheba* (Inge), 113
Comédie Française, 104
Communism, 118, 178
Connell, Mrs. Helen, 111–12
Connery, Sean, 252
Continental Shoemakers, 45, 49, 146
Cook, Peter, 312
Corsaro, Frank, 230, 232
Coward, Noël, 299
Crane, Hart, 4, 148, 317
Crawford, Cheryl, 211, 219
Crawford, Joan, 174
Cuba, 84–86, 141, 223
Cukor, George, 173–74

*Daily Worker, The,* 99
Dakin, Rose O., 14, 21, 30, 49, 50, 74, 139–40, 148, 184
Dakin, Walter Edwin, 14, 20–21, 24, 27, 30, 49, 50, 52, 79, 139–43, 158, 163, 184
Dale, Jim, 50
Dallesandro, Joe, 226, 274
"Daring Young Man on the Flying Trapeze" (Saroyan), 46
Darling, Candy, 42–44, 64, 198, 242
Davies, Marion, 98

Davis, Bette, 230
Deaconess Hospital, 270
De Beauvoir, Simone, 86–87
Deering, Olive, 222
"Delicate Prey, The" (Bowles), 200
Dellinger, Dave, 182
"Desire and the Black Masseur" (Williams), 200, 292–93
Devine, George, 253
Diaghilev, Sergei Pavlovich, 12
*Dirtiest Show in Town, The* (Eyen), 215
Doctors Hospital, 314
Doriden, 260, 264
Dowling, Eddie, 102–3, 104
Dramatists Guild, 9, 65
"Dream of Tennessee Williams, A," 280, 283
Drugs
  Inge, 110–12
  Merlo, 234
  Williams, 220, 272–73, 278, 281, 288
  Doriden, 260, 264
  Mellaril, 260, 264
  Nembutal, 217, 242, 303
  Nytol, 285
  Ritallin, 302
  Seconal, 199–200, 214, 229, 257, 266, 286
  Witherspoon, 88–89
Duff-MacCormick, Cara, ix, 295
Dunaway, Faye, 225
Dunnock, Mildred, 201
Duse, Eleanora, 108

*Elle,* 176
*Esquire,* 274, 280, 283
Evans, Professor Oliver, 132, 255
Excelsior Hotel, 226, 274

Fanning, Gene, 43, 302
Farrell, James T., 221

Faulkner, William, 215, 216
Fellini, Federico, 319
Feuillere, Edwige, 104, 223
Fitzgerald, Neil, 121–22
Fitzgerald, Scott, 225
Fleishman, Walter, 56, 59
Ford, Ruth, 197, 287–88
Forster, E. M., 186
*Four Saints in Three Acts*
  (Stein), 63
France, 24, 26, 175–76, 186–
  187, 309–11
*Frosted Glass Coffin, The*
  (Williams), 189
Fryer, Robert 197–98
*Fugitive Kind* (Williams)
  critical response to, 55
  first production, 53–55

Garbo, Greta, 173–74
*Garden District* (Williams),
  221–22
  critical response to, 222
  New York opening, 221–22
Gassner, John, 78
Gauguin, Paul 8
Gay Lib, 63
George V Hotel, 175
Germany, 26–29
Gert, Valesca, 89–90
Gibraltar, 201
Gielgud, John, 185, 186, 187,
  188
Giraudoux, Jean, 89
*Glass Menagerie, The* (Wil-
  liams), 21, 83, 105, 116,
  139, 151, 157, 172, 204,
  250
  Chicago tryout, 102–3, 107–
    110, 112–13, 114
  critical response to, 107,
    108, 114, 187–88
  Italian production, 178
  London production, 185–86,
    187–88
  New York opening, 106–7
  1973 television version, 107

Glenville, Peter, ix, 100–101,
  160, 185, 226, 242
*Gnadiges Fraulein, The* (Wil-
  liams), x, 268–69
Gordon, Ruth, 253
Gotham Book Mart, 284
Great Britain, 185–88, 221,
  252–54
*Great Gatsby, The* (Fitzger-
  ald), 225
*Great Gatsby, The* (motion
  picture), 225
Greenstreet, Sidney, 95
Group Theatre, 5, 9
Guggenheim fellowships, 4
Gwenn, Edmund, 121

Hall, Adrian, 244
Hancock, John, 254
*Hard Candy and Other Stories*
  (Williams), 36
Harris, Leonard, 296
Harris, Ralph, 261
Harris, Rosemary, 292
Haydon, Julie, 102, 103
Hayes, Helen, 173, 185–88
Helburn, Theresa, 78
Hemingway, Ernest, 81–82,
  84–86, 141, 207
Hemingway, Pauline Pfeiffer,
  81, 85, 141, 142
Henreid, Paul, 95
Hepburn, Katharine, 89
Herlie, Eileen, 289
Hickey, Bill, 43, 144
Hoiby, Lee, 297
Holiday, Billie, 265
*Homeric*, 24
Homosexuality
  McCullers, 309–11
  U.S.S.R., 12
  Williams, 12, 19, 61–64, 84,
    98–100, 105–6, 175,
    262–67
  affairs, 67–70, 74–76,
    106, 110, 138, 166–
    67, 195–212, 220,
    227–46, 251, 286–

288, 293, 297, 307, 309, 314
dancing, 117
first encounters, 31, 35–41, 52–53, 56–62
prostitution, 94–95, 177, 179–82, 184, 193–94, 292–93
sensibility and, 63
society and, 127–28, 257–58
Times Square cruising, 66
venereal disease, 95
violence, 122–24, 169–70, 171, 233–34, 272–273, 280–81
Hong Kong, 299
Hooks, David, 42
Hopkins, Miriam, 74, 77, 141, 201
Hôtel de l'Université, 186–87
Howard, Leslie, 48
Huit Clos (Sartre), 187
Hunter, Tab, 251
Hunter College, 156
Huxley, Aldous, 129

If You Don't Dance They Beat You (Quintero), 255
Iliad, The (Homer), 14
Illinois, University of, 110
Inge, William, 110–14, 208, 272–73
alcohol, 110–12
drugs, 110–12
Williams on, 110–14
Ink Spots, 139
Inman, Mrs., 133
Institute for Living, 159
International Shoe Company, 10, 16, 32, 45, 146, 156–157
International Who's Who, 2
In the Bar of a Tokyo Hotel (Williams), x, 64, 269, 273
In the Summer House

(Bowles), 201
"Inventory at Fontana Belle, The" (Williams), 197
Iowa, University of, 53–62
Isherwood, Christopher, 97, 99
Italy, 161, 176–84, 203, 204–208, 214, 226, 246–47, 253, 267, 274–76, 300
Ivanhoe Theatre, 288

Jackson, Anne, 192
Jamais Hotel, 202, 203
January Crossing (Mills), 155
Japan, 298–99
Joe Allen's, 43–44, 287
Johnson, Buffie, 191
Johnston, Spuds, 129
Jones, Margo, 99, 102–3, 116, 140, 163–68
Summer and Smoke production, 137–38, 190–92
"J.S." (river steamer), 23

Kahn, Michael, 50
Kanin, Garson, 307–8
Kappa Kappa Gamma, 34
Kazan, Elia, 114, 129, 204, 214–16, 222, 231, 246, 290
Baby Doll, 214
Camino Real, 208–11
A Streetcar Named Desire, 163–64, 165, 166, 169, 171–72
Sweet Bird of Youth, 219–220
Kazan, Molly Day Thacher, 6, 9, 163, 220, 222, 246
Kennedy, John F., 170
Kennedy, Mrs. John F., 170–171
Kerr, Walter, 267–68, 311
Kidd, Edie, 276
Kingdom of Earth (Williams), 50, 72, 208, 267–68
critical response to, 268
Kirstein, Lincoln, 97

Kramer, Mrs., 19, 37
Kramer, Florence, 20, 23, 46
Kramer, Hazel, 18–23, 31, 35–37, 46, 47, 151
Kubie, Dr. Lawrence, 218–219, 301
Kuniyoshi, Yasuo, 81

"Lady in Satin" (record album), 265
Langner, Lawrence, 78–79, 87
Lanier, Nan, 259, 267
Lanier, Reverend Sidney, 246
Lansbury, Angela, 51, 254
Lansing, Robert, 221
Last Tango in Paris (motion picture), 104
LaTouche, John, 166
Latter Days of a Celebrated Soubrette, The (Williams), 312
Lawrence, D. H., 51, 118, 129, 176
Lawrence, Frieda, 129, 132
Lawrence, Jane, 190–91
Lazareff, M., 176
Lazareff, Mme., 176
Lee, Doris, 81
Leigh, Vivien, 286
Leighton, Margaret, 268–69
Levy, Dr., 283, 285, 286
Lewis, Robert, 204, 210
Liebling, Bill, 9–13, 116, 132, 288
Liebling-Wood, Inc., 13
Life, 273
Loring, Eugene, 96, 99
Lorre, Peter, 95
Losey, Joe, 231, 252
Luce, Clare, 244
Luhan, Mabel Dodge, 131
Lutetia Hotel, 175
Lyon, Nelson, 242

Mabie, E. C., 59, 61
McArthur, Charles, 185–86
McBurney, Clark Mills, 60

McCabe, Terrence, 47
McCarthy, Joseph, 133
McClintic, Guthrie, 121
McCool, Ellen, 266
McCullers, Carson, 135–38, 201, 301, 309–11
    Williams on, 135–38
McCullers, Reeves, 136
    homosexuality, 309–11
McGovern, Eugene, 120
Machiz, Herbert, 221, 249
McIlhenny, Henry, 183
Madden, Donald, 51, 64, 244, 253, 269, 289
Madwoman of Chaillot, The (Giraudoux), 89
Magnani, Anna, xi, 77, 104, 204–8, 228, 247, 310
Malraux, André, 170–71
"Man Bring This Up Road" (Williams), 246
Mann, Eric, 301
Manning, Mary Louise, 294
Marais, Jean, 187
Marijuana, 200
Martin Beck Theatre, 219
"Mattress by the Tomato Patch, The" (Williams), 98
Maugham, Somerset, 299, 307
Mayer, Louis B., 211
Meacham, Anne, 51–221, 222, 269, 273, 276, 312
Mellaril, 260, 264
Melton, Fred, 69
Member of the Wedding, The (McCullers)
    novel, 135
    play, 136, 301
Memorial Hospital, 238, 243–244
Menotti, Gian-Carlo, 247
Merlo, Anna, 245
Merlo, Frank Phillip, 106, 138, 195–214, 219–20, 227–246, 251, 286–88, 293, 297, 309, 314

death of, 244–46
drugs, 234
financial situation, 237
physical health, 231, 233–
    234, 238–45
Merrick, David, xvi–xvii, 160,
    231, 252, 267, 272, 296
Metro-Goldwyn-Mayer, 61, 74,
    96, 97, 98, 190
Mexico, 6, 70–74, 100, 116–
    118
Miles, Sylvia, 226, 254, 274
Milk Train Doesn't Stop Here
    Anymore, The (Wil-
    liams), 51, 236–37, 246–
    254
    critical response to, 248–49,
        250
    London production, 253–54
    motion picture version, 252–
        253, 254, 265
    New York production, 248–
        250
    out-of-town tryout, 248–50
    San Francisco revival, 254
    Spoleto production, 247,
        253
    Tallulah Bankhead produc-
        tion, 250–53
Miller, Arthur, 163
Mills, Clark, 154–56
Miltown, 266
Miramare Hotel, 246
Mishima, Yukio, 299, 314
Missouri, University of, 2,
    30–34, 37–41, 44–45, 151
Moore, Dudley, 312
Moore, Virginia, 152–53
Moriarty, Michael, 50, 64
Morocco, 202–3, 236, 238, 261
Morphine, 88
Morrissey, Paul, 274
Mother Courage (Brecht), 51
Mozart, Wolfgang Amadeus,
    138
Mummers of St. Louis, 53
Murray, Don, 203

Murray, Peg, 144, 161, 271,
    303
Music Box Theatre, 200
Mutilated, The (Williams),
    268
Myers, John, 221

Nacional Hotel, 223
Nathan, George Jean, 103, 114
National Institute of Arts and
    Letters, 2
Nave Nave Mahana (Gau-
    guin), 7, 8
Nembutal, 217, 242, 303
Nesbitt, Cathleen, 222
Netherlands, the, 27–29
New Directions, 200, 216
Newman, Paul, 104, 219
New Theatre, 196, 270, 301–3
New York Drama Critics'
    Award, 213
New Yorker, The, 36, 91, 134
New York Herald-Tribune,
    The, 222
New York Times, 74, 144, 192,
    222
Night of the Iguana, The
    (Williams), x, 73, 227–
    231
    early production of, 231–
        232
    out-of-town tryout, 227–30
Nijinsky, Waslaw, 12, 68
Nixon, Richard M., 120
Norton, Elliot, 248
Nytol, 285

Ochsner Clinic, 255
"Old Men Go Mad at Night"
    (Williams), 287
Olivier, Laurence, 104
"One Arm" (Williams), 117
Orient Hotel, 299
Orme, Dick, 115, 138
Orpheus Descending (Wil-
    liams), 39, 217–18, 221
    critical response to, 218
    Philadelphia tryout, 218

*Out Cry* (Williams), 100–1, 160–62, 185, 226, 242, 271, 287

   Chicago tryout, 288–289, 295

   critical response to, 294–96

   New Haven tryout, vii–x

   New York production, 294–296

   rewrites, 306

Ozzie (nurse), 14, 319

P. J. Clarke's, 189, 199

Page, Geraldine, 104, 219, 255

*Paris Jour*, 176

*Paris Soir*, 176

Parrot, Jim, 80, 82–83

Parsons, Estelle, 267

Pasadena Playhouse, 99

*Perfect Analysis Given by a Parrot, A* (Williams), 185

Perse, St.-Jean, 204

Persky, Lester, 252, 268

Pi Kappa Alpha, 30

Pickford, Mary, 29

Pinero, Sir Arthur Wing, 76

*Pink Bedroom, The* (Williams), 173–74

Pinter, Harold, 215

Plaza Hotel, ix, 11–12

*Poker Night, The* (Williams), 139

Pollock, Jackson, 70, 316

Polyclinic Hospital, 75

Pont Royal, 310

"Portrait of Girl in Glass" (Williams), 151, 157

*Portrait of a Madonna* (Williams), 166

*President Cleveland*, 298

*Pride and Prejudice* (Austen), 56

Prostitution, 94–95, 177, 179–182, 184, 193–94, 292–93

Psychoanalysis, x, 218–219, 261, 301

Puerto Rico, 254–55

Pulitzer Prize, 213

"Purification, The" (Williams), 69

*Queen Mary*, 189–90

Quintero, José, 189, 231, 254–255, 267, 286

Rabb, Ellis, 292

Rader, Dotson, 197

Rasky, Harry, 120

Ray, Johnny, 210

*Red Devil Battery Sign, The* (Williams), 231, 296

Redgrave, Vanessa, 252

Reed, Rex, 226, 274

Rembrandt Hotel, 202

*Remembrance of Things Past* (Proust), 178

Rhodes, 261–62

Rhodes, Knolle, 50

Rhodes, Mrs. Knolle, 50

*Richard of Bordeaux*, 58, 59

Richardson, Tony, 250–52

Rimbaud, Arthur, 155, 317

Ritallin, 302

Ritz-Carlton Hotel, 249

Robert Clay Hotel, 222

Robertson, Cliff, 218

Rockefeller Foundation, 4, 10–11, 12, 79, 87

Rock Hotel, 201

Roebling, Paul, 248–50

Roebling, Mrs., 249

Romains, Jules, 155

*Roman Spring of Mrs. Stone, The*, (Williams), 177, 217

   motion picture version, 286

Rome *Daily American*, 112

*Romeo and Juliet* (motion picture), 178

Rose Arbor Players, The, 50

Rosebrough, Mrs., 52

*Rose Tattoo, The* (Williams), 203–4, 217, 237

   critical response to, 204

   motion picture version, 204

Ross, Tony, 109

Royal Court Theatre, 253
Royalton Hotel, 134

"Sabbatha and Solitude" (Williams), 304
Sagan, Françoise, 223
St. Just, Lady, 188, 226, 246, 266, 271, 274, 288, 289, 308, 312
St. Just, Lord, 188
St. Louis University, 284
St. Regis Hotel, 308
St. Vincent's Hospital, 49
Santayana, George, 184
Sardi's, 242, 268
Saroyan, William, 46
Sartre, Jean Paul, 86–87, 187
Scapino, 50
Scarlet Pimpernel, The (motion picture), 48
Schippers, Thomas, 247
Schneider, Alan, 268
Scofield, Paul, 160
Sea Gull, The (Chekov), 51
Seconal, 199–200, 214, 229, 257, 266, 286
Selznick, Irene M., 141–42, 165–66, 168–71, 203, 211
Senso (motion picture), 246
"Separate Poem, A" (Williams), 196
Sevier, John, 15
Shapiro, Bernice Dorothy, 52
Shaw, Clay, 258
Shaw, Guy, 18
Shaw, Irwin, 6
Shelton Hotel, 124
Shubert Theatre, vii, viii
Sicily, 178–226, 305
Sikes, Pinkie, 24–25
Sillcox, Luise M., 9
Singer, Louis J., 102, 103, 104
Slapstick Tragedy (Williams), 268–69
Sloane, Al, 243, 244
Small Craft Warnings (Williams), 11, 64, 119, 161, 302–3
  rewrites of, 296
  Williams appears in, 41–44, 144, 161–62, 173, 185, 189, 196–99, 242, 270–271, 302–3
Smith, Jane, 214, 271
Smith, Tippy, 34
Smith, Tony, 138, 190–91, 214, 271
Smith, William Jay, 154–56
Smith College, 79, 82
Socialism, 46, 118
Social Register, 133
Something Unspoken (Williams), 221
Sorbonne University, 155
Soule, Bobby, 244
Southwestern University, 50, 150
Spain, 200–1
Spanish-American War, 16
"Speechless Summer, The" (Williams), 236
Spender, Stephen, 49
Spiegel, Sam, 222
Spoleto's Festival of Two Worlds, 247–48, 253
Square Root of Wonderful, The (McCullers), 137
Stairs to the Roof (Williams), 74
Standard Fruit Company, 82
Stapleton, Maureen, 104, 185, 203–4, 218, 267
"Stardust" (Darling), 44
Star-Times, 112
State Asylum (Missouri), 158, 318
Stay of Execution (Alsop), 313
Steen, Mike, 264
Stein, Gertrude, 63
Stein, Jean, 215
Steinbeck, John, 211
Steinbeck, Mrs. John, 211
Stephens College, 38

Stevens, Roger, 248, 250
Stirrup, Dan, 238, 243
Stoney Lodge, 159–60, 308, 309, 317–18
*Stopped Rocking* (Williams), 285
*Story*, 46
Strand Theatre, 95–96
Strasberg, Lee, 204, 210
*Streetcar Named Desire, A* (Williams), 67, 139–42, 193, 195, 197–98, 203, 204, 297
   Italian production, 178
   New York opening, 172
   out-of-town tryout, 170–72
   preparations for New York production, 163–66, 168–69
   recent productions, 292, 306
Subber, Saint, 210
*Suddenly Last Summer* (Williams), 221–23
   motion picture version, 222–223
Sullavan, Margaret, 165
Sullivan, Brad, 42
*Summer and Smoke* (Williams), 116, 136, 137, 138, 188, 200, 202–3, 255, 301
   critical response to, 137–38, 191–92
   Margo Jones production, 137–38, 188, 190–93
*Sweet Bird of Youth* (Williams), 104, 223–24, 263
   critical response to, 223
   New York production, 219–20
   Paris production, 223

Tandy, Jessica, 165–66, 169
Tatiana, 308, 317–18, 319
Taylor, Elizabeth, 252–53, 254, 265
Taylor, Laurette, 102–4, 165, 250

   alcohol, 114
   Mrs. Edwina Williams and, 107–9
   Williams on, 108–9, 113, 114–15
Television interviews, 119–21, 269
*Ten Blocks on the Camino Real* (Williams), 128, 208–9
   Audrey Wood's reaction to, 128, 208–9
Tennessee, University of 16, 30, 32
Ter-Arutunian, Rouben, 251
*Terra Trema, La* (motion picture,) 178
Texas, University of, 47
Thailand, 297–301
Theatre Guild, 65, 74, 78–79, 87, 185
*This Is* (Williams), 296
Thomas, Dylan, 49, 137
Thomas, Norman, 46
"Three Players of a Summer Game" (Williams), 36
Torn, Rip, 219
*Tramway che se chiamo Desiderio, Un* (A Streetcar Named Desire), 178
Twain, Mark, 87
*Two-Character Play, The* (Williams), 226
"Two on a party" (Williams), 274
*Two Serious Ladies* (Bowles), 201
Tynan, Kenneth, 84–86

Union of Soviet Socialist Republics, 218
   homosexuality, 12
U. S. Corps of Engineers, 92
University City High School, 21, 29
University Theatre, 201
*Unsatisfactory Supper, The* (Williams), 125

Vaccaro, Marion, 79–80, 82–
    83, 84, 86–87, 108, 223,
    235, 238, 261–62, 319
Vaccaro, Regis, 82–83
Van Gogh, Vincent, 316
Veidt, Conrad, 120
Veidt, Viola, 120
Venereal disease, 95
"Vengeance of Nitocris, The"
    (Williams), 20
Venice Film Festival, 161, 226
Vidal, Gore, ix, 183–84, 186–
    188, 199–200
Vietnam, 120
Vinal, Harold 122
Virgin Islands, 146–47
Visconti, Luchino, 178, 246
Voices, 122
Voight, Jon, 225, 292
Von Stein, Dr. William G.,
    245
Vulcania, 200

Wallace, Mike, 121, 269
Wallach, Eli, 203–4, 208
Warhol, Andy, 226, 274
Washington University, 113,
    154
Webster, Margaret, 78
Weird Tales, 20
Wescott, Glenway, 73
Whitehead, Robert, 218, 231
Why Not Try God? (Pick-
    ford), 29
Wilder, Alec, 294
Wilder, Thornton, 170–71
Wilding, Michael, 268
Williams, Cornelius Coffin, 10,
    15–17, 20, 24, 30, 45, 60–
    61, 129, 140, 152, 156–58
Williams, Dakin, 20–21, 148,
    187, 210, 269–70, 272,
    276, 277, 279, 280, 281,
    283, 287
Williams, Mrs. Edwina, 9–10,
    15–20, 30, 116, 187, 196,
    210, 269–70, 276–78, 279

fear of Mexico, 71–72
Laurette Taylor and, 107–9
mental health, 146–47, 269–
    270, 272, 286–87
over solicitous attention of,
    15
physical health, 161, 269–
    270, 272, 306
Puritanism of, 151, 154
reaction to Rose's illness,
    153
Williams, Ernest, 319
Williams, Isabel Coffin, 16
Williams, John, 15
Williams, Rose Isabel, 10, 14,
    16, 17, 18, 19, 21, 24, 83,
    108, 145–61
debut of, 147–48
employment, 158
mental health, 21, 41, 49,
    146–60, 306, 308–9,
    317–20
    at Institute for Living,
        159
    lobotomy operation, 60,
        158, 318
    mother's reaction to, 153
    at State Asylum (Mis-
        souri), 158, 318
    at Stoney Lodge, 159–60,
        308, 309, 317–18
physical health, 41, 146,
    157
relationship with Tennessee,
    150–54
sexual repressions, 150–51
visits New York, 317–19
Williams, Tennessee
adolescence, 20–29
    first European tour, 20–
        21
    mental health, 21–22, 26–
        29
alcohol, 25, 214, 220, 233,
    245, 256, 261–62, 264,
    272, 275, 288, 293,
    299, 316

Williams, Tennessee (*cont.*)
appears in *Small Craft Warnings*, 41–44, 144, 161–62, 173, 185, 189, 196–99, 242, 270–71, 302–3, 314, 371
arrests of, 142–43, 184
background of, 15–16
on Carson McCullers, 135–138
childhood, 14–20
  physical health, 14–15
critical response to
  *Camino Real*, 209, 210–211
  *Cat on a Hot Tin Roof*, 213
  *Fugitive Kind*, 55
  *Garden District*, 222
  *The Glass Menagerie*, 107, 108, 114, 187–188
  *Kingdom of Earth*, 268
  *The Milk Train Doesn't Stop Here Anymore*, 248–49, 250
  *Orpheus Descending*, 218
  *Out Cry*, 294–96
  *The Rose Tattoo*, 204
  *Summer and Smoke*, 137–138, 191–92
  *Sweet Bird of Youth*, 223
  *You Touched Me!*, 122
on death, 305–6, 313–15
drugs, 220, 272–73, 278, 281, 288
  Doriden, 260, 264
  Mellaril, 260, 264
  Nembutal, 217, 242, 303
  Nytol, 285
  Ritallin, 302
  Seconal, 199–200, 214, 299, 257, 266, 286
education
  fraternities, 30, 31–34, 37–41, 54
  University City High School, 21, 29

University of Iowa, 53–62
University of Missouri, 2, 30–34, 37–41, 44–45, 151
egomania, 219
employment, 5, 7–8, 34–35, 45–49, 88–90, 92, 95–97, 146, 150, 151
favorite play of, 212–13, 297
financial status, x, 65, 74, 90–91, 96–98, 182–83, 319–20
  early, 2–13, 30, 33–35, 59, 60
  grants and awards, 2–3, 5–6, 9–11, 12–13, 79, 87, 213
first produced play, 50, 52
first writings, 18, 20, 29, 44–48
future plans, 293, 305–6, 315–16
heterosexual experiences, 18–24, 31, 34–37, 38–39, 44–45, 46, 47–48, 57–58, 151–52
  consummation of, 53–56
  first love, 18–23, 31, 35–37, 46, 47–48, 151
homosexuality, 12, 19, 61–64, 84, 98–100, 105–6, 175, 262–67
  affairs, 67–70, 74–76, 106, 110, 138, 166–67, 195–212, 220, 227–246, 251, 286–88, 293, 297, 307, 309, 314
  dancing, 117
  first encounters, 31, 35–41, 52–53, 56–62
  prostitution, 94–95, 177, 179–82, 184, 193–94, 292–93
  sensibility and, 63
  society and, 127–28, 257–258
  Times Square cruising, 66

venereal disease, 95
violence, 122–24, 169–70, 171, 233–34, 272–73, 280–81
on Jane Bowles, 201, 215
on Laurette Taylor, 108–9, 113, 114–15
loneliness, 125–26, 274, 287, 292
marijuana, 200
mental health, xv, 312–13
adolescence, 21–23, 26–29
collapse in the 1960s, 255–61
depression, 128–29, 255, 258–59, 263, 288
psychoanalysis, x, 218–19, 261, 301
suicidal impulse, 256
New York Drama Critics' Award, 213
origin of name, 15–16
painting by, 233, 283
physical health, vii, 124–25, 136–37, 139, 175–76, 320
cancer, 297–301
cardiovascular condition, 47–49, 53, 278, 280, 304, 311
cataracts, 93–94
childhood, 14–15
convulsions, 278–79, 280, 304
*Maecles Diverticulum* operation, 129–32
medical insurance, 183
staphylococci infection, 228–30
politics, 46, 118, 120, 145, 178
Pulitzer Prize, 213
relationship with Audrey Wood severed, 288–90
relationship with Rose, 150–154
religion, 26–29, 42, 307

shyness of, 21–25, 66, 205
on Tallulah Bankhead, 76–77
television interviews, 119–121, 269
on television reviews, 296
on William Inge, 110–14
WPA writers' project, 4, 60
writing goals, 106–7
writing style, 296–97
changes in, ix–x
Williams, Thomas Lanier I, 15
Williams, Thomas Lanier II, 15, 61
Wilson, Dooley, 95–96
Wilson, John C., 221
Windham, Donald, 69, 75, 118
*Winged Victory* (Hart), 104, 110
Winters, Shelley, 170
Wisconsin, University of, 31, 47
Witherspoon, Cora, 88–89
Wood, Audrey, 9, 13, 78, 96, 113, 116, 122, 141, 163, 166, 170, 214, 237, 244, 269, 273
neglect by, 214, 290
reaction to *Ten Blocks on the Camino Real*, 128, 208–9
relationship with Williams severed, 288–90
Wood, Grant, 81
WPA writers' project, 4, 60

Xavier, St. Francis, 15

Yale University, vii–ix
"Yellow Bird, The" (Williams), 225
Yevtushenko, Yevgeny, 11–12
York, Michael, ix, 51, 64, 274–76, 287, 295
York, Pat, 274–75
Young, John, 294
Young, Stark, 51

*You Touched Me!* (Williams
    and Windham), 99, 118,
    121–22, 124
  critical response to, 122

Zeffirelli, Franco, 178
Ziegfeld, Flo, 82
*Zoo de Vetro* (*The Glass Me-
    nagerie*), 178

## ABOUT THE AUTHOR

TENNESSEE WILLIAMS is one of America's foremost playwrights. Well known, respected and talked about, he is
probably the most produced living playwright in the
world. His plays, *The Glass Menagerie, A Streetcar
Named Desire, The Rose Tattoo, Suddenly Last Summer,
Sweet Bird of Youth, Night of the Iguana* and *Cat on a
Hot Tin Roof,* for which he won the Pulitzer Prize, are
continually revived on and Off-Broadway and throughout the country. Films made from them are constantly
revived in theaters and on TV. His other published work
includes a sceenplay, many short stories and two novels,
*The Roman Spring of Mrs. Stone* and *Moise and the
World of Reason.*

# DISCOVER
# THE DRAMA OF LIFE
# IN THE LIFE OF DRAMA

| | | | |
|---|---|---|---|
| ☐ | LOOK BACK IN ANGER  John Osborne | 2096 • | $1.25 |
| ☐ | TEN GREAT ONE ACT PLAYS  Morris Sweetkind, ed. | 2470 • | $1.50 |
| ☐ | CREATIVE FILM-MAKING  Kirk Smallman | 2623 • | $2.25 |
| ☐ | NEW PLAYS FROM THE BLACK THEATRE<br>Ed Bullins, ed. | 4790 • | $1.25 |
| ☐ | FOUR GREAT PLAYS BY CHEKHOV  Anton Chekhov | 6472 • | $1.50 |
| ☐ | THE GREAT AMERICAN LIFE SHOW<br>9 Plays from the Avant-Garde Theater<br>John Lahr and Jonathan Price, eds. | 7652 • | $2.25 |
| ☐ | AMERICAN PRIMITIVE  William Gibson | 7840 • | $1.65 |
| ☐ | THE CITIZEN KANE BOOK  Pauline Kael,<br>Herman J. Mankiewicz, and Orson Wells | 7853 • | $2.95 |
| ☐ | THE CRUCIBLE  Arthur Miller | 8148 • | $1.50 |
| ☐ | CANDLE IN THE WIND  Alexander Solzhenitsyn | 8424 • | $1.65 |
| ☐ | FOUR GREAT PLAYS BY IBSEN  Henrik Ibsen | 8625 • | $1.25 |
| ☐ | THE NIGHT THOREAU SPENT IN JAIL<br>Jerome Lawrence and Robert E. Lee | 10036 • | $1.50 |
| ☐ | THE PRICE  Arthur Miller | 10177 • | $1.50 |
| ☐ | THE LOVE-GIRL AND THE INNOCENT<br>Alexander Solzhenitsyn | 10246 • | $1.50 |
| ☐ | THE EFFECTS OF GAMMA RAYS ON MAN-IN-THE-MOON<br>MARIGOLDS  Paul Zindel | 10268 • | $1.50 |
| ☐ | 50 GREAT SCENES FOR STUDENT ACTORS<br>Lewy Olfson, ed. | 10331 • | $1.75 |

**Buy them at your local bookstore or use this handy coupon for ordering:**

# Bantam Book Catalog

It lists over a thousand money-saving best-sellers originally priced from $3.75 to $15.00 —bestsellers that are yours now for as little as 60¢ to $2.95!

The catalog gives you a great opportunity to build your own private library at huge savings!

So don't delay any longer—send us your name and address and 25¢ (to help defray postage and handling costs).